al. & Bantu considered of Asian origin

THE POLITICAL MYTHOLOGY OF *APARTHEID*

"The Taking of the Vow," a panel in the marble bas-relief frieze in the Voortrekker Monument, near Pretoria, symbolizes the key myth of South Africa. Photograph courtesy of Martin Gibbs.

THE
POLITICAL
MYTHOLOGY
OF
APARTHEID

LEONARD THOMPSON

YALE UNIVERSITY PRESS
NEW HAVEN AND LONDON

Copyright © 1985 by Leonard Thompson.
All rights reserved.
This book may not be reproduced, in whole
or in part, in any form (beyond that
copying permitted by Sections 107 and 108
of the U.S. Copyright Law and except by
reviewers for the public press), without
written permission from the publishers.

Designed by Sally Harris
and set in Meridien type by Eastern Typesetting Company.
Printed in the United States of America by
Vail-Ballou Press, Binghamton, N.Y.

Library of Congress Cataloging in Publication Data

Thompson, Leonard Monteath.
  The political mythology of apartheid.

  Bibliography: p.
  Includes index.
  1. South Africa—Race relations. 2. South Africa—
History. 3. South Africa—Historiography. I. Title.
DT763.T523   1985   305.8'00968   85-3195
ISBN 0-300-03368-0 (alk. paper)
ISBN 0-300-03512-8 (pbk.)

The paper in this book meets the guidelines for
permanence and durability of the Committee on
Production Guidelines for Book Longevity
of the Council on Library Resources.

10   9   8   7   6   5   4

CONTENTS

*Erosion of the political mythology
in the 1980s.*

v

MAPS

PREFACE

Several years ago I began to collect material showing how politicians in South Africa have made use of falsified versions of history. I soon realized that although it would be quite easy to do an elaborate hatchet job, a far more important problem lay beneath the surface. South Africans are not alone in exploiting history for political ends. Everywhere, powerful people make decisions that affect human lives and prosperity in the light of historical images that they have acquired in their youth, even though scholars know those images to be false. This book is an attempt to examine this problem, using South Africa as a test case.

In the first chapter, I place the problem in perspective. I explain what I mean by political mythology and political myth, I give examples to show that they are ubiquitous in the modern world and that they are extremely malleable, and I identify three criteria for evaluating them. The second chapter describes the context in which the mythology of the Afrikaner nationalist movement has developed and the ways in which that mythology is propagated. The third chapter describes the history of what has become the core of the mythology of the *apartheid* state: its racial ingredient. Next, I relate the history of a specific Afrikaner nationalist myth that is derived from an attempt that a few frontier farmers made to defy the government of the Cape Colony in 1815.

That is followed by an account of another specific myth, relating to events in 1838 when an Afrikaner commando defeated a Zulu army—a myth that lies behind a major public holiday in modern South Africa and provides the title for James Michener's South African novel, *The Covenant*. The last chapter shows how these myths have been affected by the changing fortunes and needs of the Afrikaner nationalist movement since it gained control of the South African state in 1948. In a brief conclusion, I raise some general questions about the role of political mythology in the light of the preceding case study, and I refer to two other political mythologies that are current in South Africa. I have added a chronological table for the benefit of readers who are not well-informed about the history of the region.

This is in some respects a pioneering study. Whereas *The Invention of Tradition*, which was recently edited by Eric Hobsbawm and Terence Ranger and published by the Cambridge University Press, is a collection of essays on traditions and customs in several societies, I have explored in some depth the history of a particular mythology. There are many aspects of the subject that warrant far more thorough investigation than I have made and more special expertise than I possess. I hope that this book may contribute to our understanding of the power of political mythology and stimulate other scholars to unravel the histories and effects of other examples.

Anyone who writes about South Africa has to cope with a terminological minefield. In identifying human groups, should we use the ethnic terms of the documents, or should we follow some modern usage? Consider the bearings of the problem when one is referring to the majority of the population of the region—the people who speak Bantu languages and are descended from farmers who have expanded into the region from the north during the last seventeen hundred years or so. At various times white people have called them Kaffirs, Natives, Bantu(s), Africans, and Blacks, or have identified them by their "tribal" names. Or consider the labels Whites have applied to the early inhabitants of the western part of the region. Until recently, Whites called them Hottentots and Bushmen (depending on whether they were stockfarmers or they depended entirely on hunting and gathering), but scholars now prefer the terms Khoikhoi and San. And what is to be done about the people whom the South African government calls Coloured—people who descend in varying degree from local Khoikhoi and San, from imported Asian and African slaves, and from Whites? How, too, is one to handle the term Black in modern southern Africa? Does it refer exclusively to the Africans (the former Bantu or Natives), or does it also include Asians and Coloureds? And what about the white population? Should we call the descendants of the early Dutch, German, and French settlers Boers, as they themselves usually did until at least the late nineteenth century, or should we call them Afrikaners, as they now prefer? And how are we to translate the Dutch or Afrikaans word *volk* in those contexts where it carries a heavier burden than the English word *people?* And what of people who have resorted to force to resist the white regime in South Africa—Freedom Fighters? Guerrillas? Terrorists?

I have tried to tread as deftly as possible through this minefield, seeking the terms that are most appropriate in their historical contexts. I sometimes use the term Black in the comprehensive sense: there are occasions when one needs a term to identify all the people who are not part of the white ruling class of South Africa, and the alternatives are unsatisfactory—it is offensive to define people negatively by calling them Non-Whites or Non-Europeans and it is cumbersome to spell out the phrase African, Asian, and Coloured.

My conceptual framework has been clarified in numerous discussions. From start to finish my colleague Robert Harms has been a stimulating and creative critic. Both John Cell, who read it for Yale University Press, and William Foltz examined the entire manuscript and made valuable suggestions. Fikile Bam, Jeffrey Butler, André du Toit, Richard Elphick, Barbara Harmel, Barney Horowitz, John Middleton and Nancy Stepan have provided me with insightful written comments on particular aspects of the work. A draft of each chapter was dealt with in a session of a seminar or workshop of the Yale-Wesleyan Southern African Research Program. There, commentators included several of the people named above, more than a dozen Yale graduate students, and also Henry Bredekamp, Stephen Clingman, Leonard Doob, Harvey Feinberg, Stanley Greenberg, Neil Lazarus, Dunbar Moodie, Dan O'Meara, Harald Sandstrom, Christopher Saunders, and Michael Savage. In addition, Norman Bromberger, Nancy Clark, Rodney Davenport, Hermann Giliomee, Keith Gottschalk, Phyllis Lewsen, Henning van Aswegen, Michael Whisson, Francis Wilson, and William Worger sent me documents and comments from South Africa. The work bears the stamp of their labor, their knowledge, and their insights.

I am grateful to the John Simon Guggenheim Foundation for awarding me a fellowship for the year starting in July 1982, which became a critical period in my reading, research, and preliminary drafting; to the National Endowment for the Humanities, under whose auspices I conducted a seminar for college teachers on the political mythology of race in the summer of 1983; and to that endowment, the Ford Foundation, and the Open Society Fund, which have supported the Yale-Wesleyan Southern African Research Program. Special thanks are due to William Carmichael of the Ford Foundation for his commitment to the program since its inception in 1977, and to Pamela Baldwin, the administrative assistant of the program.

Like others who have worked on African subjects at Yale, I am indebted to J. M. D. (Moore) Crossey, the curator of the African collections in the university library. If a book or a pamphlet on an African subject exists in North America, he has either made sure that it is in the library, or he will run it down and make it available.

All translations from the Dutch and Afrikaans are mine; some were amended by André du Toit or Pamela Kriger. The maps were made by Robert L. Williams; the index by Lynn Berat. The title of chapter 4 was inspired by C. Vann Woodward's classic *The Strange Career of Jim Crow.*

It is a pleasure to be working again with the staff of the Yale University Press—not least with the history editor, Charles Grench, who repeatedly contributed doses of energizing encouragement and creative criticism.

1
POLITICAL MYTHOLOGY
IN THE MODERN WORLD

I

This book deals with political myth and political mythology. By a political myth I mean a tale told about the past to legitimize or discredit a regime; and by a political mythology, a cluster of such myths that reinforce one another and jointly constitute the historical element in the ideology of the regime or its rival.

Some political myths are stories that illustrate an aspect of an ideology and that may be discarded without seriously weakening the ideology itself. For example, American textbooks inculcated patriotism in generations of American children by telling the tale of George Washington and the cherry tree, according to which

> George Washington, as a little boy, was given a hatchet for his birthday. Tempted by his shiny new tool, George went out and practiced chopping on one of his father's cherry trees. When the tree was found dead . . . , George was asked by his father if he had done it. " 'I can't tell a lie, Pa; you know I can't tell a lie. I did cut it with my hatchet.' 'Run to my arms, you dearest boy,' cried his father in transports."[1]

Influential though this tale has been as an illustration of the integrity of the Founding Fathers, American patriotism is not weakened by its gradual withdrawal from the lexicon.

Similarly with British patriotic myths. For example, generations of British children were taught to believe that during the night of 20 June 1756 Siraj-ud-Daula, nawab of Bengal, murdered 123 British captives in the Black Hole of Calcutta. Geoffrey Moorhouse has explained what happened:

> The young Nawab may have been arrogant but he was not a bloodthirsty monster and all he did with the British captives was to relieve them of their valuables and have them locked up for the night in the brig at Fort William, which had always been known by the British as the Black Hole, though it was nothing worse than a room with a window opening onto a verandah. Unfortunately, the night of June 20, 1756 was probably the most oppressive of that year, because the monsoon broke the following day. When the brig was unlocked in the morning many of the prisoners had suffocated or died of heat exhaustion—perhaps 43 out of 64, which was bad enough but not nearly as bad as the Black Hole's self-appointed hero, John Zephaniah Holwell, made out in subsequent accounts. He claimed that 146 people had gone in, of whom 23 survived, and those figures still tend to circulate in some British history books though they have long been proved a nonsense.[2]

The effect of the myth of the Black Hole of Calcutta is to illustrate the cruelty of "the lesser breeds without the law." British patriotism can survive the abandonment of that myth.

Other political myths are much more than mere stories about the past. They are also indispensable, integral parts of a regime's ideology. Take the case of Joseph Stalin's *History of the Communist Party of the Soviet Union: A Short Course,* which was published in 1938, printed in millions, and became "a manual of ideology completely binding on all citizens" until Stalin's death in 1953. As described by Leszek Kolakowski,

> The historical conclusions are simple: the Bolshevik party, under the brilliant leadership of Lenin and Stalin, unswervingly pursued from the outset the faultless policy which was crowned by the success of the October Revolution. Lenin is always depicted in the forefront of history, and Stalin directly after him. A few individuals of the second or third rank who were lucky enough to die before the great purges are briefly mentioned at appropriate points in the story. As for the leaders who actually helped Lenin to create the party, carry out the Revolution, and found the Soviet state, they are either not mentioned at all or are shown as double-dyed traitors and wreckers who crept into the party and whose whole career consisted of sabotage and conspiracy. Stalin, on the other hand, was from the beginning an infallible leader, Lenin's best pupil, his truest helper and closest friend.[3]

So long as Stalin lived, that version of the history of the Communist Party was the Soviet equivalent of sacred writ. It constituted a core myth for the Soviet system in the Stalin era, as distinct from peripheral myths, such as that of the Black Hole of Calcutta.

One can also distinguish between conservative and radical myths. Conservative myths often narrate events leading to the foundation of a state; they correspond with Malinowski's charters legitimizing the social order in primitive societies. There was an elaborate foundation myth in classical Rome. In Virgil's version in the *Aeneid*, written in the imperial Augustan age, Aeneas was the founder of the city and he was

the instrument of a providential purpose—the greatness of
Rome and its universal empire.[4]

American
Foundation
Myth

There are similar foundation myths in modern countries,
expounded in textbooks and popular literature, and deeply
embedded in the public consciousness. James Oliver Robertson has described the American version:

> What is specifically American in American nationalism
> is the widespread belief in the unique origins of the
> nation. Americans are a *new* people, formed out of a
> migration of people seeking freedom in a *new world.* The
> nation was founded in a revolution which was both the
> first war of liberation and the first lasting overthrow of
> an *ancien régime.* That revolution created a *new* nation
> dedicated to the spread of freedom and democracy and
> equality. The history of that people and nation has been
> the struggle, physically and geographically as well as
> morally and ideally, to spread freedom across the con-
> tinent and throughout the world.[5]

Radical myths are created and propagated by domestic or
foreign opponents of a regime, to discredit it and promote
its downfall. These myths, like conservative myths, often
concern past events, as with the myth that was used to
discredit the Weimar Republic, according to which Germany
lost the First World War not because the army was defeated
by the enemy but because it was stabbed in the back by
politicians on the home front. Similarly, in the United States
radicals counter the conservative mythology that American
history is the story of the creation of a land of plenty and
equality with the myth of a capitalist conspiracy against the
deluded masses. Other radical myths are eschatological pro-
jections into the future. Millennial obsessions abounded in
medieval Europe and promoted the disastrous Children's
Crusade of 1212. In 1856 South Africa was the scene of a

devastating millennial movement. After white farmers and British regular troops had defeated the Xhosa people in a series of frontier wars and deprived them of much of their land, thousands of Xhosa destroyed their very means of subsistence—their cattle and their crops. A prophet had told them that that was the will of their ancestors; and that if they obeyed, their ancestors would provide them with bountiful crops and magnificent herds of fat cattle and make the white people disappear from their country. The result was catastrophic: famine and mass starvation.[6] Today, the most widespread millennial myth is the myth of the proletarian revolution, which is to end all revolutions and create a classless society.[7]

The most remarkable example of the operational use of a radical myth is the *Requerimiento*. This was a document drawn up at the Spanish court in 1513, on the advice of Dominican friars, for use by conquistadors. It included a summary of the history of the world since its creation. The crucial event is the appearance of Jesus Christ, who has the entire world under His jurisdiction. Jesus transmitted His power to Saint Peter, and through Him to the succession of popes. In 1493 Pope Alexander VI issued bulls that delegated papal authority over most of the newly discovered American continent to the Spanish monarchs, who thereby acquired God-given sovereignty over the lands and their inhabitants. Conquistadors were to read this remarkable document to Indians before attacking them. If the Indians accepted it, they would become serfs of the Spaniards; if not, the document continued,

> with the help of God, we shall forcibly enter into your country and shall make war upon you in all ways and manners that we can, and shall subject you to the yoke and obedience of the Church and of their Highnesses;

we shall take you and your wives and your children,
and shall make slaves of them as their Highnesses may
command; and we shall take away your goods, and we
shall do all the harm and damage that we can as to
vassals who do not obey and refuse to receive their lord,
and resist and contradict him.[8]

This document was actually used on several occasions, without the Indians being given the slightest means to understand
what was going on. The conquistador Oviedo reported that
in one case Indians were seized and, "after they had been
put in chains, someone read the *Requerimiento* without
knowing their language and without any interpreters."[9]

Many other myths have been put to nefarious purposes.
Ernst Cassirer, writing soon after he migrated from Germany
to the United States during the Second World War, observed:
"The power of mythical thought" is "perhaps the most important and the most alarming feature in this development
of modern political thought."[10] Cassirer traced the history
of mythical thinking in Western philosophy from the Greeks
onward, leading up to a review of the origins and substance
of Alfred Rosenberg's Nazi tract, *The Myth of the Twentieth
Century*. Hegel, Carlyle, and Gobineau all prepared the way
for the Nazi synthesis, which was precipitated by the threat
of the collapse of the German social and economic system.
In modern societies, wrote Cassirer, "myth has not been
really vanquished and subjugated. It is always there, lurking in the dark and waiting for its hour and opportunity.
This hour comes as soon as the other binding forces of man's
social life, for one reason or another, lose their strength and
are no longer able to combat the demonic mythical
powers."[11]

In similar vein, Geoffrey Barraclough contends that history
should be a myth-free science. So long as history continues

to include mythical elements, it will be an instrument for chauvinism: "Unless history can emancipate itself from mythology, in the way that sciences such as astronomy or chemistry have done, unless it can break once and for all time with its mythological roots, as astronomy has emancipated itself from astrology and chemistry from alchemy, the chances of history breaking out of the vicious circle in which its past has imprisoned it, are not great."[12]

Views such as these are products of wishful thinking. Myth cannot be eradicated from human culture, because it performs a necessary function. Nor is it to be regarded as inexorably evil. Bronislaw Malinowski emphasized the function of myth in "primitive societies":

Malinowski on myth.

Myth fulfils in primitive culture an indispensable function: it expresses, enhances, and codifies belief; it safeguards and enforces morality; it vouches for the efficiency of ritual and contains practical rules for the guidance of man. Myth is thus a vital ingredient of human civilization; it is not an idle tale, but a hard-worked active force; it is not an intellectual explanation or an artistic imagery, but a pragmatic charter of primitive faith and moral wisdom.[13]

Psychologists believe that myths serve a necessary function in contemporary societies. There is support for this point of view from political scientists. Henry Tudor says, "Myth-making is characteristic of culture as such and is no more a reversion to 'the first rudimentary stages of human culture' than are dancing, painting and architecture."[14] The *Oxford English Dictionary* has lent its authority to this trend. Whereas the original *OED* volume containing the letter *M*, published in about 1908, defined myth as "a purely fictitious narrative," the 1976 *Supplement* includes a quotation from the

British Journal of Sociology, defining myth as "a tale which is told to justify some aspect of social order or of human experience."[15] I agree. Myth, including political myth, is an ineluctable human product.

II

Some critics who excel in exposing the factual errors in political myths treat them as though they were fixed and unchanging.[16] They fail to show that myths are historical phenomena. Myths originate in specific circumstances as a product of specific interests, and they change with the changing interests of successive generations and successive regimes. They vary in intensity: they may be dormant, they may flourish, they may decline, they may die out. Myths also change in substance and meaning. They may serve one interest at one time and another interest later on, or they may be manipulated to serve more than one interest at the same time.

Henry Tudor demonstrates some of these qualities in his account of the Roman foundation myth, which changed in substance and meaning with the shifts in the structure of the Roman polity and in the relationship between Rome and the rest of the Mediterranean world.[17] More recently, Marina Warner has produced a striking example of the dynamic qualities of myth in her study of Joan of Arc. First, she describes what is known of the historical Joan on the basis of the available evidence. She then shows how, after Joan's condemnation as a heretic had been rescinded in 1455, French people came to regard her as a heroic figure. Since then, successive generations and diverse interest groups have appropriated her, making her image correspond with their interests and their perceptions of the heroic. In the great nineteenth-century French controversy between church and state each claimed her as its own; and since 1902 there have been two statues in her birthplace, the village of Domremy. One is

a white marble group showing Joan, exalted and radiant. She is enfolded in the fleur-de-lysé mantle of a queenly figure, who, wearing a pearl-embroidered coif on her looped hair, represents France in its medieval form, the fifteenth-century realm. With her help, Joan lifts to the sky an avenging sword.[18]

The other sculpture, at the entrance to the Domremy basilica,

makes the exactly opposite point: Joan, dressed as a peasant, kneels in an attitude of alarm and humility, one hand shielding her face, the other outstretched in wonder before her three voices, who are raised high above her on a brick wall and are cast in precious bronze in contrast to her white marble. Catherine holds out a sword, Margaret a helmet, and Michael, slightly higher than the others and spreading tremendous wings, raises himself to his full height, points with his index finger of his right hand toward heaven and holds aloft her cross-banner in his left. Joan here is God's humble instrument. Thus the opposing power blocs contending for Joan's patronage confided their quarrel to imperishable stone in her very homeland.[19]

Now, however, having been canonized in 1920, Joan has come to be "a safe symbol of the country's grandeur" and "to represent the nation to [all] French men and women."[20]

Most political mythologies are linked with the state because it is the dominant institution in the modern world. Every state exerts a profound effect on popular consciousness through its use of official symbols and rituals. Moreover, the politicians and bureaucrats who control the state at any given time frequently modify those symbols and rituals to suit their

Not necessarily true.

interests. One could give an accurate account of a country's political mythology and history by studying the development and the usage of its flag, its national anthem, its postage stamps, its coins, and its official holidays and festivals. States differ, however, in the degree to which they dominate the institutions that create, propagate, and modify myths: churches, schools and universities, printing presses (especially those that publish textbooks), and radio and television programs. There is a great difference between the mythologies that prevail in states where there is freedom of teaching and publication and those in states with censorship and standardized, ideological instruction. The former mythologies are weak, diluted, and subject to public dispute; the latter are strong, uniform, and incontestable. In the time of Stalin, says Kolakowski, "The *Short Course* was not merely a work of falsified history but a powerful social institution— one of the party's most important instruments of mind control, a device for the destruction both of critical thought and of society's recollections of its own past."[21]

As has been vividly portrayed by George Orwell in *1984*, mythologies of totalitarian regimes are particularly malleable. "A totalitarian system," writes Kolakowski, "cannot survive without constantly rewriting history, eliminating past events, personalities, and ideas and substituting false ones in their place."[22] Moreover, sooner or later a revolutionary totalitarian regime finds it expedient to incorporate elements of the prerevolutionary national mythology. Initially, for example, the Soviet mythology made a clean break with the imperial Russian tradition; but Russian nationalism soon made an intrusion and during the Second World War, when the Soviet Union was fighting for survival against German invaders, Stalin's mythology was as nationalist as it was communist.

Contemporary Romanian mythology is a striking synthesis of core elements that were originally contradictory: the conservative mythology of the prerevolutionary monarchical regime and the socialist mythology of its opponents. The conservative mythology rooted Romanian nationalism in pre-Christian times, justified Romania's historic claims to possession of Transylvania, Bessarabia, Bukovina, the Banat, and Dobrudja, and vindicated the political structure of the kingdom. No matter that this mythology was not supported by evidence, it was propagated and it was widely believed. For some years after its installation in 1944, the communist regime lacked commitment to the Romanian national tradition and ignored the entire prerevolutionary mythology. By the mid-1950s, however, the government was facing such widespread internal opposition, including resentment of Soviet pressure, that the leaders found it expedient to appropriate the nationalist elements in the old tradition and combine them with the communist mythology. In the words of a scholarly commentator, President Ceauşescu's supporters, searching for legitimacy, then rewrote the history of Romania, identifying the president with "historic figures of Romania's past . . . 'national heroes' who, in their own way, stood for social justice and preservation of the Romanian patrimony and civilization against hostile foreign imperialists."[23] Ceauşescu and his wife became "hailed as executors of a glorious historic tradition characterized by centuries of struggle for the achievement of true national independence and social justice which began in the fourth century B.C. during the reign of Burebista."[24]

Nevertheless, there are limits to the adaptability of myths. We have the example of the Aryan myth, which, in various forms, had been deeply rooted and widely accepted in European culture.[25] It reached a climax in the Third Reich, for which Alfred Rosenberg's *Myth of the Twentieth Century* was an official doctrine. In Rosenberg's version, Aryans were responsible for all the great civilizations of antiquity. The Nordic peoples, especially the Germans, were their modern heirs. Jesus Christ was an Aryan and he was a martial person rather than the gentle Christ of the ecclesiastical tradition. That myth was used to justify the Holocaust.[26] However, since the Nazi regime was overthrown, so universal has been the revulsion among Germans as well as foreigners that the Aryan myth has ceased to be used as a prop for racist· behavior.

III

In assessing political myths, we may apply three criteria. One is the special province of the historian, who is a technician in the handling of historical evidence.[27] If a myth is compatible with the evidence, it passes a crucial test. If it distorts the evidence, it fails the test and is bad history—and to that extent an implausible myth.

Historical research is a cumulative process. Narratives, analyses, and interpretations that were consonant with the evidence available yesterday may be discredited by evidence that has been brought to light by fresh research today or tomorrow. A historian should therefore consider the extent to which a myth is an accurate account of an actual historical event or process, in the light of all the relevant evidence that is available. He has a professional obligation to apply this procedure; in a reasonably free society, failure to do so loses him the respect of his peers and prejudices his career. However, the historian's technical criticism may merely reveal errors of sorts that do not affect the substance of the myth. Perhaps the myth includes faulty dates, or fresh research has turned up warts in heroic figures or some other historical "facts" that leave the essence of the myth intact. In other cases, the historian's technical criticism may discredit the essence of the myth by showing that what happened cannot fairly be used to support the effects which the myth produces.

Even then, as in the Romanian case, the myth's political impact may be unimpaired, especially in countries where the public is sheltered from the free exercise and dissemination of historical scholarship. There, politicians may continue to exploit myths long after competent historians have revealed their fundamental falseness and discarded them on the dust heap.

*

One may also assess a political myth in terms of its scientific probability. Scientific knowledge, like historical knowledge, is subject to a process of accumulation, and in the last few centuries the rate of accumulation has been exponential. But scientists as well as historians have been guilty of manipulating evidence to produce conclusions that confirm their prejudices.

Central to the theme of this book is the change in the use which scientists have made of the concept *race*.[28] In one form or another, racist mythology was compatible with much mainstream Western science deep into the twentieth century. As Darwinian evolutionary theory gradually penetrated the scientific community, scientists related it to the earlier concept of a great chain of being, with white people at the top and black people at the bottom of the human part of the chain, close to the orangutans at the top of the nonhuman part. The result was a synthesis in which many scientists agreed that racial differentiation had occurred very early in human evolution, and racial differences were still taken to be fixed, deep, and culturally significant. Between the two world wars, scientific racism was still being endorsed by various influential specialists. The work of craniologists, who had claimed that their measurements of the size and shape of human skulls demonstrated the superiority of white people, was being discredited; but psychologists were claiming that tests measuring human "intelligence" were yielding similar results, and politicians were making use of their findings to further their own interests. For example, intelligence tests were used as the justification for giving preferential admission to the United States to people from northwestern Europe in the Immigration Restriction Act of 1924, which Stephen Jay Gould calls "one of the greatest victories of scientific racism in American history."[29]

Scientific racism was a perfect fit with the global political economy of the period of white hegemony. It was used to justify white hegemony in North America and in the European empires in Africa, Asia, and the Caribbean.

Ever since the turn of the century, however, some Western scientists had expressed doubts about the validity of the racist paradigm. As early as 1897, John Mackinnon Robertson, a British sociologist, denied that there was a correlation between race and culture. In 1911 Franz Boas, a German-born American anthropologist, published *The Mind of Primitive Man*, in which he rejected the linear, evolutionist classification of societies that had been compatible with racism in favor of a pluralist approach which stressed the integrity of each culture, regardless of race. Boas and his successors, Ruth Benedict, Margaret Mead, and Alfred Kroeber, went some way toward purging cultural anthropology of scientific racism. By the 1930s the British biologists Lancelot Hogben, J. B. S. Haldane, Ronald Fisher, and Julian Huxley also were challenging the premises of scientific racism; and in 1935 Alfred Haddon and Julian Huxley published *We Europeans: A Survey of "Racial" Problems*, in which, using nonspecialist language, they denounced German racism—the concept of "pure races," the correlation between intelligence and physical type, and the myth of Aryan superiority.[30] Even so, racist ideas were by no means expunged from scientific circles in the West before the Second World War. Haldane himself had endorsed the eugenics movement for selective human breeding during the early 1920s, and, as Francis Jennings has demonstrated, Kroeber's emphasis on Indian "savagery" contributed to the decimation of the American Indian population north of the Rio Grande.[31]

During and after the Second World War, however, the reaction against racism gathered momentum among scientists and nonscientists alike. Initially, it was mainly a response of people in the Allied countries to the ideology of an enemy; but as the news of the Holocaust spread it precipitated a deeper and more widespread aversion to the consequences of racism. This was a gradual and uneven process. At various times the Dutch, Belgian, French, British, and Portuguese governments tried desperately to maintain control of specific colonial territories. Nevertheless, the British relinquished control of India in 1947 and of Kenya in 1963, the French withdrew from tropical Africa in 1960 and from Algeria in 1962, and the Portuguese surrendered to local movements in Angola and Mozambique in 1975. By then, too, substantial steps had been taken to dismantle discriminatory laws and practices in the United States, and, with their vast majority in the United Nations, the Asian, African, and Latin American states were transforming the character and the policies of the organization.

During this postwar generation, Western scientists gradually abandoned the paradigm of a hierarchy of races that had been current for more than a century. Changes in the distribution of power coincided with changes in the world view of scientists. By the 1980s, most scientists had rejected the racial interpretations of intelligence tests. In physical anthropology the view gained ground that the very concept of *race* was scientifically irrelevant. As Nancy Stepan puts it in *The Idea of Race in Science:*

End of Scientific Rationalism.

> The fundamental unit of analysis in the old racial science was the human race or racial "type." Races were defined anatomically and morphologically, in terms of the phenotype—that is, by detailed measurements of the shape of the skull, the dimensions of the post-cranial skeleton, by stature, and by skin colour. The features measured were taken to be on the whole stable in character, and therefore a good indication of racial identity and affinity. The unit of analysis in the new biology was, by contrast, not the race but the "population," defined not morphologically or behaviourally but genetically and statistically.[32]

By the 1980s a new biological science, purged of the old racial paradigm, was dominant in scientific circles in the West. Stepan goes so far as to claim that "a tradition of scientific racism which had lasted from the early nineteenth century until the end of the Second World War if not later, has at long last been laid almost to rest."[33] The discrediting of scientific racism is one of the most significant intellectual transformations of the last generation. Nevertheless, Stepan is too optimistic. The process is incomplete and potentially reversible. There is resistance among scientists such as Arthur R. Jensen, H. J. Eysenck, and John Baker.[34] There is more general resistance among the white public and many successful politicians. As Stepan herself points out, the shift in scientific opinion was not easily translated into nonscientific language, nor was it readily injected into the popular consciousness, where deep-rooted racial prejudices gave ground at a much slower rate.[35] In Europe they were fostered by the tensions arising from postwar immigration from Africa, Asia, and the Caribbean; in the United States they were a

Race in the U.S. is a cultural category.

response to immigration from Central and South America as well as the Caribbean, and also to court-ordered plans to desegregate schools.

Time lags always exist between the findings of specialists and their incorporation in the basic knowledge of the general public. For many white people in Europe and America as well as South Africa the old racist paradigm is still an extremely attractive way of explaining the world and justifying white power and privilege; its attractions may increase in response to the threat of Insecurity created by political and economic crises. When they have served the interests of autocratic regimes, political myths have often been resilient enough to survive the derision of mainstream scientists as well as historians. That was the case in the Soviet Union, where the biological ideas of Trofim Lysenko, who rejected Mendelian genetics, became dominant in the 1930s and achieved a complete monopoly in 1948, when the Central Committee of the Communist Party decreed that they were correct. It was not until 1964, and especially after the fall of Khrushchev, that they became totally discredited.[36]

Despite all this, however, with laws, political rhetoric, newspapers, radio and television programs, and school and college textbooks abandoning racism, on balance the Western mentality has been moving in the direction pioneered by the scientists. In particular, in most social settings in the West young people have been growing up with less racial prejudice than their parents.

*

The third criterion for assessing political myths is utilitarian. In applying this criterion, one asks not whether the myth is technically an accurate account of events, nor whether it is compatible with scientific knowledge, but whether its effects are good or bad. The answer to this question will vary with

the values of the respondent. Peoples' values differ profoundly. The mind set of a person is formed in part by the
culture in which he or she was reared and exists, and in part
by his or her own specific status and experiences in that
culture.

The realization that political myths may have good effects
goes back at least to the Greek philosophers. To Plato, truth
was a vital virtue; but he made one exception. The ruler of
his model Republic should create and propagate an official
mythology—a "royal lie," an "audacious fiction"—to ensure
that the citizens would act for the good of the country, defend
it against attacks, and trust their fellow citizens. "The fos-
tering of such a belief," according to Plato, "will make them
care more for the city than for one another." Those effects
may seem to be unexceptionable. However, Plato's "royal
lie" went on to include a rigid system of closed classes:

> Citizens, we shall say to them in our tale, you are broth-
> ers, yet God has framed you differently. Some of you
> have the power of command, and in the composition
> of these he has mingled gold, wherefore also they have
> the highest honour; others he has made of silver, to be
> auxiliaries; others again who are to be husbandmen and
> craftsmen he has composed of brass and iron; and the
> species will generally be preserved in the children. But
> as all are of the same original stock, a golden parent
> will sometimes have a silver son, or a silver parent a
> golden son. And God proclaims as a first principle to
> the rulers, and above all else, that there is nothing which
> they should so anxiously guard, or of which they
> are to be such good guardians, as of the purity of the
> race. . . . For an oracle says that when a man of brass
> or iron guards the State, it will be destroyed.[37]

Plato was by no means exceptional in endorsing the class divisions of ancient Greece. Aristotle provided an elaborate rationalization for slavery. "It is clear," he wrote, "that some men are by nature free, and others slaves, and that for these latter slavery is both expedient and right."[38]

As Plato indicated, political mythologies may contribute to the general welfare by projecting sound moral principles and promoting domestic and international harmony. Insofar as political mythologies use history to establish the highest standards by which people may judge the performance of their contemporaries, they fulfill a useful and beneficial function and meet the third criterion for the assessment of mythologies. However, the passages cited from the Greek philosophers also illustrate the extent to which values have changed over time. Today, scarcely anyone would accept Aristotle's endorsement of slavery; and Plato's system of fixed, reproductive classes corresponds to no contemporary political order and certainly to no official ideology except the South African.

Values vary from place to place as well as over time. There are vast gulfs between the values that prevail in different parts of the contemporary world, as a result of the differences in their political institutions, their class systems, their productive capacities, and their relationships to the global economy. To be reared in a totalitarian state, with its propaganda, its censorship, its educational institutions, and its harassment of dissidents, is to acquire very different values from those of people who are brought up in Western Europe or North America; and still other values predominate in societies that are overwhelmingly poor, nonindustrial, and dependent.

In an ideal world, a political mythology would satisfy all three criteria. It would conform to the evidence, it would be scientifically valid, and its effects would be wholly beneficial. Providing models of human personality and behavior, it would help humanity to profit from the achievements and avoid the errors of previous generations. In the real world, political mythologies fall short of satisfying one or more of these criteria, and many mythologies have nefarious effects.

IV

In *Political Myth*, Henry Tudor has stressed the differences between the roles of the mythmaker and the historian:

> The view of the world that we find in a myth is always a practical view. Its aim is either to advocate a certain course of action or to justify acceptance of an existing state of affairs. Myths are, therefore, believed to be true, not because the historical evidence is compelling, but because they make sense of men's present experience. They tell the story of how it came about. And events are selected for inclusion in a myth, partly because they coincide with what men think *ought* to have happened, and partly because they are consistent with the drama as a whole.

Tudor claims that if a myth is "a plausible story" and if it "casts real light on the experience of its audience, then it is likely to be received as a true account, regardless of what the professional historian might say." In short, says Tudor, "Where the historian deploys current knowledge in an attempt to elucidate the past, the myth-maker does so in order to make a point of practical importance to his contemporaries. And between the two there is a world of difference."[39]

The implication of Tudor's persuasive reasoning is that the roles of the mythmaker and the historian are incompatible. The historian should stick to his last. It is difficult enough to collect evidence, to sift it, to compose an accurate narrative, and to place it in a logically coherent framework. If

historians allow their political or social predilections to influence their professional work, they will corrupt it.

Such a conclusion smacks of hubris. It ignores the fact
that none of us is a specially privileged, objective observer
of humanity. Like every other human being, historians are
enmeshed in humanity. In our professional work we cannot
insulate ourselves from our national and ethnic culture, our
class interests, and our personal experience. Technical expertise should be dominant during the stage when we are
collecting and analyzing evidence; but there are two other
stages in the complex process of historical reconstruction.
Evidence does not dictate our choice of a subject; nor does
evidence alone determine the context in which we place our
work. It is one thing to demonstrate whether x murdered y;
that is the function of a jury, which is charged solely to pass
upon a preselected question in the light of evidence presented
to it. It is another thing to understand why x may have
murdered y; that is the function of historians, whose explanation may take us far beyond the particulars of the case
into a study of the social and economic conditions that gave
rise to the particular killing. However skilled we may be in
handling evidence, our use of it is bound to reflect our values.
The historian who believes that he is a special sort of com-
puter that has the gift of producing "history" from data
automatically fed into it is out of touch with reality.

Many historians attach so much weight to satisfying the
demands of technical expertise that they confine the scope
of their work within narrow limits. In addition, they often
write in jargon that is readily intelligible only to a particular
intellectual clique. Such people fail to do much to prevent
false and bad myths from circulating and prevailing in the
public consciousness. As William McNeill puts it: "Historians' assaults on myth are themselves based on myth: the
faith that facts speak for themselves, that infinite detail

somehow organizes itself into meaningful patterns without the intervention of human intelligence, and that historical truth resides in faithful transcription of recorded words and deeds." McNeill goes further. He contends that, since "communities live by myths," historians have a duty to create and disseminate good myths:

> Indeed, the principal reason for studying the past is that it promotes the formulation and reformulation of useful myths about the conduct of public affairs, creates and confirms peoples' identities, and offers models of behavior for leaders and followers alike, to help to guide us through present complexities. . . . The American (and world) people badly need new visions, new generalizations, new myths, global in scope, to help us navigate in our tightly integrative world. If historians fail to advance suitably bold hypotheses and interpretations, then politicians, journalists, and other public figures will continue as now, to use unexamined clichés to simplify the choices that must be made.[40]

McNeill is justified in drawing attention to the lack of substantial communication in the West between historians and public figures. His advice is acceptable provided it is interpreted as meaning that, *in addition* to rigorous handling of evidence and scrupulous respect for scientific knowledge, historians should make their findings intelligible to nonspecialists and demonstrate with the utmost clarity how they relate to the contemporary needs and interests of mankind. Failure to do so has contributed to the lack of historical perspective among electorates, the rise of politicians who carry superficial and misleading images of the past, and the adoption of catastrophic policies, as by the French and British in their Suez enterprise of 1956 and by the Americans in Vietnam in the 1960s.

On the other hand, McNeill's advice is not acceptable if it is interpreted as meaning that historians should at all times be dealing with subjects of immediate and obvious concern to contemporary politicians, or propounding grand historical generalizations. Microscopic examination of a problem that seems to have little apparent relevance for today may prove to be invaluable to policy-makers tomorrow. This applies particularly to the work of foreign area specialists. What American politician cared about Islamic fundamentalism in Iran before the oil crisis of the 1970s? How many American politicians are informed about the racial problems of southern Africa today, though they may become a threat to international peace tomorrow? In the long run, moreover, Plato's prescription of a rigid class system is a warning that our judgments about social relations are influenced by the technological and cultural conditions of our time and may cease to be appropriate when those conditions have changed.

To sum up: Myths are an ineluctable part of human culture. Political mythologies—sets of political myths—legitimize or discredit political systems, especially state regimes in the contemporary world. They are extremely flexible. Classes which control social institutions may manipulate them and modify them to suit their changing interests. They wax and wane in intensity, and their content varies as a result of changes in the structure of local and global societies. They can accommodate a great deal of factual and scientific error; but myths that are peripheral to the ideology may disappear when dominant classes perceive that they ceased to serve their interests, whereas myths that are integral to the ideology are far more tenacious.

Historians have a responsibility to discredit false and noxious myths and, with rigorous regard for truth, to respond to the general public's doubts about the utility of their specialized skills and knowledge—doubts that were expressed most crudely by Henry Ford I in his well-known dictum that "history is bunk." Human society is never completely static: it is always in motion. One cannot understand the present without some awareness of the momentum that it carries with it from the past. Historians, as specialists in knowledge of the past, have an obligation to communicate their knowledge to other people as effectively as possible. If that means making myths—that is to say, describing exemplary events powerfully—then historians should indeed be mythmakers.

2

AFRIKANER
NATIONALIST MYTHOLOGY

1

Every political mythology bears the stamp of its context.[1] In South Africa, the mythology of the Afrikaner nationalist movement reflects the fact that the Afrikaner people have never amounted to a numerical majority of the population in any specific territory. At the time of a census that was taken in 1980, the total population of the Republic of South Africa, including the ten "Homelands," numbered nearly 29 million. According to the official racial classifications, 72.4 percent of the total were Black (i.e., indigenous Africans), 15.7 percent were White, 9.1 percent were "Coloured" (i.e., people of mixed descent), and 2.8 percent were Asian. Of the Whites, 56.9 percent spoke Afrikaans as their home language and 37.2 percent spoke English.[2]

The Afrikaners are descended from Dutch, German, French, and other north Europeans who settled at the Cape of Good Hope under the auspices of the great Dutch East India Company in the seventeenth and eighteenth centuries. They have experienced two challenges to their group and individual interests. One challenge came from the British government and British people. Great Britain wrested the Cape Colony from the Dutch at the beginning of the nineteenth century. For the next hundred years and more, the

Afrikaners remained an overwhelmingly rural people. In deed, they often referred to themselves as Boers, meaning farmers. Meanwhile, British, Jewish, and other new immigrants from Europe dominated the region's towns and villages—its trade, commerce, and professions. Such people also dominated the industrial and financial enterprises that began to transform the region after the discovery of diamonds in 1867 and gold in 1885. Although there were wealthy Afrikaners and poor British settlers, the ethnic division in the white population corresponded quite closely with occupational and class differences. Then, at the turn of the twentieth century the British government conquered the republics which Afrikaners had created in the interior and made a serious effort to denationalize the Afrikaners.

The second challenge came from the indigenous peoples. By the end of the nineteenth century, Afrikaners, British settlers, and British regular troops had conquered the local populations and deprived them of most of their land, and had begun to incorporate them as a working class in the capitalist economy. Africans resisted white domination from the very beginning; but their resistance was less formidable than the imperial challenge until deep into the twentieth century, because the successive Dutch and British colonial regimes could always be counted on to side with the Whites in the event of serious black resistance. The context was transformed after the Second World War. Great Britain ceased to be an imperial power; Afrikaner nationalists gained control of the South African state in a general election in 1948; and the African inhabitants, encouraged by the decolonization of the territories farther north, sought to obtain an effective say in the affairs of the country.

Consequently, there have been two main themes in the Afrikaner nationalist mythology. The first was mobilization, with a strong liberatory motif. In the late nineteenth century, clergy, politicians, and authors began to articulate the concept of an Afrikaner nation. Their purpose was to mobilize all the descendants of the Europeans who had settled in the Cape Colony during the Dutch period, whether they lived in British colonies (the Cape Colony and Natal) or Afrikaner Republics (the Transvaal and the Orange Free State), against British imperialism and its local potential allies, the white settlers of British origin. In addition to descent, the hallmarks of the nation were use of the Afrikaans language (which had become distinct from the Dutch of the Netherlands) and membership of a Dutch Reformed Church. Politicians and cultural leaders expanded this theme throughout the first half of the twentieth century, creating an effective mobilizing mythology.

The second theme was racism. Afrikaner nationalist my- 2) Racism
thology has always included a racist ingredient. Most Afrikaners have believed that human abilities are determined by race, that Europeans are a superior race, and that the different races are incompatible. However, before the second half of the twentieth century Afrikaner mythology was able to assume racism rather than to elaborate it, since similar racist views prevailed in Europe and America and among other white South Africans. Moreover, British imperialism seemed to constitute a greater threat to Afrikaner interests than black resistance. Afrikaner nationalists resented South African participation on the Allied side in the two world wars, which they regarded as imperialist wars of no concern to South Africa. After 1948, however, with the Afrikaner National Party in control of the government, Britain transferring political power to the inhabitants of her African colonies, and the Third World acquiring a strong voice in international organizations, the Afrikaner nationalist ideology concentrated on providing legitimacy for the racial policies of the government.

The mobilizing theme in the Afrikaner mythology is comparable with major themes in the mythologies of other for-

mer colonial peoples—Americans as well as Asians and
Africans. Great Britain figures as the oppressor of the Afrikaner nation and the British settlers as its Trojan horse. Stress
is placed on the events of the 1830s, when several thousand
Afrikaners left the Cape Colony to cast off British rule; and
those of the decade 1895–1905, when Joseph Chamberlain,
British colonial secretary, and Alfred Milner, high commissioner in South Africa, in collaboration with British and
Jewish mining capitalists, exploited the presence of the *Uit-
lander* (foreign) community on the Witwatersrand to pro-
voke a war of conquest. The spotlight lingers on the methods
used by the British army to overcome the resistance of the
Boer commandos, which included removing women and
children from their farms and placing them in camps where
more than twenty thousand died of dysentery and other
diseases, and on Milner's attempt to denationalize the Afrikaners by swamping them with British immigrants and
educating them into a British mold.

The racist theme in the Afrikaner mythology has been far
more tenacious than elsewhere, largely for reasons of political arithmetic. Most nationalist movements mobilize a people who are the numerical majority of the population in the
territory that they aspire to control, and their historic role
has been to weld their people together into a self-conscious
solidarity, to eliminate foreign rule, and, perhaps, to struggle
with their neighbors over the delimitation of boundaries.
When foreign rule has been eliminated, however, rival ethnic
communities often compete for control. There are two main
types of such situations. One is exemplified by Quebec,
where the rivals are the products of two successive migrations from Europe. The other exists in many countries in
tropical Africa, such as Nigeria, where two or more indigenous ethnic communities compete for power.

The Afrikaner nationalist movement is the product of a
unique environment. Like Quebec, South Africa contains

two distinct white communities; but it also contains an indigenous population of vastly superior numbers. To legitimate the policy of *apartheid* (separateness) or "separate development," the mythology presents the African inhabitants as a totally distinct subspecies of humanity. They are deemed to have arrived in South Africa no earlier than the first Dutch settlers and to have blindly resisted the spread of "civilization," which is regarded as an exclusively "White" and "Christian" achievement. Furthermore, to legitimate the policy of dividing them among ten different "homelands," they are deemed to comprise ten distinct "nations."

Like other mythologies, this one is dynamic: it changes with changing circumstances. Initially, it included a strong neo-Calvinist element. Afrikaners were a Chosen People with a God-given destiny. As formulated by J. C. van Rooy, chairman of the Afrikaner Broederbond, in 1944,

[handwritten margin note: Neo-Calvinism; Afrikaners, a chosen people.]

> In every People in the world is embodied a Divine Idea and the task of each People is to build upon that Idea and to perfect it. So God created the Afrikaner People with a unique language, a unique philosophy of life, and their own history and tradition in order that they might fulfill a particular calling and destiny here in the southern corner of Africa. We must stand guard on all that is peculiar to us and build upon it. We must believe that God has called us to be servants of his righteousness in this place. We must walk the way of obedience to faith.[3]

This neo-Calvinist element was crucial throughout the mobilizing phase of the mythology. It has declined, but by no means disappeared, during the second half of the century as Afrikaners have become an urban and a more secular people. Similarly, the liberatory thrust was extremely potent so long as British imperialism seemed to be a serious obstacle to

Afrikaner autonomy, but the racial element surpassed it as British imperialism waned and African resistance grew. This transition was completed after the Second World War, when the Afrikaner National Party gained control of the state machinery and eliminated the last vestiges of British legal authority over South Africa, only to find that the era of white hegemony was drawing to a close everywhere else in the world. Segregation was on the way out in America; colonization was ending in Asia and tropical Africa; and local Africans were mounting a serious challenge to the white regime and denying that it was legitimate.

II

The first attempt to formulate a distinctive Afrikaner historiography was made by residents of Paarl, a small town in the old colonial agricultural belt about thirty-five miles from Cape Town. Led by S. J. du Toit (1847–1911), a minister of the Dutch Reformed Church, they founded the Genootskap van Regte Afrikaners (Society of true Afrikaners) in 1875, launched a newspaper called *Die Patriot* in 1876, and published *Die Geskiedenis van ons Land in die Taal van ons Volk* (The history of our country in the language of our people) in 1877. Du Toit and his colleagues were reacting against cultural domination by the British colonial regime—the use of English as the only official language and the imperial bias of the school textbooks. They based their own history on publications by European authors who were critical of British imperialism and on private correspondence and interviews with fellow Afrikaners. Though this was simple, naive history, it was a pathbreaking achievement. It was the first book published in Afrikaans—the spoken language of the people—as distinct from Dutch, from which it had grown apart in the South African milieu by simplifying the syntax, changing the vowel sounds, losing vocabulary items that were not relevant, and incorporating loan words from the other languages that were spoken at the Cape in the eighteenth century—Malay, Portuguese creole, and Khoikhoi. It was the first book to treat all Afrikaners, dispersed as they were among British colonies and independent republics, as a single people. It was, too, the first book to set out the rudiments of a national mythology, with the overt purpose of encouraging Afrikaners to think of themselves as forming a distinct people with a common destiny and to resist the pressures for assimilation into British culture.[4]

The seeds planted by the Paarl authors did not bear much fruit so long as Afrikaners were divided between colonial and republican regimes. Most of them were more concerned with processes in their particular territories than with identifying with an ethnic community that transcended the political boundaries. In the Cape Colony the most effective Afrikaner politician, Jan Hofmeyr, sought to advance the material and cultural interests of his community by working for concessions within the colonial system, whereas the primary goal of the leadership of the Orange Free State and the Transvaal was to sustain the independence of their republics. Nevertheless, Paul Kruger, president of the South African Republic (the Transvaal) from 1881 until the British conquest in 1902, gave his immense prestige to a vital element in the embryonic Afrikaner mythology: the Calvinist concept of national calling and destiny.[5]

Kruger belonged to the smallest and most conservative of the Dutch Reformed churches in South Africa—the Gereformeerde Kerk van Suid-Afrika. Its members were known as Doppers, because, it is said, they believed in extinguishing the light of the Enlightenment, the Dutch word *domper* meaning an extinguisher. Their first ministers came from the Christelike Afgescheiden Gereformeerde Kerk in the Netherlands, which had seceded from the state church in 1834, rejecting its liberal theology and its evangelical emphasis on personal devotion and experience. The core of Dopper theology was the Calvinist conception of the sovereignty of God in every aspect of life and acceptance of the Bible as the only source of belief and practice. The Doppers exerted strict control over the moral behavior of their members; they wore distinctive old-fashioned clothes; they forbade the singing of hymns; and they held aloof from others, going so far as to censure church members who attended communion services of other Reformed denominations.[6] Kruger was a sincere Dopper believer. So sure was he that the earth was flat that when an American traveler was introduced to him as being on a voyage around the world, Kruger retorted, "You don't mean *round* the world . . . it is impossible! You mean *in* the world."[7] This formidable president laced his speeches with explicit comparisons between the history of the biblical Israelites and the history of the republican Afrikaners and with assertions that the People (*Volk*) are the elect of God with a God-given destiny, and that the voice of the People is the voice of God.[8]

By 1899 several authors had published historical works in the tradition initiated by S. J. du Toit, though most of them wrote in Dutch rather than Afrikaans. In *De Geschiedenis van het Afrikaansch Geslacht van 1688 tot 1882* (The history of the Afrikaner race from 1688 to 1882), C. P. Bezuidenhout declared that du Toit's was the only history of South Africa worth being read by an Afrikaner, and that he too was writing to rebut lies spread by English authors.[9] In 1882, F. Lion Cachet wrote a history of *De Worselstrijd der Transvalers* (The struggle of the Transvalers), extolling their victory in the recent war in which the Transvalers had regained their independence from Britain: "Ever since the Cape was taken over by England the Boers struggled with England, not for honor or gold, but for life, political life, to exist as an independent people."[10] Others followed in similar vein. J. F. van Oordt, C. N. J. du Plessis, and J. C. Voigt eulogized the achievements of the republican Afrikaners and denounced the British.[11] The polemics of Afrikaner anti-imperialism came to a head soon after the outbreak of the South African War in 1899, with the publication, in Dutch and English versions, of a brilliant tract, *A Century of Wrong*, which was written by Jacob Roos and Jan Smuts and issued by F. W. Reitz in the name of the South African republic. "Brother Afrikanders!" it read, " . . . the struggle of now nearly a century, which began when a foreign rule was forced upon the people of the Cape of Good Hope, hastens to an end." Then, after a bitter rehearsal of the behavior of perfidious Albion, it concluded: "Whether we conquer, whether we die, liberty will rise in South Africa like the sun rises from the morning clouds, and like it rose in the United States of America, and then it will be from the Zambesi to Simons Bay—'AFRICA FOR THE AFRIKANDER.' "[12]

In 1902, when the war ended, it seemed likely that Afrikaner nationalism was being crushed, once and for all. The republics were overthrown; their white people were impoverished. Afrikaners were divided among the Transvalers, Free Staters, and Cape colonials; and among the *bittereinders* (bitter-enders), who had fought to the end, *hensoppers* (hands-uppers), who had passively accepted British rule, and National Scouts, who had collaborated with the British. In fact, the opposite occurred. The very excesses of British imperialism evoked and enhanced a sense of national consciousness among a high proportion of the people of Afrikaner descent in all parts of the country. As one Afrikaner said in 1906: "Milner has made us a nation."[13]

The Afrikaner revival was initiated by *predikants* (clergy) of the three Dutch Reformed churches, the most powerful

[margin note: Role of the Church]

Afrikaner institutions that had survived the war. *Predikants* had ministered to the commandos during the war, and after the peace they used their immense prestige to resist anglicization by preserving Afrikaans culture and identity. In 1904, speaking at the funeral of ex-president Paul Kruger in Pretoria, the moderator of the Nederduits Gereformeerde Kerk in Suid-Afrika (the principal Dutch Reformed Church) said that "Paul Kruger was dead, but his people were not dead. Neither was his spirit dead, and they could go along the lines that he had laid down under the flag that now waved over them, and still be true to it, but they would always remain Afrikanders, God helping them."[14]

Predikants of the Gereformeerde Kerk were particularly prominent in the resistance to anglicization because the neo-Calvinist theology that they shared with the conservative, separatist church in the Netherlands encouraged isolation. Building on the traditional Calvinist doctrine of the sovereignty of God in every aspect of life, Abraham Kuyper (1837–1920), who eventually became prime minister of the Netherlands, distinguished different spheres of human activity and deemed each sphere to be autonomous under God. The state is one such sphere, and social spheres such as the family and other private associations are justified in opposing the encroachment of the state.[15] This doctrine was highly appropriate to the needs of people who wished to assert their national identity in the presence of a hostile state. (Later, in the transformed context of the second half of the twentieth century, it would be a serious embarrassment to an Afrikaner nationalist regime with totalitarian tendencies.)

Predikants of all three churches organized resistance to Milner's educational policy in the Transvaal and the Orange Free State, founding private schools for Christelijk-Nationaal Onderwijs (Christian National Education). These CNO schools emphasized the Calvinist tradition, promoted an Af-

[margin note: Christian National Education]

[handwritten note: Also promote Calvinist tradition, Afrikaner National consciousness, Dutch.]

rikaner national consciousness, and used Dutch as well as English as media of instruction.

In addition, the clergy and lay public resumed the attempt to create a literature in Afrikaans as distinct from Dutch. Their writings were passionately nationalist in tone and substance. As Jan Celliers put it in 1907: "But it is clear to every Afrikaner that only our own literature, steeped in the Afrikaner spirit and intelligible to Afrikaners, through and through in language and content, that only such a literature is really calculated to hit the mark here. Who wants to help us build up such a literature for our people? We have a people to serve, we have a nation to educate; we cannot wait!"[16]

Among the most influential of these Afrikaans poets was the Reverend J. D. du Toit (Totius) (1877–1953), the son of the Reverend S. J. du Toit.[17] A minister of the Gereformeerde Kerk, Totius studied at the Dutch center of conservative Calvinism, the Free University of Amsterdam, and in 1911 he became professor of theology at the Gereformeerde seminary in Potchefstroom. His poetry was written in simple, colorful Afrikaans; its themes were episodes in Afrikaner history such as the Great Trek and the wars against Africans and the British; and it made frequent use of Old Testament analogies. The underlying motif was that suffering and oppression purify a People, "led forward by God's plan."[18] For example, Totius's poem *Ragel* (Rachel, mother of Joseph) is a tribute to the sufferings of the Afrikaner women in the war. It concludes:

> Thus I think of
> the Rachels of my land,
> who without home or house
> were cruelly surprised—burnt
> out of their homes,
> pushed out into the veld.[19]

Willem Postma (1874–1920), Totius's brother-in-law, wrote Afrikaans prose works explicitly portraying Afrikaner history as the history of a Chosen People, denouncing the anglocentric teaching of history in the government schools and treating anglicized Afrikaners as traitors.[20]

The language struggle was fruitful. By 1908 there was a vigorous nationalist movement among the Afrikaner students at the embryonic University of Stellenbosch, where D. F. Malan, who would become the principal architect of the political victory of the National Party in 1948, encouraged them to "raise the Afrikaans language to a written language, make it the bearer of our culture, our history, our national ideals, and you will raise the People to a feeling of self-respect and to the calling to take a worthier place in world civilization."[21] In the same year, Afrikaner members of the National Convention that created the constitution for the Union of South Africa ensured that Dutch should be an official language of the Union, equal to English; and in 1925 the constitution was amended so that Afrikaans supplanted Dutch.

Two authors were preeminent in the molding of Afrikaner mythology in the first half of the twentieth century: Gustav S. Preller (1875–1943) and C. J. Langenhoven (1873–1932). Preller, a Transvaler, was captured by the British in 1902 and sent to India as a war prisoner. Returning to Pretoria, he became a journalist and a prolific writer on historical themes, using primary sources to create subjective, sentimental portrayals of Afrikaner historical personages as heroic figures. He was largely responsible for making the Great Trek the centerpiece of Afrikaans historiography, with biographies entitled *Piet Retief* (1906) and *Andries Pretorius* (1937) and six volumes of *voortrekker* documents (1918–38).[22] Whereas Preller wrote mainly in Dutch, his contemporary Langenhoven wrote in Afrikaans from an early stage in his career.

Langenhoven lived at Oudtshoorn in the eastern Cape province, where he produced a stream of prose and poetry, much of it extremely sentimental in tone, that made him the most popular Afrikaans writer of his generation. His works included a volume of historical verse, *Eerste Skoffies op die pad van Suid-Afrika* (First stages on the path of South Africa) (1921), which dealt with nineteenth-century episodes such as the Slagtersnek rebellion of Afrikaner fronticrsmen in 1815 and the Great Trek, when several thousand Afrikaners left the Cape Colony to become independent from Britain.[23]

Afrikaner resentment toward the symbols of British imperialism led to a series of disputes among white South Africans during the 1920s and 1930s, when J. B. M. Hertzog was prime minister.[24] In 1910, *God Save the King* automatically became the official anthem by virtue of South Africa's membership in the British Empire, much to the discomfiture of many Afrikaners. Eight years later, Langenhoven published a sentimental poem that rapidly became popular as *Die Stem van Suid Afrika* (The voice of South Africa), especially after it was set to music in 1921. During the 1930s, the South African Broadcasting Corporation began to use it in addition to *God Save the King;* and in 1938 the government had it played at the opening of parliament, as well as the official anthem. *Die Stem van Suid Afrika* resonates with a white and specifically Afrikaner mythology, as is shown by the reference to wagons in the first verse, which reads, in English translation:

> Ringing out from our blue heavens, from our deep
> seas breaking round;
> Over everlasting mountains where the echoing
> crags resound;
> From our plains where creaking wagons cut their
> trails into the earth—

Calls the spirit of our Country, of the land that
   gave us birth.
At thy call we shall not falter, firm and steadfast
   we shall stand,
At thy will to live or perish, O South Africa dear
   land.[25]

There was a particularly bitter dispute over a national flag.
When the Union of South Africa was founded in 1910, its
national flag was the British Red Ensign, with the insertion
of the Union Coat of Arms in a lower corner. In 1926 the
Hertzog government pressed ahead with its decision to create
a new flag for South Africa. The battle was joined on ethnic
lines. Many Afrikaners were deeply attached to the old republican flags—the Transvaal *vierkleur* (flag of four colors)
and the Free State orange and white—while many British
South Africans became choleric at the thought of losing British symbols. After a year of intensely emotional conflict,
parliament approved a national flag consisting of three hor-
izontal sections of orange, white, and blue (the Netherlands
driekleur of 1572–1650), with three small insertions in the
middle (the *vierkleur*, the Free State flag, and the Union
Jack); and parliament also decreed that the full Union Jack
was to be flown alongside the new flag on official buildings
and at special occasions.[26]

Throughout the 1930s, under the spell of people such as
Langenhoven and Preller, British imperialism was still the
great historic enemy, despite the fact that the Statute of West-
minster (1931) and the Status of the Union Act (1934) made
South Africa a sovereign state and vested full powers in its
parliament and cabinet. The imperial factor received a final
fillip in the Second World War. Although Jan Smuts brought
the country into the war by a majority vote in the South
African parliament in September 1939 and won a decisive

victory for his war policy in a general election in 1943, many Afrikaners considered that South Africa had no real interest in siding with Britain—some, indeed, hoped for a German victory—and regarded Smuts and his associates as imperial lackeys—traitors to the *volk*.

The most dramatic event in the upsurge of Afrikaner nationalism was the symbolic ox-wagon trek of 1938, which celebrated the centenary of the Great Trek.[27] Eight wagons, named after *voortrekker* heroes such as Piet Retief, Hendrik Potgieter, and Andries Pretorius, traversed South Africa by different routes, to be welcomed by enthusiasts in practically every white town and village in the country, before they converged on a prominent hill overlooking Pretoria. There, on 16 December 1938, the centenary of the Battle of Blood River, which marked the defeat of the Zulu Kingdom, more than 100,000 Afrikaners—perhaps one-tenth of the total Afrikaner people—attended the ceremonial laying of the foundation stone of the Voortrekker Monument. Men grew beards, women wore *voortrekker* dress, for the occasion. Their intense fervor was captured by a journalist: As wagons passed through Johannesburg, "men and women gazed at the cumbersome vehicles that had cradled a nation, and were silent with adoration. . . . The Afrikaners on the Rand had made a pilgrimage to a new symbol of nationhood." In Pretoria, when torches brought by relays of boys from Cape Town and the site of Dingane's headquarters arrived, "women rushed forward and burned the corners of their handkerchiefs and *kappies* [bonnets] in the flame of the two torches, to keep as mementos of the great event." And on the hill above, "women knelt in silent prayer in the darkness round the bare foundations of the Voortrekker Monument."[28] The ceremony concluded with the singing of *Die Stem van Suid Afrika; God Save the King* had been excluded. The magazine *Die Huisgenoot* published a special number for

[margin note: Importance of ritual intensification in defining identity.]

the occasion, including a message from Daniel François Malan, leader of the "Purified" National Party:

> Genuine religion, unadulterated freedom, and the pure preservation of one's white race and civilization are essential requirements for our own People's existence. Without this the South African people can have no soul and also no future.

[margin note: Great Trek gave our people their nationhood.]

> If that is true, then the Great Trek was the most important, most decisive, and all-overshadowing event in our People's history. The Great Trek gave our People its soul. It was the cradle of our nationhood. It will always show us the beacons on our path and serve as our lighthouse in our night.[29]

III

[margin note: National symbols are "nationalized" National deep.]

After 1948, the anti-imperial and ethnic elements in the Afrikaner nationalist mythology became far less relevant than the racial element. Great Britain ceased to be a major power and British symbols were removed from South Africa. Images of South Africans succeeded those of British sovereigns on stamps, coins, and paper money. Honors such as the Cape of Good Hope Decoration and the Order of the Star of South Africa replaced British awards such as the Victoria Cross and the Distinguished Service Order. Settlers' Day, Kruger Day, and the Day of the Covenant took the place of Empire Day and the Queen's Birthday. *Die Stem* became the national anthem. The national flag created in the 1920s became the only official flag. To crown it all, in 1961 South Africa became a republic and left the British Commonwealth.[30] Furthermore, the National Party won election after election. Its old rival, the United Party, collapsed in 1977 and by the 1980s considerable numbers of English-speaking voters were voting Nationalist.[31]

Race had always been a vital factor in the Afrikaner mythology. However, until the Second World War it took second place to the imperial element and was partially subsumed by it. Nearly all white South Africans, English-speakers as well as Afrikaners, assumed that any sensible, civilized person knew that Africans were a culturally inferior race and should be treated accordingly—an assumption that corresponded with the global distribution of power and wealth and was still endorsed by reputable Western scientists. Among the white South African electorate there was virtually no demand for the removal of the ubiquitous color bars, for example, for the admission of Africans, or Coloured people, or Asians to parliament. Disputes over racial policy were frequent; but they took place within a much narrower framework, and the movement was toward greater, not less, discriminatory legislation. There was, for example, a prolonged dispute over the question whether the few thousand enfranchised Africans who met the qualifications for the franchise in the Cape Province—a legacy from the colonial period—should be allowed to continue to vote for white candidates in their general electoral districts, or whether they should be removed from the common voters' rolls and, regardless of their numbers, entitled to elect only three white people to represent them in the House of Assembly. The outcome of the dispute was that the change did eventually take place, in 1936. Moreover, before the Second World War opposition to the South African racial order was generally disunited and nonviolent, and the government was able to suppress, often quite brutally, any black activities that looked as if they would threaten white hegemony.[32]

In these circumstances, the racial element formed a pervasive background to the Afrikaner mythology. It stressed

Racial element - pervasive background to the Afrikaner mythology.

the courage of the *voortrekkers* in their conflicts with Africans
and ridiculed the British missionaries and the occasional
British officials who had criticized the racial structure of
South African society and sought to introduce major reforms.
John Philip, superintendent of the London Missionary Society in South Africa from 1819 to 1851, who had cam-
paigned with some success for the repeal of laws that bound
the Khoikhoi ("Hottentots") in the Cape Colony to their
white masters in a serf-like status, and for the moderation
of the colonial government's warlike policy toward the Africans in the eastern frontier zone of the colony, was singled
out for disparagement as a naive and prejudiced meddler
in affairs he did not understand.[33] This was a typical link
between the imperial element and the racial element in the
mythology.

The racial element became more autonomous during the
period 1934–48, when D. F. Malan's second and more radical Afrikaner Nationalist Party was in opposition to the
United Party administrations of J. B. M. Hertzog and J. C.
Smuts.[34] This was a period of great industrial growth in
South Africa. Africans were flocking from their reserves—
scattered, impoverished territories where most of them could
not produce a subsistence—to the towns, where wage labor
was available in the burgeoning manufacturing industries as
well as the gold mines. Despite the existence of stringent
pass laws, the government was unable to control this movement and white people became fearful of its consequences.

In the same period, there was an infusion of radical nationalist ideas from Germany. Several talented young Afrikaner intellectuals returned home with doctoral degrees
from German universities. Attracted by the cruder elements
in German national socialism, they laid special stress on the
supremacy of the nation over the individual. During the early
stages of the Second World War, when the Third Reich

seemed poised for victory, they published numerous articles, pamphlets, and books, some for academic audiences, others for popular consumption. Nicholaas Diederichs, who was destined to become minister of finance and then president of the Republic of South Africa, wrote a treatise on nationalism as a world view, attacking individualism and liberal democracy and exalting the nation: "Nationalism rejects this concept of freedom . . . on the grounds of its doctrine that the individual in itself is nothing, but only becomes itself in the nation as the highest community."[35] Piet J. Meyer, later to become head of the Broederbond and chairman of the South African Broadcasting Corporation, informed a meeting of enthusiastic students: "The Afrikaner accepts his national task as a divine task, in which his individual life-task, and his personal service to God has been absorbed in a wider, organic context."[36] J. Albert Coetzee started a pamphlet with the statement: "The history of South Africa is really the history of the origin of a new nation—of how, from different European nations, groups, and individuals it was separated, cut off, differentiated and specialized to form a new *volksgroep*, with its own calling and destiny, with its own tradition, with its own soul and with its own body."[37]

Crude racism also emerged in the lexicon, as in a pamphlet by G. Eloff on *Rasse en Rasvermenging* (Races and race mixing), where distinct white, black, and yellow races are described, each with specific spiritual as well as biological characteristics, and which declares: "The preservation of the pure race tradition of the *Boerevolk* must be protected at all costs in all possible ways as a holy pledge entrusted to us by our ancestors as part of God's plan with our People. Any movement, school, or individual who sins against this must be dealt with as a racial criminal by the effective authorities."[38] This line of thought led a sociologist, G. Cronjé, to elaborate a policy of *apartheid* (literally, separateness) or complete separation of the races in *'n Tuiste vir die Nageslag: Die Blywende Oplossing van Suid-Afrika se Rassevraagstukke* (A home for posterity: The permanent solution of South Africa's racial questions). "The more consistently the policy of apartheid could be applied, the greater would be the security for the purity of our blood and the surer our unadulterated European racial survival . . . total racial separation . . . is the most consistent application of the Afrikaner idea of racial apartheid."[39] Here was a dramatic intensification of the racial element that had always been part of the Afrikaner world view. A mythology that had been originally articulated for the purpose of resisting British imperialism and checking the trend toward anglicization had developed into a mythology for the reversal of the most dynamic forces in modern South African history—forces that were creating an industrial society out of people of diverse backgrounds and traditions.

These ideas were prominent in the minds of leaders of the National Party that came into power in 1948. The man most responsible for putting them into practice was Hendrik Frensch Verwoerd, who had studied in German universities in the 1920s. As minister of native affairs from 1950 to 1958 and prime minister from 1958 until his death in 1966, Verwoerd led South Africa out of the Commonwealth and wrote apartheid, or "separate development" as he preferred to call it, into the statute book. In his election statement in 1961, he denounced the proposition that South Africa should be treated as a "multi-racial nation with one multi-racial Parliament." "True unity in a racial group can only develop amongst its own people, separated from the others. The only national unity for the whites is unity amongst the whites."[40] Just as the Whites had the right to national existence and self-fulfillment, so had the several black communities, and more particularly the "Bantu" communities, which were embryonic nations:

We do not only seek and fight for a solution which will mean our survival as a white race, but we also seek a solution which will ensure survival and full development—political and economic—to each of the other racial groups, and we are even prepared to pay a high price out of our earnings to ensure their future. . . . We want each of our population groups to control and to govern themselves, as is the case with other Nations. Then they can cooperate as in a Commonwealth—in an economic association with the Republic and with each other. In the transition stage the guardian must teach and guide his ward. This is our policy of separate development. South Africa will proceed in all honesty and fairness to secure peace, prosperity and justice for all, by means of political independence coupled with economic interdependence.[41]

Successive South African administrations proceeded to give effect to this grand racial design. However, the results were anything but peace, prosperity, and justice for the vast majority of the population. Going far beyond previous laws and practices, the government made racial segregation and discrimination pervasive and unescapable; it suppressed dissent with the utmost rigor; and it ensured that most Africans would live in squalid poverty by limiting their rights to land ownership and citizenship to the former reserves, which, in Orwellian style, it redesignated as "Homelands." In those scattered and impoverished territories, African communities could survive only by sending their healthy adults out to earn wages as laborers in the "white areas"; but the government tried to ensure that no more Africans should exist in the white areas than those whom white employers needed to work in their homes, on their farms, and in their industries. In these circumstances, the Afrikaner nationalist mythology deemphasized the old anti-imperial and ethnic elements and concentrated on providing legitimation for the racial policies of the government. This was a difficult task. Inside and outside South Africa, *apartheid* became a byword for racial oppression.

IV

The Afrikaner nationalist mythology has been propagated through an elaborate network of religious, educational, and communications institutions. Not only has it dominated the historical consciousness of most Afrikaners, but it has also been imposed on the minds of other sections of the South African population, especially since the National Party won control of the state machinery in 1948.

A remarkable organization—the Afrikaner Broeder-bond—has been largely responsible for this achievement.[42] Founded by a tiny group of zealots in 1918, the Broederbond became a secret society in 1921 and gradually built up an extensive cell organization throughout southern Africa. By 1977 there were 810 cells with twelve thousand members. Afrikaners are recruited who "are wholly devoted to the service of the Afrikaner nation" and who may be relied on to "cling to the Christian national viewpoint of the Afrikaner."[43] One of its goals has been to dominate every aspect of South African society. As Hendrik Frensch Verwoerd, later prime minister, put it in 1943: "The *Afrikaner Broederbond* must gain control of everything it can lay its hands on in every walk of life in South Africa. Members must help each other to gain promotion in the Civil Service or any other field of activity in which they work with a view to working themselves up into important administrative positions."[44] In this, the Broederbond has been remarkably successful. Since 1948, all South African prime ministers and nearly all cabinet ministers have been Broeders; so have nearly all the heads of the Afrikaans universities and churches, and of the great state corporations (including ISCOR [the South African Iron and Steel Corporation], SABC [the South African Broadcasting Corporation], SASOL [the South African Coal, Oil, and Gas Corporation], and ARMSCOR [the Armaments Corporation of South Africa]). Two-way flows of information within the Broederbond have enabled its executive council to find out what the cells are thinking on relevant issues and to transmit to them its recommendations, which then bear fruit in the actions of influential Afrikaners in all walks of life—national and local politicians and administrators, police and military officers, editors and journalists, clergy and businesspeople, professors and schoolmasters.

After the Nationalists came into power, the Broederbond was able to exert a profound influence over public opinion through the South African Broadcasting Corporation, which has a monopoly of radio and television services throughout the country. The SABC is a public corporation and the government appoints all the members of its board. Founded in 1936, it was used by the Smuts government to support South Africa's participation in the Second World War on the Allied side. After 1948 it became an instrument of the National Party, largely under Broederbond direction. The radio news broadcasts give great prominence to announcements and explanations of government policies by cabinet ministers, and political commentaries are invariably slanted in the official direction. Elements of nationalist mythology are often emphasized, especially on national holidays, and never challenged. In the Afrikaans and English programs, very little time is given to the views of opposition political parties, and virtually none at all to the views of black South Africans, except to collaborators such as the Matanzima brothers, who rule the "independent" Transkei under South African patronage and protection. Since 1952 the SABC has also broadcast programs in the principal African languages of the region—including Sesotho, Zulu, and Xhosa.[45]

Despite the country's advanced technology, the government was for many years wary of television, lest it should result in the use of imported programs that would promote anglicization and undermine the established racial norms. However, after careful preparation, the SABC introduced television to South Africa in 1976. Its news services and commentaries, like those on the radio, are thinly disguised government propaganda. Although the SABC is obliged to use a great deal of foreign entertainment material, it avoids featuring black and white people in egalitarian social situations—especially anything that hints at interracial sex, though an exception was made for the BBC production of *Othello*, with Laurence Olivier playing the part of the Moor.[46]

Besides being continually exposed to nationalist propaganda on radio and television, many Afrikaners limit their reading to Afrikaans newspapers, all of which are closely identified with the government, notably *Rapport*, a Johannesburg weekly, and dailies such as *Die Burger* (Cape Town), *Die Transvaler*, *Die Vaderland*, and *Beeld* (Johannesburg), and *Die Volksblad* (Bloemfontein). The Afrikaans press conducts vigorous debates among Afrikaners about Afrikaner politics, but it pays little attention to the interests and achievements, the problems and opinions, of other white people, and scarcely any attention to noncollaborating black South Africans.[47]

Most of the English newspapers support opposition political parties. They often criticize the government's most blatant excesses; the *Rand Daily Mail* has been especially critical. Nevertheless, they are loath to confront the racist core of the nationalist mythology; partly because most of their readers are themselves caught in the web of racism, but also because the government has created a spate of legal restrictions on the press, it has detained numerous journalists, and it has appointed commissions to devise further constraints. The government has been especially severe on African journalists and independent publications for Africans. In 1977 it banned the *World*, Johannesburg's main newspaper for Africans, and detained its editor, Percy Qoboza. By the 1980s no newspapers in the country were owned by Blacks, and the press that catered to the growing black readership had become quite bland, concentrating on reporting black social and athletic activities rather than stories illustrating the tragedy of being black in South Africa. Furthermore, the government's Department of Information issues numerous publications aimed at specific races and classes at home and abroad, where the fundamental tenets of the political mythology are reiterated.[48]

The Broederbond has always given the highest priority to educational issues. Initially, its principal aim was to thwart British cultural imperialism by ensuring that the Afrikaans language received equal treatment with English in the public schools and the civil service, and then by placing Afrikaner children in exclusively Afrikaans schools, where, insulated from contamination, they would develop a strong sense of Afrikaner identity. As expressed by a *predikant* in 1943, "God has willed it that there shall be separate nations each with its own language, and . . . mother-tongue education is accordingly the will of God. The parent should accordingly have no choice in this case."[49] Much attention was also devoted to creating among Afrikaner teachers a nationalist spirit that they in turn would inculcate in the children. In 1943 a school inspector told a Broederbond-inspired congress:

The Afrikaner teachers will then demonstrate to Afrikanerdom what a power they possess in their teachers' organisations for building up the youth for the future republic. I know of no more powerful instrument. They handle the children for five or more hours daily, for five days each week, while at hostels and boarding schools the contact is continuous for longer periods. A nation is made through its youth being taught and influenced at school in the tradition, customs, habits and ultimate destination of its *volk*.[50]

Step by step, these goals have been attained. In 1925 a constitutional amendment made the Afrikaans language, rather than European Dutch, one of the two official languages of the country. There followed an intense struggle for control of the education of white children between those who favored mixing them in dual or parallel medium schools and those who wished to separate them in unilingual institutions.[51] The latter view was summed up in a document produced in 1948. White children were to be compulsorily divided into two sets of schools, English-medium and Afrikaans-medium; and in the Afrikaans schools a "Christian-National" philosophy was to prevail. They were to be "imbued with the Christian-National spiritual and cultural material of our nation. . . . We wish to have no mixing of language, no mixing of cultures, no mixing of religions and no mixing of races." History was to be taught as a revelation of the purposes of God, who has "willed separate nations and people."[52]

Before the National Party came to power in 1948 the outcome of this struggle was inconclusive and, because white education was a provincial matter under the South African constitution, it differed from province to province. After 1948, parliament legislated the nationalist program. One law gave the central executive wide powers over the provincial educational authorities and created a National Education Advisory Council, whose members were nominated by the government. Another law empowered the minister of education, after consultation with the council and the administrators of the provinces (who are also government nominees), to "determine the general policy which is to be pursued in respect of education in schools . . . within the framework of specified principles." Education was to have "a Christian character" and "a broad national character," and the mother tongue, English or Afrikaans, was to be the medium of instruction. A ministerial proclamation provided that in doubtful cases the final decision as to which of the two languages was to be the medium of instruction lay with the inspector of education, not the parent.[53] The result was that all white children became corralled into ethnic institutions throughout their entire school career, with the sole exception of the few whose parents placed them in private schools—and even that was made unlawful in the Transvaal.[54]

In their ethnic schools, Afrikaner children are subjected to powerful indoctrination. The bureaucrats who man the national education department and the provincial education departments in the Transvaal, the Orange Free State, and the Cape are loyal government appointees, as are the vast majority of the school inspectors and Afrikaner teachers. The teachers owe their appointments to local school committees elected by the parents. Predikants, most of whom are ultra-conservative nationalists, dominate the rural committees and continue to exert considerable influence in the urban committees, so that Afrikaners who fail to conform to Christian-National norms are excluded. The Afrikaner teachers are organized in unilingual professional associations which are among the most reactionary forces in South African society.

Besides dividing white children into two sets of schools and propagating a narrow nationalist spirit in the Afrikaans schools, the government transformed the system of school education for the African, Coloured, and Asian people.[55] Until 1948 only a small proportion of the black population of South Africa received any schooling at all, and most of the education that was available to them was provided by mission institutions, which received small amounts of state aid.[56] From the Afrikaner nationalist point of view the system was dangerous because most mission schools were run by non-Afrikaners whose norms were inappropriate. As Verwoerd put it: "Good racial relations are spoilt when the correct education is not given. Above all, good racial relations cannot exist when the education is given under the control of people who create wrong expectations on the part of the Native himself. . . . It is therefore necessary that Native education should be controlled in such a way that it should be in accord with the policy of the State."[57]

Accordingly, in 1953 Parliament passed a Bantu Education Act, which was followed by similar legislation for Coloured and Indian education. These laws withdrew state subsidies from the mission schools and made it unlawful for anyone to conduct a school without a license. As a result, nearly all the mission schools closed or were taken over by the central government, which acquired control of the entire educational system for black South Africans. By the 1980s most blacks as well as white children were receiving some schooling, but whereas more than one-third of the white pupils were in postprimary classes (standards 6 to 10), only about one-sixth of the black children were above the primary level. The facilities for black and white pupils were not only separate but grossly unequal. Black school buildings and equipment, black teachers' qualifications and salaries, and black teacher:pupil ratios were all greatly inferior to those for whites. This was largely a result of differential subsidies. In 1979 the government spent R724 per white pupil, R357 per Indian pupil, R225 per Coloured pupil, and only R71 per African pupil—a differential of ten to one between Whites and Africans.[58] The quality of black education was also affected by the high level of unemployment among black South Africans and the government's capacity to have "disloyal" teachers dismissed. The system promoted rote learning from prescribed textbooks within the framework of prescribed syllabuses, in preparation for official examinations.

South African school syllabuses and examinations have been standardized within narrow limits ever since 1918 by the statutory Joint Matriculation Board, composed of representatives of the four provincial educational departments, the universities, and the teaching profession. The board controls university entrance examinations and exerts a great influence over school syllabuses at all levels. From the beginning, history had a prominent place in the curricula and was an examination subject for most matriculants. The history syllabuses concentrated on the history of Europe and the history of white people in South Africa. During the Afrikaner nationalist regime, history, geography, and "civics" were conflated into a subject called social studies in the elementary and primary levels through standard 4 (equivalent to the American grade 6) in white schools and through standard 7 in black schools, and the history syllabuses for the higher standards were modified to give more time to South African history than to the history of the rest of the world. All syllabuses contain a common core drawn up by a national committee, to which the provincial education departments may add up to 30 percent to take account of local circumstances.[59]

Schools select their textbooks from a short list—usually numbering no more than three books per course—that has been approved by their provincial education department. Most textbook authors are people with experience as teachers or school inspectors. This work is profitable for authors and publishers, especially since successful texts are published in both official languages. Two large groups—Nasionale Pers, publisher of *Die Burger* and *Beeld,* and Perskor, publisher of *Die Transvaler* and *Die Vaderland*—produce most textbooks that originate in Afrikaans. Independent firms, notably Maskew Miller and Juta of Cape Town, publish most of those that originate in English.

More than half the white South African schoolchildren, and more than half the African schoolchildren outside the "homelands," are in the Transvaal. Consequently the decisions of the Transvaal education department have the greatest effect. In 1958, that department circulated a list of "aims" with the history syllabus for standards 6 to 8 (American grades 8 to 10). It began as follows:

> In the teaching of history one seeks to attain several objectives. There is the knowledge which is imparted of one's own and of others, knowledge which leads to a better understanding and which enriches man spiritually with matters which few other subjects can offer him. Therefore, in the study of this subject one notices how God leads a nation to pious deeds, how character formation takes place and how a Divine plan with a nation is carried out. This is a religious aim. But as the historical heritage is a spectacle of courage, sacrifice and loyalty but also of cowardice, disloyalty, treachery and selfishness, it also remains of value for the ethical forming of man. For the shaping of nationalism in contrast with chauvinism, and as a result of this the bringing about of a genuine social attitude, this subject is of incalculable value.[60]

V

The ultimate source for much of the structure and content of these textbooks may be traced back to one of the most productive historians of all time—George McCall Theal (1837–1919).[61] A Canadian by birth, Theal migrated to South Africa at the age of nineteen. In the Eastern Cape Colony and Kimberley, he tried his hand as a teacher, a bookkeeper, an editor, a journalist, a diamond digger, and a "native administrator" before becoming a clerk in the Native Affairs Department of the colony. In that appointment he was allowed to follow his natural bent, and between 1896 and 1905 he scoured the archives for South African materials in London, Paris, and Rome. Although he had no formal historical training, his output included three volumes of *Basutoland Records* (1883), thirty-six volumes of *Records of the Cape Colony* from 1793 to 1831 (1897–1905), and nine volumes of *Records of South Eastern Africa* translated from the Portuguese (1893–1903). He also wrote numerous historical syntheses, including what eventually became an eleven–volume *History of South Africa*. These syntheses, which were completely devoid of footnotes identifying his sources, were chronicles—summaries of official records, illuminated by his own experience and his knowledge of the Dutch, Xhosa, and Portuguese languages and interpreted through his world view as a member of the dominant white minority in a racially stratified society. He believed implicitly in the purity of his motives and the definitiveness of his judgments, claiming in a 1915 preface: "To the utmost of human ability I have striven to write without fear, favour, or prejudice, to do equal justice to all with whom I had to deal. I can, therefore, without laying myself open to the accusation of vanity, place my work confidently before the public as not alone the only detailed history of South Africa yet prepared, but as a true and absolutely unbiassed narrative."[62]

The virtue in Theal's perspective is that he did not succumb to the jingoism that was rampant in the late Victorian age. In large measure he succeeded in steering a judicious course between British imperialism and Afrikaner parochialism. In this respect, his work was a healthy antidote to the imperialist excesses that pervaded the textbooks that had previously been used in the Cape Colony and Natal and those that poured forth from British presses before, during, and after the South African war of 1899–1902. However, Theal's reconciliation of Boer and British historical experiences was achieved at a cost. Although he had lived among Xhosa people, spoke their language, and took an interest in recording their traditions, he identified fully and exclusively with white South Africans, interpreting the racial conflicts of the eighteenth and nineteenth centuries as clashes between civilization and barbarism. Moreover, the fact that nearly all his sources were official colonial records or other documents written by white people strengthened his natural tendency to see the world through white eyes. In all this, he was a creature of his upbringing, his culture, and his age. Theal was a settler historian par excellence. Consider, for example, his explanation for the decision of the Dutch authorities in 1708 to stop owners from manumitting their slaves unless they gave security that they would not become a charge on the poor fund for at least ten years:

> As time wore on, it became apparent that in most instances emancipation meant the conversion of a useful individual into an indolent pauper and a pest to society. Habits of industry, which in Europeans are the result of pressure of circumstances operating upon the race through hundreds of generations, were found to be opposed to the disposition of Africans. Experience showed that a freed slave usually chose to live in a filthy hovel upon coarse and scanty food rather than toil for something better. Decent clothing was not a necessity of life to him, neither did he need other furniture in his hovel

than a few cooking utensils. He put nothing by, and when sickness came he was a burden upon the public. Such in general was the negro when left to himself in a country where sufficient food to keep life in his body was to be had without much exertion.[63]

Subsequent historians of South Africa, including textbook writers, have drawn heavily on Theal's prodigious output. Indeed, he set the tone for a mainstream white South African historiography, devoid of the extreme aberrations of Afrikaner nationalism as well as those of British imperialism, that endures to the present day. It was not until after the First World War that trained historians such as William Miller Macmillan (1885–1974), Cornelis de Kiewiet (1903–), and Johannes Stephanus Marais (1898–1969) began to examine Theal's treatment of specific episodes and to question his perspectives, and found him wanting in both respects. Marais, for example, found that on crucial issues Theal got his facts wrong, with the effect invariably of tilting the balance in favor of the Whites against the Blacks.[64] Nevertheless, there is always a time lag between the publication of the results of research and their incorporation in school textbooks; the time lag is extended when, as in this case, the findings run counter to the perceived interests of dominant social classes.

The Theal tradition pervaded a series of matriculation textbooks that were written by C. de K. Fowler and G. J. J. Smit, history teachers in the high schools in the Cape peninsula. This series dominated the market in the Cape Province from 1931 to 1975, when approximately fifteen thousand copies were printed each year, about half in English and half in Afrikaans.[65] Comparison of four of these texts, published in 1932, 1945, 1956, and 1969, shows a considerable continuity; most of the substantial changes that were made re-

sulted from alterations in the syllabus (e.g., advancing the
terminal date) rather than the incorporation of information
that shed light on the experiences of black people. Like Theal,
Fowler and Smit wrote from a settler perspective. Typically,
the first South African chapter in the 1932 text, entitled
"Social and Economic Conditions at the Cape (1771–
1795)," started with thirteen pages devoted exclusively to
the white population, before giving three pages to the slaves
(who outnumbered the whites), six lines to the free Blacks,
and just over one page to the "Hottentots" (Khoikhoi) and
"Bushmen" (San)—the indigenous inhabitants of the Cape
Colony as then constituted. The passage on the slaves resembled Theal's treatment of the subject and contained this
unproven—and, as we now know—false assertion: "The
slaves at the Cape were much better treated than in any
other slave-owning country in the world."[66] In the 1969
version, the first South African chapter complied with the
syllabus by dealing with "the settlement of the Cape Colony
by the Dutch" and achieved the feat of completely ignoring
the presence of slaves. Also, like the 1932 text, it only mentioned the indigenous peoples as obstacles to white
interests.[67]

As Afrikaner nationalists gained control of the political
machinery, they used it to intensify the ethnic as well as the
racial bias in education. In 1965 F. E. Auerbach published
a study of the textbooks that were being used in Transvaal
high schools. He found much evidence of the impact of Christian National ideology, especially, but not exclusively, in the
books used in Afrikaans schools. A standard 7 (grade 9) text
described the Cape Colony law of 1828 that removed the
legal restrictions on the movements of "Hottentots" as "the
notorious Fiftieth Ordinance" and linked it with the modern
Afrikaner nationalist denunciation of liberalism: "In this law
we can see liberalism for it was designed to improve the lot

of the coloured British subjects in South Africa." The law caused "great dissatisfaction among the Boer population because of this equalisation [*gelykstelling*]."[68] Scrutinizing the ways in which the textbooks dealt with the history of early contacts between Whites and Africans on the eastern frontier of the Cape Colony, Auerbach noted an element of negro- *Nothing* phobia in nearly all of them. Several used emotive words in *unusual* describing Africans—"wily and cunning Xhosa," "openly *about this* hostile natives," a "warlike race" with "covetous eyes" who "robbed" and "murdered."[69] He also demonstrated that nearly all the textbooks "perpetuate errors which historians have corrected by diligent research twenty and more years ago," so that children were induced to regard the Xhosa people "as thieves and possibly murderers," and the white farmers who were intruding into their territory as blameless.[70] The ethnic element was particularly pronounced in the texts that were available only in Afrikaans. One such standard 6 text declared that "the Lord planted a new nation at the Southern tip of Africa."[71] Auerbach also examined the books that were being used for the Race Studies syllabus and found that they presented "Bushmen," "Hottentots," and "Bantu" as essentially tribal people, so that "pupils can be expected to gain the impression that the Africans' . . . way of life is inherently and permanently of a primitive tribal nature . . . and that, where that way of life has changed, this is represented as a danger to White South Africans."[72] Moreover, the standard 8 guidance textbook included a section on "The Sin of Blood Mixture."[73]

In conclusion, Auerbach showed how prominent officials had endorsed the use of schools for indoctrination in negrophobia and illiberalism. F. H. Odendaal, administrator of the Transvaal Province, had told a meeting of school principals and vice-principals that "we must strive to win the struggle against the non-White in the classroom rather than lose it on the battlefield." In 1960 G. J. Potgieter, president of the Transvaal Afrikaans teachers' association, had sent a circular to schools saying: "Principals are urged to act as field-generals in a campaign against liberalism and materialism . . . no separate lesson is required; inculcate a little with each lesson."[74]

During the 1970s and early 1980s, there was no discernible increase in objectivity in the school textbooks. One text was written by Professor Floris van Jaarsveld, the most prolific and influential Afrikaner historian of his generation.[75] It justified the pass laws that were abolished in 1828 in terms that evoked parallels with the pass laws that are applied to modern Africans; it presented the *voortrekkers* as heroic figures whose "task was to tame the wilderness" and whose "only textbook was the Bible"; it claimed that they migrated into "empty land"; it used nineteenth-century history to imply that foreigners could not ever understand South Africa's problems; and it emphasized the dichotomy civilized-uncivilized. In short, Professor van Jaarsveld, who was in a position to know better than the teachers and school inspectors who write most South African history textbooks, wrote history for schools in such a way as to provide support for the racial policies that the Afrikaner nationalist regime has pursued since 1948.

A textbook by C. J. Joubert that has circulated widely in both English and Afrikaans editions in white schools in the Transvaal, adheres very closely indeed to the nationalist interpretation of South African history.[76] Its central theme is the rise of Afrikaner cultural and political nationalism. It also gives extensive and favorable attention to the doctrine of separate development of the different South African "nations," including the ten African "nations" identified by the government. It lauds the achievements of nationalist prime ministers; it is sympathetic to the Afrikaners who raised a rebellion when the government decided to participate in the First World War in 1914; it says little about English-speaking White South Africans; and it treats Blacks as natural sub-ordinates of Whites. This text also explicitly vindicates the racial division of the labor force into well-paid, skilled, and relatively secure white workers and poorly paid, unskilled, and insecure black workers, without suggesting that it has had anything to do with dispossession, taxation, curbs on black mobility, and pervasive discrimination; and it attri-butes dissent exclusively to external forces, especially inter-national communism. Its passage on tropical Africa concentrates on the setbacks that have followed decoloniza-tion and accounts for them in terms of black backwardness and the communist threats to Africa.

Such texts are also remarkably selective in what they say about Nazi Germany. The passage on Adolf Hitler and the Third Reich in *History in Perspective* for standard 7 by E. H. W. Lategan and A. J. de Kock might almost have been writ-ten by Hitler himself. It introduces him as a brave recipient of the Iron Cross in the First World War. It says that he persecuted Jews and placed them in concentration camps but does not suggest that any of them were killed there. While admitting that the loss of personal liberty was a high price to pay for the restoration of German national "pride," it makes the democracies fully responsible, for "it was ac-tually only the logical result of the mistakes made by the West at Versailles in 1919."[77]

In 1981 a British research team at the University of Leices-ter Centre for Mass Communication Research, commis-sioned by UNESCO, completed another study of South African textbooks. After analyzing forty-two secondary text-books, they concluded that the syllabuses were designed to cultivate attitudes favorable to the system of white suprem-acy and that the textbooks served the same ends, sometimes directly, as in their descriptions of *apartheid*, usually indirectly, in encouraging values that underpin the system. They found that the books glorified nationalism as a major theme in European as well as South African history, treated the past as a model for the present, perpetuated wholly inaccurate myths, discredited counterideologies, and stereotyped black people as incompetent, primitive, ignorant, unintellectual, warlike, and, indeed, innately and permanently inferior.[78]

The effect of textbooks such as these is enhanced by the classroom situation. The Broederbond has always exerted a powerful influence over Afrikaner teachers; for many years their professional associations have been deeply committed to the nationalist cause. There can be no doubt that this affects their classroom behavior. Many of them adhere closely to the textbooks and embellish them with ethnic and racial slurs and anecdotes. A skillful ideologue, with the fervor of absolute conviction, makes a deep and enduring impression on the young mind. J. A. Heese provides a striking example of this in his study of the Slagtersnek rebellion of Afrikaner frontiersmen in the Cape Colony in 1815. He records that his history teacher made him hero-worship a certain Freek Bezuidenhout, whose behavior, as we shall see in chapter 4, was in fact not heroic by Afrikaner nationalist norms or any other norms.[79]

VI

White children who were not Afrikaners acquired a political mythology that differed in important respects. To some extent, this was an inevitable consequence of the historical background: the distinct origins and cultures of two fragments of European society that migrated to South Africa at different times, and the imperial conflicts that culminated in the war of 1899–1902. However, Afrikaner nationalist policies prolonged and accentuated these differences by corralling the two communities into separate schools. In the English-medium schools for white children there was an element of Anglo-chauvinism and a less rigid racism. These differences were most marked in some of the private schools conducted by Anglican, Methodist, and Roman Catholic churches, where many of the teachers were themselves born or educated overseas, usually in Britain. Nevertheless, the differences were limited. All South African schools were using similar history syllabuses and preparing students for similar examinations. In many cases, probably the majority of cases, the English-medium schools and the Afrikaans-medium schools used the appropriate edition of textbooks that were published in both languages, such as the books by Fowler and Smit that have been discussed on pages 57 and 58. In other cases they used books that were available only in English. Texts by A. N. Boyce and M. S. Geen, for example, were distinctly less favorable to the anti-British element in the Afrikaner mythology and distinctly less committed to the government's racial policies. The senior textbook by Boyce that was current in the early 1980s drew heavily on the work of liberal historians and provided a summary of the principal *apartheid* laws; but it said virtually nothing about the state's treatment of political dissidents or the conditions of life of more than 80 percent of the population of the country: their poverty and insecurity, and their daily struggle for survival. The white pupils in the English-medium as well as those in the Afrikaans-medium schools, cocooned in their privileged, segregated world, lacked elementary information about what it meant to be black in South Africa.[80]

The textbooks that are approved for use in African schools are perhaps the most remarkable of all. The use of textbooks to indoctrinate subject races in South Africa—as in colonial

situations elsewhere—is nothing new. Long before the National Party came into power in 1948, white South Africans
were producing textbooks for African use that were tenden-
tious, not only as a result of the authors' ignorance and
insensitivity, but also as a matter of policy. One such was
the 1932 *South African History for Natives*. The author, P. A.
W. Cook, a member of the staff of the Wesleyan teacher
training college at Healdtown in the Cape Province (now
the Ciskei), declared in the introduction: "The language has
been simplified . . . and chapters have been included to make
the point of view of European people more intelligible to
the native child."[81] His entire book is permeated with paternalism and prejudice. Of the people for whom he was
writing, he said: "Naturally there were wars most of the
time, for the tribes were all striving to secure the best land
for themselves."[82] In the concluding chapter, "The Progress
of South Africa," Cook defined civilization as "the ways of
living in large numbers, peacefully and happily," implied
that this was the white man's gift to the natives, and listed
four attributes of civilization: "everybody must learn how
to work and be willing to work"; he must work for his
neighbor's benefit; he must cooperate; and he must live for
his country.[83]

In the early 1980s, a series of social studies textbooks was
being used by African students in standards 5, 6, and 7.[84]
To comply with the syllabuses the central government had
laid down for African schools, these three books contain
sections on geography, general history, South African history, and civics. The general history sections start in standard
5 with Egypt, Greece, and Rome and in standard 7 get as
far as the Reformation and Counter-Reformation, with additional chapters on recent developments in transport, communication, and medical science. The South African history

sections, too, form a chronological series. They are nothing more than a potted version of the history of white settlement and expansion in South Africa from 1652 to the 1670s (standard 5), to 1771 (standard 6), and to the 1830s (standard 7). Africans, as distinct from "Bushmen" and "Hottentots," do not appear at all in the standard 5 or standard 6 historical sections, and in the standard 7 book they emerge only at the end of a chapter on the white stockfarmers, where they figure merely as participants in frontier wars that are described from the white point of view. Africans do appear, however, in the civics sections of all these books, where they are presented as distinct nations benefiting from the political dispensation provided by a generous civilized government. These are the only written versions of history or civics that many African children will ever see. Indeed, this series seems to have a virtual monopoly of the farm school market, at least in the Orange Free State and the Transvaal. Moreover, the farm school teachers themselves are heavily dependent on the texts because they have had very little training and are responsible for teaching children of all school-going ages in several subjects.[85]

In some cases, especially when nearly all black education was in the hands of European missionaries, the indoctrination was effective. For example, Silas M. Molema (1891–1965), who was born in Mafikeng (in modern Bophuthatswana), wrote a book called *The Bantu Past and Present* while he was a medical student in Scotland during the First World War. Molema's account of the major processes in the precolonial history of southern Africa is scarcely distinguishable from the accounts of his white contemporaries. The precolonial Bantu were "primitive," and "backward and degraded." They were not savages because they cultivated the soil, used domesticated animals, had "a rudimentary knowl-

expresses hegemonic viewpoint. Has internalized dominant viewpoint.

edge of metals and of working them, and had a form of government, etc." Nevertheless, wrote Molema,

"progress" as ideology.

> it would seem that so long as they were left to themselves their history of progress was *nil;* it could be written in one word—"stereotypy" or "stagnation." Through these long centuries, in which other nations have risen and fallen, the Bantu seem to have remained an indolent, lethargic, and dreamy race of men, and their history one dull, dreary, featureless scene of barbarism and incompetence, with only enough knowledge to provide for the barest and most immediate necessities of life.[86]

However, most black pupils either ignored racist value judgments or rejected them. Molema himself probably changed his mind in later years. He became an active member of the African National Congress and served as its treasurer from 1949 to 1953, when the South African government banned him.[87] In 1918 Z. K. Matthews, an African who was to cap a distinguished political and academic career by serving as Botswana's first ambassador to the United States, was in the matriculation class at Fort Hare Native College. Later in life, he recorded:

> Our history, as we had absorbed it from the tales and talk of our elders, bore no resemblance to South African history as it has been written by European scholars, or as it is taught in South African schools, and as it was taught to us at Fort Hare. The European insisted that we accept his version of the past and what is more, if we wanted to get ahead educationally, even to pass examinations in the subject as he presents it. . . . The syllabus for matriculation emphasized South African history, so with Miss Noppe [an Afrikaner] we struggled

counter-ideology.

through the white man's version of the so-called Kaffir Wars, the Great Trek, the struggles for control of Southern Africa. Indeed, we studied this history not merely in the white man's version—which was invariably loaded with bias against the non-white—but in a distinctly pro-Boer version. It was as though we were American boys compelled to study the events of 1776 in a version dictated by Englishmen, and ultra-Tory Englishmen at that. If it was difficult for us to accept the white man's account of his own past doings, it was utterly impossible to accept his judgements on the actions and behaviour of Africans, of our own grandfathers in our own lands. Yet we had to give back in our examination papers the answers the white man expected.[88]

As Matthews indicated, black students could not be expected to believe in the white mythology. Their personal experience rebutted it; so did their knowledge of events outside South Africa. They were never wholly insulated from external influences. For example, there was a continual infusion of ideas from America, as in 1923, when Sol Plaatje returned from an extensive tour of Britain and North America, where he had encountered a broad spectrum of black opinion from the members of the Tuskegee Institute to Dr. W. E. B. Du Bois and Marcus Garvey.[89]

Foreign influences became still more subversive of the racial order in South Africa after the Second World War, with the decolonization of tropical Africa and the growth of the civil rights movement in the United States. By the 1950s, people were reacting to the government's attempts to control their minds by standing the white racist mythology on its head and replacing it with a mythology of black virtue and white vice. Coloured teachers in Cape Town schools were dictating two sets of notes to their classes: one headed "For examination purposes only," the other "The truth."[90] In 1952, using pseudonyms, two authors surreptitiously published pamphlets with the arresting titles: *The Role of the Missionaries in Conquest* and *Three Hundred Years: A History of South Africa*, volume 1, *Tribalism and Slavery*, volume 2, *Dispossession*, and volume 3, *Colonial Fascism*.[91] Although the government regularly banned works of that sort, copies circulated inside South Africa.

After 1959, when the government created segregated colleges for African, Coloured, and Asian students, its attempts to use its monopoly of black education as an instrument of thought control became a boomerang. With European missionaries ousted from the process, the African schools and colleges became places where young people gained an apprenticeship in politics and formulated a Black Consciousness movement with a liberatory mythology.[92] In chapter 6, we shall consider some of the consequences of the failure of the government to win the battle for the minds of the black population of South Africa.

3

UNASSIMILABLE RACES

I

The political mythology that legitimizes the South African social order rests on a core assumption about humanity. The core assumption is that *races* are the fundamental divisions of humanity and that different races possess inherently different cultural as well as physical qualities. In the modern South African context, white people, as Christians, have a God-given destiny to preserve their distinction from other races. In numerous elaborate speeches, Hendrik Frensch Verwoerd (1901–66), as minister of native affairs and then as prime minister of South Africa, was the most authentic exponent of this assumption:

> We send this message to the outside world and say to them . . . that there is but one way of saving the white races of the world. And that is for the White and non-White in Africa each to exercise his rights within his own areas. . . .[1]

> We have been planted here, we believe, with a destiny— destiny not for the sake of the selfishness of a nation, but for the sake of the service of a nation to the world of which it forms a part, and the service of a nation to the Deity in which it believes. . . .[2]

> If meddlesome people keep their hands off us, we shall in a just way such as behoves a Christian nation, work

out solutions in the finest detail and carry them out. We shall provide all our races with happiness and prosperity.[3]

This core assumption is buttressed by a specific myth. Africans are said to be quite recent immigrants into South Africa; therefore, they have no greater historical claim to dominion over the land than Whites. South African propaganda makes much of this myth. In its extreme form, it runs like this: "When the whites came to Africa in the 16th century, there were no native blacks in South Africa—only some nomadic tribes, including the Hottentots, who were of Arabic origin. So whose country is it by virtue of original settlers?"[4] This myth has penetrated deeply into the historical consciousness of white South Africans. In 1981 it repeatedly confronted members of the American Study Commission on U.S. Policy toward Southern Africa, chaired by Franklin A. Thomas, president of the Ford Foundation. As enunciated by an Afrikaner builder in Johannesburg:

> The black guy is hard to understand. His views are totally different from ours. He'll agree with you one time and he'll be totally against you the next. Most of the blacks I've met say this is their country. But when you get down to facts, there were only Bushmen in South Africa when the whites landed at the Cape. The blacks were in Rhodesia. Basically, we came here more or less at the same time. We both belong to South Africa. There is no one black man who can say that this is his country more so than a white. We belong here as much as they do.[5]

*

This chapter describes the peculiar history of South African racism. Derived from a seventeenth-century fragment of European society, the people who became known as Afrikaners developed racial ideas that were adapted to their experience and their needs in the South African context. Until the Second World War those ideas differed in detail but not in essence from ideas that were current in Western Europe and North America. Then, however, they began to diverge. Outside South Africa, thought and action began to move away from racist suppositions. Inside South Africa, leading politicians, official television and radio services, newspapers, teachers, and textbooks propagated a modified, Verwoerdian version of a racist mythology to legitimize a racist regime.

II

By the time the directors of the Dutch East India Company decided to create a supply station at the Cape of Good Hope in the mid-seventeenth century, Europeans thought themselves vastly superior to Africans. They were predisposed to despise people who were so unlike themselves in physical appearance and social behavior; and for the Dutch this predisposition was confirmed by participation in the Atlantic slave trade along the West African coastline. Throughout northern Europe, Africans were stereotyped as idolatrous and licentious, thieving and lying, lazy and dirty. The stereotype persisted throughout the eighteenth century, spiced by reports of wars and massacres, and allegations of cannibalism and sexual relations between apes and Africans. Abolitionists as well as defenders of the slave trade had no doubt that Africans were inferior to Europeans. Explanations for African inferiority varied. Environmental determinism was a common explanation: tropical heat combined with the alleged abundance of tropical natural conditions was responsible. Nevertheless, few Europeans doubted that Africans were members of the human species. They were im-

[handwritten margin note: Belief in innate African inferiority.]

mature people, to be treated like children. They were lagging a thousand years or more behind Europeans. This line of thought led to justifications of slavery. Europeans could save Africans from the degradations of their own societies by taking them to the Americas, where hard work and civilized discipline would be a step toward maturity.[6]

By 1652, the Dutch also had at their disposal a quantity of information about the Cape of Good Hope. Since Vasco da Gama's epoch-making voyage to India and back in 1497–98, the passengers and crews of numerous Portuguese, Dutch, English, French, and other European ships had landed in Saldanha Bay, Table Bay, or False Bay on passage to and from southern Asia, and several of them had published their impressions.[7] Nearly all these accounts drew attention to the human inhabitants of the region, whom they called Hottentots, emphasizing the strangeness of their speech, their physical appearance, their clothing, their mode of life, and their customs. Many authors, who may or may not have made their own observations, repeated what their predecessors had written, and by the middle of the seventeenth century the word Hottentot was becoming a symbol of human degradation in European literature—far lower than the Africans of the Guinea coast. Jacobus Hondius summed up the stereotype in his *Klare Besgryving van Cabo de Bona Esperanca* in 1652. His verdict was a typical jumble of physical description and value judgment:[8]

> The natives in the vicinity of the Cape of Good Hope are generally called Hottentots by us on account of their speech, which sounds very much like stuttering and, in fact, they even refer to themselves as Hottentots. . . . They have very ugly countenances. . . . They have everything in common with the dumb cattle, barring their human nature, from which, occasionally, some

co-ordination of the senses may bring forth a spark of intelligence. . . . So far as clothing is concerned, they usually wear nothing but a small skin, as wide as a hand, and as long as a span, which serves to cover their private parts; both men and women being otherwise entirely naked. . . . Since they hang the entrails of animals round their legs and neck as containers to hold odds-and-ends of things . . . (fresh as well as stale), dripping with fat, and plaited twice or thrice, they all smell fiercely, as can be noticed at a distance of more than twelve feet against the wind, and they also give the appearance of never having washed. . . . They are thus very dissolute and in every way like animals, for they are wild, rough, and unclean in their habits. . . . There are no signs of Belief or Religion to be found among them and it is for this reason they are called Cafres, Caferes, or, according to Marmol, Quefreres, in keeping with the name of their country Quefrerie.[9]

Some of the reports included additional allegations. For example, a member of the 1595 Dutch fleet commanded by Cornelis Houtman (the first Dutch expedition to make the round trip to Asia via the Cape) suspected that the "Hottentots" were cannibals, and this charge was taken up by later writers: "As far as we could perceive they were cannibals," read a 1609 account.[10] Thus, the founders of the Dutch settlement were prepared to deal with a degraded people—human indeed, but "beast-like."[11] However, sixteenth- and seventeenth-century European mariners and traders were not much given to grand philosophical theories. They did not speculate about the historical antecedents of the people they found in southern Africa, or their relationships with other human beings. It was sufficient to describe them as they perceived them and to evaluate them in the light of their experience.[12]

There were exceptions to the predominantly adverse portrayal of the "Hottentots" by Europeans, most notably by two Dutchmen who had spent over a year at the Cape after the *Haerlem* was wrecked there in 1648. Having got on well with them, they denied that the local people were "brutish and cannibals," and declared that when clashes had occurred with the Europeans, the fault had lain with "the uncivilized and ungrateful conduct of our folk."[13] Nevertheless, the derogatory stereotype continued to prevail in Europe. In 1657 Johann Schreyer called Hottentots "false by nature, inconstant, revengeful, thievish, lazy and slow to work, nearly always gay [cheerful]";[14] throughout the eighteenth century " 'Hottentot' was a widely accepted symbol for irredeemable savagery and the very depths of human degradation";[15] and as late as 1899 the *Oxford English Dictionary* defined *Hottentot* as, figuratively, a "person of inferior intellect or culture."[16]

Meanwhile, in 1652 the report of the *Haerlem* survivors prompted the directors of the great Dutch East India Company to establish a staging post at the Cape of Good Hope to service their fleets on the long passage to and from the East Indies, since as many as 50 percent of the members of a crew were dying of scurvy in a single voyage. During the ensuing century and a half, while the staging post grew into a loose-knit colony nearly as large as France, the European officials and colonists deprived most of the Khoikhoi communities (the "Hottentots") of their means of independent subsistence, driving some survivors beyond the colonial boundaries and incorporating others under their hegemony.

In a pathbreaking study of white South African racial attitudes published in 1937, I. D. MacCrone, a psychologist, contended that during the seventeenth century the Europeans at the Cape had no sense of innate racial superiority over the indigenous peoples but that they felt justified in subduing them because they were not Christians and also because their appearance and behavior resembled those of wild beasts rather than civilized humans.[17] A distinctly racial attitude first emerged, according to MacCrone, among the trekboers—those white colonists who, during the eighteenth century, moved beyond the Cape peninsula and its immediate hinterland, where the rainfall was sufficient for arable farming, into the arid interior, where they became semi-nomadic, self-sufficient pastoral farmers. Subsequently, historians have modified MacCrone's perspective, demonstrating that the Dutch East India Company itself took crucial decisions that determined that the structure of the colonial society should be a racial one, by prohibiting interracial marriages, appointing only white people as local officials, and making it increasingly difficult for people who were not white to own land.[18]

The Dutch East India Company imported slaves to the Cape Colony by sea from Madagascar, Southeast Asia, and tropical Africa. In South Africa, as in European colonies in the Americas, the enslavement of dark-skinned people promoted racist assumptions among the colonists. Conflicts with the indigenous peoples accentuated that trend. After some fighting in 1659–60 and again in 1673–77, the Whites subdued the pastoral Khoikhoi (whom they continued to call Hottentots) quite easily; but bands of San, whom the whites called Bushmen and who were genetically akin to the Khoikhoi but lived exclusively by hunting and collecting, defended their territory and their way of life by hit and run raids on trekboer livestock and herders, making life precarious for Whites and their dependents throughout the northeastern region of the colony until well into the nineteenth century. The trekboers retaliated by forming commandos—hunting expeditions designed to exterminate the Bushmen.[19] Men bragged about their bag of Bushmen as fishermen boast about their catch.

During the eighteenth century Cape colonial society became increasingly stratified along racial lines, and by the time the British gained possession of the colony in 1806 the colonists had acquired an idiosyncratic world view as a result of their experiences in an isolated milieu. Most of them were speaking a language that had deviated considerably from Dutch by simplifying the syntax and incorporating loan words from their Asian slaves. Some of them were calling themselves by a distinctive name: Afrikaners. Moreover, despite substantial differences, nearly all of them held the conviction that they were an innately superior part of the population. Experience had conditioned them to a way of life in which slaves, Khoikhoi, and people of mixed descent, most of whom were physically distinguishable from themselves, did the menial work on their land and in their homes. They were steeled to coping with the utmost severity with the slightest sign of insubordination by members of the subject races. In this the Dutch officials had set an example by perpetrating horrendous tortures on slaves, whereas they took legal action against colonists for mistreating their slaves only if they had committed the most outrageous crimes.

As they gained experience the colonists modified the precolonial stereotype of the Khoikhoi. They dropped the charge of cannibalism. They found that Khoikhoi whom they dispossessed of their land and their livestock could become capable and loyal herdsmen and domestic servants—albeit "lazy";[20] and many eighteenth-century *trekboers* had no compunction in indulging in sexual intercourse with Khoikhoi women, although they rarely assumed responsibility for the offspring.[21]

Most Dutch officials and Cape colonists showed scarcely any curiosity about the historical antecedents of the Khoisan peoples. Taking them as they perceived them, they apparently assumed that they had lived in the region from time immemorial; there is certainly no evidence that they sought to justify their own occupation by claiming that the Khoisan themselves were recent immigrants. The occasional European visitor did indulge in romantic speculations on the subject. One such was Peter Kolben, who resided in the colony from 1704 to 1713 and was employed for part of that time as secretary to the district officer (*landdrost*) in Stellenbosch. Subsequently, Kolben wrote that there was a Hottentot tradition that their first ancestors came to their country through a window or door and that the name of the male ancestor was Noh. Kolben then proceeded to equate Noh with the Noah of the Bible, "who descended by a Window or Door from the Ark," and to suggest that the Hottentots descended from Noah via the Troglodytes: "Upon the whole, their Customs referring their tradition so clearly to *Noah*, if they are not descended of the *Troglodytes*, History will help us no farther; and we have Room to suppose (as strange as it may seem) that they have remain'd where they are ever since the Deluge."[22]

Impact of Biblical tradition with local tradition.

III

Initially, the officials and colonists at the Cape knew very little about the people who would become the ancestors of the majority of the inhabitants of modern South Africa. These were Bantu-speaking farmers, who occupied the country to the east of the Cape Colony, where there was sufficient rainfall for them to grow millet and sorghum as well as to herd cattle. Some Whites seem to have been scarcely aware of their existence; others did not clearly distinguish between them and the Khoisan peoples, or could add little to the general statement that they were culturally and physically different from the Khoisan. In his official journal, Commander Jan van Riebeeck noted that Khoikhoi informants had referred to a place or a ruler called Chobona. He equated this with Monomotapa and sent several fruitless expeditions to try to find it. Van Riebeeck was aware that some such kingdom was the source of gold for the Portuguese and Arab trading stations on the east African coast, but he was not well-informed about the location of Mwenemutapa in modern Zimbabwe.[23] He seems to have known virtually nothing about the Bantu-speaking farmers who lived in what are now the Ciskei, the Transkei, Natal, and KwaZulu, despite the existence of several Portuguese publications with a wealth of information about them. These were accounts written by or about survivors of Portuguese shipwrecks; for example, survivors of the *Santo Alberto*, which foundered in 1593 near the mouth of the Mthatha River, and the *Sao Joao Baptista*, which was wrecked in 1622 near the mouth of the Keiskamma, who had struggled northeastward to Portuguese bases at Lourenço Marques (Maputo) and Sofala.[24]

This ignorance was soon remedied, at least in official circles, as survivors of Dutch shipwrecks began to find their way to the Cape. On 16 February 1686 the *Stavenisse* was wrecked on the Natal coast, and during the following three years several bands of survivors arrived in Cape Town. There they provided the government with details of their experiences, including accounts of their lives among the Nguni.[25] Their treatment had varied with their own behavior, and also from chiefdom to chiefdom. Some had been robbed and beaten; others had been given hospitality and assistance. One group listed the chiefdoms they had traversed, including four names that are readily identifiable as those of modern ethnic communities: Mpondomisi, Mpondo, Thembu, and Xhosa.[26] Summing up in a report to the directors of the company, Governor Simon van der Stel described them as a "civil, polite and talkative" people, living in peaceful, stable polities under chiefs who were "much respected and beloved by their subjects," in an "exceedingly fertile and incredibly populous" country, swarming with "cows, calves, oxen, steers, and goats" as well as "elephants, rhinoceroses, lions, tigers, leopards, elands, and harts," and producing "three sorts of corn," many vegetables and wild fruits, and iron.[27] Van der Stel, who was no sentimentalist, added: "It would be impossible to buy any slaves there, for they would not part with their children, or any of their connections for anything in the world, loving one another with a most remarkable strength of affection."[28]

Regular interaction between Cape colonists and Bantu-speaking Africans began early in the eighteenth century. Initially, expeditions composed of white colonists, their Khoikhoi clients, and perhaps a few slaves visited Xhosa country as hunters and traders and, in at least one case, as marauders. During the 1770s, outlying members of the two societies were beginning to compete for land on either side of the Fish River. This was the start of a century of conflict between the white and the African societies throughout southern Africa. Many Africans vigorously resisted white expansion. The Xhosa fought eight wars between 1779 and 1878; the Zulu defied Afrikaner migrants in 1838, and in 1879 they destroyed an entire British regiment at Isandhlwana; the southern Sotho outmaneuvered the commandos of the Orange Free State in 1858; the Venda drove Boers out of the northern Transvaal in the 1860s; the Pedi defied the South African Republic in 1876; and the Ndebele resisted the British South Africa Company regime in Rhodesia in 1893, and again in 1896–97, when many Shona joined them in revolt.[29] Nevertheless, Whites were able to overcome African resistance. They had superior firepower, discipline, and logistics. They did not allow their own disputes to override their common interests as Whites; British troops as well as Afrikaner commandos took part in the conquest, and Afrikaners were always able to obtain arms and ammunition from Britain or the European continent. On the other hand, Whites were able to exploit the endemic cleavages within African societies by playing off chiefdom against chiefdom and segment against segment. Indeed, in every military encounter with Africans, Whites had Coloured or African allies.

Moreover, Africans themselves had paved the way for white expansion. The principal white thrust into southeast Africa—the Afrikaner Great Trek of the 1830s—took place when many of its African communities had been disrupted by internal warfare. Between 1818 and 1828 Shaka's Zulu regiments had conquered the large area stretching from the Drakensberg Mountains to the Indian Ocean, and from the Pongola River in the north to the Tugela in the south. They had also devastated neighboring territories, while offshoots had invaded areas still farther afield and would eventually carve out military states as far north as modern Tanzania and Zambia.[30]

By the end of the nineteenth century, South African society possessed many of its modern characteristics. Though conquered, Africans were still an overwhelming majority of the population of the region. Whites controlled its principal resources—the bulk of the arable land and the rich deposits of gold and diamonds—which they exploited with black labor. Africans, left with insufficient land for their own subsistence and required to pay taxes to white governments, were obliged to send out family members to earn wages by working for white people. The British colonial governments in the Cape Colony and Natal, and the Afrikaner republican governments in the Transvaal and Orange Free State encouraged this process. The lands left in African occupation were becoming labor reservoirs for white farmers and industrialists. In urban industry, the labor force was divided by a color bar. White workers were well-paid, privileged, and deemed to be skilled. Black workers were poorly paid, underprivileged, and deemed to be unskilled, and most of them shuttled to and fro between their rural homes and their places of employment, where they worked for a year or so at a time. White hegemony, comprising a virtual monopoly of the instruments of coercion and an inordinate share of the wealth of the region, survived the war of 1899–1902, when Whites fought one another. When the Union of South Africa was founded in 1910, its constitution included a political color bar. Only white men were eligible for membership in the sovereign, central parliament. Only white men could vote in the Transvaal and the Orange Free State provinces. Whites formed an overwhelming majority of the electorate in Natal and the Cape Province.[31]

When the process of conquest began, the Afrikaners who moved into territories inhabited by Bantu-speaking Africans had expectations that were derived from their experiences in the racially stratified Dutch Cape Colony. African resistance accentuated the Afrikaners' sense of racial solidarity, and they became caught up in the endless task of trying to reconcile two contradictory impulses: their reliance on black labor and their search for security. Most of them were not much given to putting pen to paper. However, several of the leaders of the organized groups of Afrikaners who left the colony in the 1830s wrote long letters to Cape colonial newspapers and to the Cape government to justify their behavior and establish their claim to independence from Great Britain. The best-known example is Piet Retief's letter to the editor of the *Grahamstown Journal*, which included a statement of intent, carefully designed to satisfy British officials in the aftermath of the emancipation of the slaves in the British Empire: "We are resolved, wherever we go, that we will uphold the just principles of liberty; but, whilst we will take care that no one shall be held in a state of slavery, it is our determination to maintain such regulations as may suppress crime, and preserve proper relations between master and servant."[32]

A far more elaborate record of the emigrants' attitudes to Africans is to be found in the printed proceedings of a commission that the British colonial government of Natal appointed in 1852.[33] More than half the witnesses were Afrikaners, including nine of the nineteen commissioners, and they apparently spoke with complete candor. They were unanimous in their assessment of the Africans, whom they called Kaffirs: lazy and unintelligent, inveterate liars, incapable of gratitude, ignorant of their own true interests. They should be compelled to work for Whites. As J. H. Hatting put it:

> The Kafirs are lazy by nature and accustomed to do their work under the influence of fear; they are protected in this district, they live on land for nothing, and as they have little wants in their condition of life, they can live without working. Their own work must be done by their women, who they treat as slaves. But I consider it with respect to their civilization, as well as to their own improvement, as an act of justice to the white inhabitants that they should be compelled to go into the service of the Boers.[34]

There was a consensus among the Afrikaner witnesses on the need for coercion. According to Solomon Maritz, "there is no mode of dealing with them except that of compulsion or severity."[35] J. du Plessis declared: "There are no other means to rule the Kafirs but by fear; and Kafirs will not work for the white men unless they know that they will be punished when they refuse."[36] Making the same point, Dewald Johannes Pretorius harked back to the good old days before the British conquered the Cape Colony: "I would make a law for the Kafirs that every man having a Kafir should be allowed to flog him when he misbehaved, of course in a moderate way. If this was known by the Kafirs it would become almost unnecessary to inflict the punishment. . . . When this law was in force in the old colony the farmers had plenty of hands, and then the Hottentots were comparatively rich."[37] Asked by a commissioner whether, "in discussing any plan for the disposal of the Kafirs, we should allow ourselves to be guided in the smallest degree, by the views, or feelings of the Kafirs themselves on the subject under our consideration, further than those views may appear to affect the practicabilities of our measures," Pieter Albertus Ryno Otto replied, "No; for a Kafir does not even know his own true interests."[38] The Afrikaner witnesses also stressed the security theme. Dewald Johannes Pretorius was of the opinion that "the black and white races in large masses cannot live together in peace and safety in the same land."[39] Christoffel Lotter, a local official (field cornet), sought to reconcile the search for security with the demand for labor: "All the Kafirs should be removed from amongst us, and the farther the better, but not beyond the boundaries of the English territories; that they shall pay the necessary taxes, and go into service, so that the farmers can get more laborers."[40]

All the Afrikaner witnesses who gave evidence to the Natal commission expressed themselves in practical, secular terms. None of them attempted to justify their views on theological or philosophical grounds; nor did they invoke history to validate their claims. They expressed no doubt that African farmers had occupied much of southeastern Africa for innumerable generations (though they were not necessarily aware that central Natal had been quite densely settled by Africans before the time of Shaka), nor did they make distinctions of an ethnic sort among Africans. In short, they

were espousing the hard core of what was to become the
policy of segregation or even *apartheid*, but without a trace
of the paternalist hypocrisy that would accompany segregation, or of the ideological and mythical underpinnings of
late twentieth-century *apartheid*.

By the end of the nineteenth century republican Afrikaners
and their colonial and European sympathizers were building
on the reactions of the emigrants, now known as *voortrekkers*.
To S. J. du Toit, the author of the influential *Die Geskiedenis
van ons Land in die Taal van ons Volk* (1877), it was self-
evident that all the precolonial inhabitants of South Africa
were savages. That required no explanation. Some people,
he wrote, say that the Bushmen are not human; that was
not true; nevertheless, the Boers could do nothing else but
shoot them dead. The Kaffers are more human than the
Bushmen, but their customs stamped them as savages: by
practicing witchcraft, buying women with cattle, and making
the women do all the work.[41]

In 1882 F. Lion Cachet, a Dutch theologian who had lived
in South Africa from 1858 to 1880 and put the *Nederduitse
Gereformeerde Kerk*, the principal Dutch Reformed Church,
on a firm basis in the Transvaal, published an elaborate defense of the Kruger regime. Cachet explained, ''The most
reliable informants agree that the Kaffers are sons of Ishmael
who, in relatively recent times, have reached the South coast
of Africa over land.'' He cited physical, cultural, and linguistic
evidence for this conclusion. The linguistic passage reads as
follows:

> They call themselves with one general name, Amakafula
> . . . in which Kafula is not an original Kaffer word but
> a corruption of Kafir. Now since that name is given by
> the Arabs to everyone who rejected Mohamed's doc-
> trine, it is very likely that the present Kaffer tribes earlier
> trafficked with the Arabs and are of Arabian origin. Not

too risky even is the interpretation that Kaffers were originally fugitives who, unwilling to submit to Mohamed, had to escape persecution and, trekking in a southeasterly direction, eventually found an uninhabited country between Delagoa Bay and the Fish River, where they could settle, or out of which they could drive the weaker tribes of Hottentots and Bushmen, who previously lived there.[42]

In 1898 J. F. van Oordt, a prolific Afrikaner writer, published a book on Paul Kruger and the rise of the South African Republic. Van Oordt's book contained an exposition of Afrikaner race attitudes that must be taken seriously; he was supporting the republican cause in the growing dispute with Great Britain:

> If there is anything that has always distinguished the Afrikaner Boers from the so-called more civilized Englishmen, it was the treatment of the coloureds. According to the Boer idea, the Kaffer, the Hottentot, the Bushman belong to a lower race than the Whites. They carry, as people once rightly called it, the mark of Cain; God, the Lord, destined them to be "drawers of water and hewers of wood," as *presses* subject to the white race. . . . People can only control a Kaffer or a Hottentot through fear; he must always be kept in his place; he was not to be trusted; give him only a finger and he will take the whole hand. The Boer does not believe in educating him; yes, I do not believe that I go too far when I express my feeling that the Boers as a whole doubt the existence of a Kaffer- or a Hottentot-soul. Among the frontier Boers, whose lives were a continuous struggle with the Kaffer tribes, this feeling existed more deeply than among the Western Boers.[43]

Nine years later, van Oordt published his views about the origins of the Bantu-speaking people. Their "real original home," he wrote, was "the peninsula of Malacca," as demonstrated by linguistic evidence which showed that the Bantu language belongs to "the *Ugro-Altaic* group," which has arisen from "a mixture of Hamitic and Turanian elements."[44]

Meanwhile, on the eve of the South African War, in a vehement attack on British policy toward the Transvaal republic, J. C. Voigt, a Cape colonial doctor, explained that the Kaffirs were a single race from South Africa to Somaliland, as demonstrated by their language and their customs, notably circumcision: "It is a curious fact that circumcision was, and still is, prevalent among all the Kaffir nations. This seems to show that the original cradle of the race must have been somewhere not very far removed from the influences of the ancient Egyptian civilisation and its customs; for it is well known that the rite of circumcision spread from Egypt to Syria, Palestine and Arabia."[45] Voigt then repeated the theory that Cachet had expounded about the origins of the Bantu-speaking people, as refugees from "aggressive Mahometanism."[46] Voigt's world view was a vulgar social Darwinian view. He castigated Great Britain for refusing "to believe that in the struggle for existence between nations and races, as between individuals, the weakest goes to the wall."[47]

IV

The Afrikaner tradition was by no means unusual before the second half of the twentieth century. Its basic concepts were compatible with, and often derived from, works by foreigners and British South Africans. John Barrow, who served on the staff of a British governor during the first British occupation

of the Cape Colony in 1797 and 1798 and traveled exten-
sively in the region, was quite sympathetic toward Africans.
However, he wrote that he was convinced that the Africans
were of "Arabic" origin:

> Their pastoral habits and manners, their kind and
> friendly reception to strangers, their tent-shaped houses,
> the remains of Islamism discoverable in one of its strong-
> est features, the circumcision of male children, univer-
> sally practised among the Kaffer hordes, all denote their
> affinity to the Beduin tribes. Their countenance also is
> Arabic; the colour only differs, which in some tribes
> varies from deep bronze to jet black, but most generally
> the latter is the prevailing colour. Nor can I suppose
> they owe this colour to their connection with those
> blacks which are usually called Negroes, as they have
> no resemblance, in any part of the body, to the pecu-
> liar conformation of this race of human beings. To the
> Ethiopians or Abyssinians they have a much closer
> resemblance.[48]

[handwritten margin note: Speculation of origins.]

Barrow also referred to the Great Chain of Being, according to which different types of human beings stood at different places at the upper end of a hierarchy of living things,
from the most simple to the most complex—a concept that
became fashionable in the late eighteenth and early nineteenth centuries among some Europeans who were trying
to make sense of their observations without relying on the
Old Testament as an infallible guide.[49] Barrow himself was
skeptical of its applicability to the people of South Africa,
perhaps because Great Chain theorists relied on the shapes
of skulls, and the southern Africans did not come "low"
enough on that scale:

> The comparative anatomist might be a little perplexed
> in placing the skull of a Kaffer in the chain, so ingen-

iously put together by him, comprehending all the links
from the most perfect Europeans to the Ourang-Outang,
and thence through all the monkey-tribe. . . . In short,
had not Nature bestowed upon him the dark-colouring
principle that anatomists have discovered to be owing
to a certain gelatinous fluid lying between the epidermis
and the cuticle, he might have ranked among the first
of Europeans.[50]

In the century before Darwin, many educated Europeans
were prepared to accept explanations that hinged on the
theory that human societies were liable to "degenerate" over
time. They were also inclined to see causal connections
between societies that had similar customs and rituals. From
those premises, they could readily endorse the hypothesis
that Bantu-speaking Africans were people of Arabian origin
who had "degenerated" during the centuries since their detachment from Asia. Thomas Pringle, a relatively liberal
member of the first considerable group of British settlers who
migrated to South Africa in 1820, put it as follows:

> In their customs and traditions, there seem to be indi-
> cations of their having sprung, at some remote period,
> from a people of much higher civilisation than is now
> exhibited by any of the tribes of Southern Africa; whilst
> the rite of circumcision universally practised among
> them without any vestige of Islamism, and several other
> traditionary customs greatly resembling the Levitical
> rules of purification, would seem to indicate some for-
> mer connection with a people of Arabian, Hebrew, or,
> perhaps, Abyssinian lineage.[51]

Dr. Andrew Smith, who led a major official expedition
from the Cape Colony to the interior plateau in the years
1834 to 1838, applied another common European criterion

of analysis, classifying people in degrees of civilization, opposing "civilized men" (i.e., Europeans, preferably Englishmen) to "savages."[52] Richard Godlonton, an 1820 settler
who edited the *Grahamstown Journal*, repeated the degeneration theme, citing as evidence "the barbarous state of
nudity in which they are found at the present day" plus
various "disgusting and sensuous vices" associated with the
relics of customs which clearly indicate "a much higher state
of morals."[53] William Cornwallis Harris, a British military
officer on leave from India who conducted a hunting expedition north of the Vaal River in 1836–37, was an extreme
racist. In explaining why Afrikaners (later known as *voortrekkers*) were leaving the Cape Colony, he denounced the
British government for having failed to deal severely with
the Xhosa people on the eastern frontier of the colony. It
should "not long ago have seen the imperious necessity,
dictated alike by reason, justice, and humanity, of exterminating from off the face of the earth, a race of monsters,
who, being the unprovoked destroyers, and implacable foes
of Her Majesty's Christian subjects, have forfeited every claim
to mercy or consideration."[54]

The British witnesses who gave evidence to the Natal commission in 1852 and 1853 had a wider range of views than
the Afrikaner witnesses, but most of them stereotyped Africans in much the same way. Benjamin Blaine declared that
"their position on the scale of civilization . . . is almost as
low as humanity has fallen to since the creation of man. . . .
They are crafty and cunning, and at the same time indolent
and excitable; averse to labor, but when their passions are
roused bloodthirsty and cruel, and are apparently unaffected
by those influences which tend to raise barbarism to civilization."[55] Theophilus Shepstone, who had been born and
raised on a Methodist mission station in the Cape Colony
and had become secretary of native affairs in Natal, was more

guarded: "I do not think them wanting in capacity or intelligence. In moral feelings they are necessarily so, as compared with civilized and educated Europeans. I see no
absolute bar to their civilization or to their usefulness, in any
position in which their intelligence and capacity may here-
after place them."[56] One witness stood out from all the rest.
This was G. R. Peppercorne, a recent British immigrant to
Natal, who submitted a written document that differed fundamentally from the negrophobic mainstream:

> To designate these people as "unreclaimable savages,"[57]
> is the libel and pretext of those who seek to rob them
> of their birthright as human beings; and expect to obtain
> from them, in return, the qualities of gratitude, respect,
> and attachment—upon compulsory terms. . . . It would
> be difficult, indeed, to find, in Europe, a more peacable
> or well disposed peasantry, considering their numbers,
> than the native population of Natal. . . . When prepos-
> terous apprehensions, and false accusations, are mixed
> with an eager and insatiable desire to control and en-
> force their gratuitous labor, I think that very little further
> comment is needful on what is called the deficiency of
> Native Labour.[58]

As these examples show, British settlers were more inclined to place the debate in a comparative perspective than
Afrikaners. Some of them also referred to the historical background of the African population. Theophilus Shepstone
thought it was "the opinion of men who have investigated
this subject more than I have, that most of them have a
common origin."[59] Henry Fynn, who in 1824 had been one
of the first British traders in Natal, was convinced that they
had all "formed originally one nation." Perhaps Fynn had
read Barrow's book, for he also speculated that "the Kafir
tribes" had degenerated from an earlier higher state of civi-

lization and that their customs showed that they were related to the Jews.[60]

Later in the nineteenth century, three immigrants began to make the first sustained studies of the precolonial history of the southern African region: W. H. I. Bleek, a philologist, G. W. Stow, a geologist and collector of oral traditions, and G. M. Theal, whom we have already encountered as a great historical compiler and synthesizer. Bleek's studies led him to the conclusion that the Bushman, Hottentot, and Bantu languages were fundamentally different from one another; that the Bushmen must have been isolated from all other races for many millennia; that the Hottentots had formerly lived in Egypt; and that the Bantu-speaking people originated in Malaya or Polynesia.[61] Using similar diffusionist logic, Stow called the Bushmen the only true aborigines of the country. Stow regarded the Hottentots as comparatively recent immigrants, and the Bantu-speaking people as having invaded South Africa in a number of successive "waves" from Central Africa, driving the Hottentots before them.[62]

Bleek

In his highly influential publications, Theal integrated and amplified the work of his predecessors, within a world view that combined Eurocentricity with social Darwinism and a strong reliance on migration as a dominant explanatory factor.[63] In particular, Theal tied cultural characteristics directly to physical characteristics. The "Bushmen" were an "unimprovable race," "one of the lowest, if not the very lowest, of all the races on the face of the earth."[64] Acknowledging debts to Bleek and Stow, Theal had the "Hottentot race" originating in Somaliland as a mixture of "Hamites" with Bush women, who then were driven southward to the Great Lakes area and later displaced from there by "Bantu tribes."[65] The "Bantu," according to Theal, were of Asian origin, as suggested by Bleek and van Oordt. They entered North Africa at some time "not exceedingly remote" and,

Bantu → Asian origin.

after various vicissitudes, three Bantu "hordes" arrived in southern Africa, one having traveled southeastward from the Guinea coast ending up in the Transkei and Natal, another migrating southward from the Great Lakes reaching the South African highveld, and the third from the Congo basin settling in South West Africa.[66] Bantu individuals, said Theal, differed in intelligence more or less in proportion to the amount of white "blood" they had acquired in North Africa: "With blood of such different origins in their veins, some are far more intelligent than others, but the opinion of those who have most to do with them now—four hundred years after their first contact with Caucasian civilisation—is that occasional individuals are capable of rising to a high standard, but that the great mass shows little aptitude for European culture."[67] Adopting a metaphor that was popular in Europe in the nineteenth century, Theal declared that the intelligence of an African child stops developing at about the age of puberty: "The growth of his mind, which at first promised so much, has ceased just at that stage when the mind of the European begins to display the greatest vigour."[68] As for the impressive stone buildings at Great Zimbabwe and elsewhere that were "discovered" by white travelers in the 1870s, Theal lent his authority to the current view that they were the work of representatives of some advanced, alien civilization. Africans could not possibly have created them; they were the work of "invaders," whose disappearance is "an unsolved mystery."[69]

Ideas such as these percolated into the textbooks that were current in the Cape Colony in the late nineteenth century, with an increasing emphasis on the laboring role of Blacks. The major textbook writer was Alexander Wilmot, a Cape Town politician and a fellow of the Royal Geographical Society. Wilmot's perspective stressed racial solidarities, migrations, and conquests by a succession of races. According to Wilmot, white racial superiority justified white political supremacy and white exploitation of "coloured" labor:

> The existence of the coloured races is an immense benefit, as, by means of them, cheap labour is obtainable, and large agricultural supplies can be constantly procured; but Southern Africa, although its population chiefly comprises the descendants of stalwart nomadic races who have migrated from a northern part of the continent, is eminently a white man's country, where homes can be found for millions of the overflowing population of Europe.[70]

The work of people like Wilmot and Theal formed the basis for the spate of publications on South Africa that flowed from the British presses after the discovery of gold in the Transvaal. James Bryce, who had written an important book on American democracy and would later serve as British ambassador in Washington, was a sophisticated exemplar of the racism that permeated the British ruling class in the high imperial age. In his *Impressions of South Africa*, published in 1897 after he had toured the country for several months, there were pungent descriptions of the "inferior races."

> Here in South Africa the native races seem to have made no progress for centuries, if, indeed, they have not actually gone backward; and the feebleness of savage man intensifies one's sense of the overmastering strength of nature. . . . When the Portuguese and Dutch first knew the Kafirs, they did not appear to be making any progress toward a higher culture. Human life was held very cheap; women were in a degraded state, and sexual morality was at a low ebb. Courage, loyalty to chief and tribe, and hospitality were the three prominent virtues. War was the only pursuit in which chieftains sought

distinction, and war was mere slaughter and devasta-
tion, unaccompanied by any views of policy or plans of
administration. The people were—and indeed still are—
passionately attached to their old customs . . . and it
was probably as much the unwillingness to have their
customs disturbed as the apprehension for their land
that made many of the tribes oppose to the advance of
the Europeans so obstinate a resistance. . . . Their minds
are mostly too childish to recollect and draw the necessary inferences from previous defeats, and they never
realized that the whites possessed beyond the sea an
inexhaustible reservoir of men and weapons.[71]

Like Theal, Bryce was sure that the stone ruins in Zimbabwe
were the product of "a more advanced race" than "the Kafirs." "Whoever these people were, they have long since
vanished."[72]

Republican Afrikaners might have agreed with everything
that Bryce wrote about the "native peoples" of South Africa,
but they must have been dismayed to find how he applied
the degeneration theory to themselves. The Afrikaans language, according to Bryce, was "a debased dialect" that
"practically disqualified" them from "literary composition."
The Transvaal Boers were "unlike . . . any European people
or . . . the people of the United States. Severed from Europe
and its influences two hundred years ago, they have, in some
of the elements of modern civilization, gone backward rather
than forward." They are "strangely ignorant and backward
in all their ideas."[73]

Another influential British product of the high imperial
age was a Clarendon Press series, *A Historical Geography of
the British Colonies*, to which C. P. Lucas contributed the
South African volume, published in 1897. It contained the
established stereotypes: Bushmen were "the outcasts of

South Africa, untameable savages"; Hottentots were "a desultory race, with little capacity except for loafing and for minding cattle"; Kaffirs were much more primitive than American Indians—they invaded South Africa quite recently, "raiding, exterminating, clearing the ground of its human products." They had no valid claim to the land: "The ownership which the Bantu tribes could claim had no deep roots in the past. It was won by force, and as it was won and as it was upheld, so it could with no glaring injustice be swept away."[74]

V

As I have demonstrated in chapter 2, throughout the first half of the twentieth century the framework of the precolonial history of southern Africa, as established by Theal and his predecessors, prevailed in virtually all the publications that dealt with the subject, with minor variations and amplifications. It was present in books aimed at an exclusively Afrikaner readership. It was to be found in books written for English-speaking white readers. It affected books derived from African oral traditions. It was embodied in textbooks published in both Afrikaans and English versions for school-children, such as the successful series by C. de K. Fowler and G. J. J. Smit. It even dominated the first book on South African precolonial history by an African, Silas Molema.[75]

The school and college textbooks gave short shrift to the history of the region before the arrival of Van Riebeeck's expedition in 1652. They picked up the local inhabitants as they came within the purview of the Whites and described them from the white perspective. In these descriptions there was no explicit suggestion that Whites and Blacks were separate species (polygenism), or that Whites were at the top of a Great Chain of Being, with Blacks forming the bottom link in the human series, next to the most advanced animals. Nevertheless, they were all based on the assumption that human races were distinct populations, each with specific and enduring cultural as well as physical characteristics, and each at a given place on a scale of civilization.

The textbooks identified three principal races in precolonial southern Africa: Bushmen, who were true savages, on the lowest level of all; Hottentots, who were slightly higher; and Kaffirs, who were barbarians rather than savages because they grew crops and worked iron. Kaffirs were commonly introduced as a cruel and warlike people. The textbooks also usually contained a historical sequence: the Bushmen were the oldest race in the region; the Hottentots came later from the north; the Kaffirs originated in Asia and "trekked" southward in comparatively recent times.

Morgan

In light of the Verwoerdian policy of treating Africans as members of ten distinct "nations" and dividing them among ten separate "homelands," it is interesting to observe that in pre-1948 Afrikaner thought the stress was still on races as populations with common qualities, rather than on differences within each race. For example, in his nationalist polemic entitled *Boer en Barbaar* (Boer and Barbarian), J. H. Malan cited van Oordt's theory that "the original Country of the Bantu was the peninsula of Malacca," and stressed the cultural unity as well as the "barbarity" of the Africans. From Central Africa, one tribe "bulged out to the south," and, after many years, "the nation broke up into great sections and splattered further southwards out of each of them on account of new streams from the north." "[A]ll the Kaffir tribes from Ovamboland to the Keiskamma in the east earlier belonged to one nation"; the similarities in their customs and dialects "constitute irrefutable grounds for that conclusion."[76] Likewise, an Afrikaans history textbook by D. J. J.

de Villiers and others published in about 1920 had the usual three distinct races, each treated as a single entity, and introduced the "Kaffers" as "a warlike race."[77] Another such textbook by W. Fouché included a variant, derived from distinctions made by early Dutch officials. Fouché added to the usual three races a predecessor of the Bushman, "Strandlopers" (Beachwalkers), describing them as "black people" who belonged to "a very low human race" and have subsequently disappeared.[78] They were followed by Bushmen, who came from "the center of Africa," Hottentots from the north of Africa, and Bantu, who probably lived first in Asia and then in central Africa, from which they "trekked" southward to their present homes. The Bantu "were bloodthirsty and cruel, and some tribes tortured and killed their captives in the most horrible ways."[79]

Some English language textbooks were less negrophobic. In Natal, for example, where British South Africans controlled the educational system, the principal textbook used in schools during the late nineteenth and early twentieth centuries was by Robert Russell, a superintendent of education in the colony. Russell distinguished the usual three races and had the "Kafirs or Bantus" coming down from north Africa, "driven south by Hamitic tribes from Western Asia."[80] However, unlike most contemporary authors, Russell who had probably read the accounts of the *Stavenisse* survivors in Bird's *Annals of Natal,* described the "Kafirs" as "an intelligent, talkative, laughter-loving people, brave and cruel in war, and kind and hospitable in peace," who had been living "in the midst of plenty" and "in perfect amity" down to the time of Shaka.[81] Commenting on this book, Theal took Russell to task for painting Africans in favorable hues: "As soon as one gets beneath the surface of Bantu traditions anywhere in South Africa, it becomes certain that the normal condition of things was pillage and bloodshed."[82]

During the first half of the twentieth century, two European missionaries wrote books based on African oral traditions that they had collected over many years. One was a
History of the Basuto: Ancient and Modern, which was an English translation of a manuscript by D. F. Ellenberger, a veteran of the Paris Evangelical Missionary Society who had
arrived in Lesotho in 1861. Citing Bleek, Ellenberger regarded Hottentots as "an entirely different race" from Bushmen; and he had "the Bantu race" originating in Egypt or
Ethiopia and ejecting offshoots southward from the center
of the continent, "like swarms of bees always in search of
new country wherein to settle and multiply."[83] The other
work derived from oral traditions was *Olden Times in Zululand
and Natal* by A. T. Bryant, a British Catholic missionary who
had arrived there in 1883. Bryant classified mankind into
"races," "divisions," and "families," and so on down to
"clans," "septs," and "nepts." Negroes constituted a *race* ("a
generally recognized primary variety of the human species
distinguished by special physiological peculiarities"), of
which "the Bantu" formed a *division* ("geographically, lin-
guistically and culturally distinct"), and the Nguni, Sotho,
and Tonga were the three South African *families* ("specialized
sections" of the division).[84] Both Ellenberger and Bryant
were Eurocentric and paternalistic, and yet deeply committed to their projects. As Bryant put it, "For us, the more
richly endowed Caucasic race, we hold it an altruistic duty
to our unlettered Negro brother to rescue him from final
oblivion, before too late, such of his simple traditions as are
still recoverable, whatever be their worthlessness to us."[85]
Bryant went on to complain of lack of public support: "So
far as we know . . . no public fund or South African Government . . . has ever considered the systematic collection
and preservation of Native history as worth the outlay of
one brass farthing or the expenditure of one hour's labour—

a grim reflection, indeed, of the Whiteman's consistent and deliberate neglect of Native interests in the past."[86]

In 1937, thirteen authors, most of them connected with the relatively liberal English-medium South African universities, summed up white South African scholarship of the period before the Second World War in *The Bantu-speaking Tribes of South Africa*. Raymond Dart, professor of anatomy at the University of the Witwatersrand, contributed the first chapter, which was entitled "Racial Origins."[87] His work rested on the assumption that pure races had once existed, and that each such race had distinct physical characteristics and a distinctive cultural level. In contemporary Africa, according to Dart, there were three races: "Bush," "Brown or Hamitic," and "Negro," each of which had originated in Africa. None of the existing races was pure, as a result of "mongrelization" over time, but impurities could be identified and gauged by measurement of skulls. The amount of Asian infusion, for example, could be determined by applying "Retzius's anthropological weapon, the cephalic index,"[88] since all three African races are longheaded (dolichocephalic) and most Asians are broadheaded (brachycephalic). The impurities in each African race, and in each segment of the Negro race, could be identified by applying an elaborate scheme worked out by Italian anatomists, according to which skulls could be classified in no fewer than eighteen different categories.[89] Correlating his physical data with linguistic and cultural information, Dart had Bush people entering South Africa from the north and eliminating the earliest inhabitants, whom he called Boskop people; and then members of the Bantu branch of the Negro race, who had already mixed with Brown or Hamitic people in East Africa, entering South Africa in a series of waves and mingling with the Bush people. Dart did not assign dates to these events, beyond suggesting that Bantu began to move

southward from the Great Lakes region at the end of the
sixth century A.D. and eventually entered South Africa "by
a series of inroads separated by centuries."[90] Nor did Dart
speculate on the relationships between the physical and the
mental or cultural qualities of human beings. However, it is
abundantly clear that he believed that such relationships
existed and that the "Nordic" (or white) race was the climax
of human development. The Negro skull, wrote Dart, "is
infantile in form"; the Bush skull is "foetal" and the Bush
"retain primitive features in the lower jaw."[91]

In another chapter in *The Bantu-speaking Tribes of South
Africa*, N. J. van Warmelo, a government ethnologist, contended that it was not possible to recover anything substantial concerning the history of the African population before
the time of Shaka (the early nineteenth century). Referring
specifically to the work of Bryant, van Warmelo wrote that
"as regards origins we are up against a wall we are not as
yet prepared to scale. The theories hitherto put forward are
not worth repeating here: they appear to be fanciful, and
hardly meet the case."[92] Van Warmelo cannot be faulted for
deriding the theories that were current in the first half of the
twentieth century concerning the origins of the precolonial
inhabitants of southern Africa. However, although he was a
zealous recorder of African traditions, he failed to foresee
that archaeologists, anthropologists, and historians would
soon begin to provide a less fanciful, though still far from
complete, account of the early history of the region.

The persistent influence of Theal over textbook writers,
and the contributions of scholars such as Dart to *The Bantu-
speaking Tribes of South Africa* indicate that before 1948 there
were no fundamental, generic differences between the racial
assumptions of Afrikaners and those of other white South
Africans. Indeed, it is likely that such differences as existed
were more a matter of occupation, class, and regional milieu
than of ethnicity. To nearly all white South Africans, it

seemed obvious that they themselves were members of a race that was superior to all other races in Africa. This was demonstrated to their satisfaction in every facet of contemporary life: religion, technology, politics, and the arts, as well as the vast difference in power and wealth. As Bryant pointed out, Whites were generally indifferent to the precolonial history of the region. The chronology of African migration meant nothing to them; and they laid much more stress on the common qualities of the "natives" than on the differences among them. This is not to say that there was no core mythology to endorse the racial order, but rather that the core mythology did not include specific historical details. White South Africans took it as given that races were static, self-perpetuating entities with fixed cultural and linguistic as well as physical characteristics, and that they themselves represented the summit of human achievement.

The racial mythology that prevailed in Europe and North *key point.* America in the first half of the twentieth century was very similar to that prevailing in southern Africa. We have seen how liberal British statesmen such as James Bryce dealt with the problem of race at the turn of the century. Views such as his persisted in Europe and North America, not only in political and popular circles but also among reputable scientists. If craniology, as espoused by Dart, was becoming old-fashioned, support for racism was provided by the eugenics movement that flourished in the early twentieth century. Eugenicists contended that mankind should be *eugenics* improved through the adoption of genetic policies, for example, through fiscal measures encouraging childbearing by allegedly superior human types. For a time eugenics attracted scientists as renowned as J. B. S. Haldane and Julian Huxley, William McDougall and John Maynard Keynes. When eugenics began to be discredited in the 1920s, scientific racism continued to receive indirect support from the hereditarian theory of IQ, which was adopted by scientists in America at the end of the nineteenth century and developed there by people such as H. H. Goddard, Lewis M. Terman, Robert M. Yerkes, and Charles Spearman. In England, it was given a great boost by Cyril Burt. Stephen Jay Gould has shown how all such scientific props for racism were the products of inadequate methodology and false logic; in many cases, a scientist's unconscious assumptions determined his methodology, which in turn ensured that the conclusions vindicated the assumptions. In at least one case a scientist willfully falsified the evidence. Sir Cyril Burt, who stood at the pinnacle of the psychological profession in England and was knighted for his work, concocted data to show a high correlation between the IQ scores of identical twins who had been raised apart, thus "proving" that hereditary factors were more influential than environmental factors in determining achievement—frauds that were not exposed until after Burt's death in 1971.[93]

C. G. Seligman, a leading British anthropologist, wrote a textbook entitled the *Races of Africa* that was regarded as authoritative in Britain for many years. It was first published in 1930, and revised editions were issued in 1939 and, after his death, in 1957, when it was still being recommended for use in the London School of Oriental and African Studies. Seligman's ideas were fully compatible with white South African norms. There is the same conceptualization of races as ideal types, which he implied had an actual existence before they were confused by migrations. The precolonial history of Africa was essentially a history of interaction between intrusive "Hamites" and local Negroes and Bushmen. "The Hamites . . . are 'Europeans,' i.e. belong to the same great branch of mankind as the Whites,"[94] and they were responsible for every significant achievement in Africa:

> Indeed it would not be very wide of the mark to say
> that the history of Africa south of the Sahara is no more

than the story of the permeation through the ages, in different degrees and at various times, of the Negroes and the Bushmen by Hamitic blood and culture. The Hamites were, in fact, the great civilizing force of black Africa from a relatively early period, the influence of the Semites being late and in the main confined to the "white" areas north of the Sahara inhabited by Hamitic peoples.[95]

And again:

Apart from relatively late Semitic influence—whether Phoenician (Carthaginian) and strictly limited, or Arab (Muhammadam) and widely diffused—the civilizations of Africa are the civilizations of the Hamites, its history the record of these peoples and of their interaction with the two other African stocks, the Negro and the Bushman, whether this influence was exerted by highly civilized Egyptians or by such wider pastoralists as are represented at the present day by the Beja and the Somali.[96]

In European colonial circles, the myth of white racial superiority persisted to the very end of the imperial era. In 1939, a French professor in Algeria published an article in an American medical journal purporting to prove that native Algerians were biologically inferior. They were, he argued, deficient in that part of the brain that distinguished mankind from animals—the cortex: "The native of North Africa, whose superior and cortical activities are only slightly developed, is a primitive creature whose life, essentially vegetative and instinctive, is above all regulated by his diencephalon."[97] This meant that Algerians were doomed to remain mentally puerile people. As late as the 1950s Dr. A. Carothers, an expert employed by the World Health Organization, found another biological reason for coming to the same conclusion about Africans. In 1954 he published a study showing that "the African" was the equivalent of a European who had had a frontal lobotomy—an operation that was known to have serious personality effects. Appointed by the British government to investigate the so-called Mau-Mau rebellion in colonial Kenya, Carothers produced a report that attributed the rebellion to the psychiatric atavism of the "natives" and that justified placing captives in special prisons and subjecting them to a cruel program of "psychological rehabilitation."[98]

Carothers was an exceptional case. Nevertheless, his program was a logical, if extreme, expression of the racism that pervaded Western thought throughout the imperial era. Indeed, the core of the political mythology of race—the assumption of innate white superiority—prevailed in the consciousness of most white people, wherever they lived, well into the second half of the twentieth century. Reflecting the power relationships of the time, it was shared by white people of all social classes. In South Africa, it validated the structure of a capitalist state where the fundamental cleavage was perceived in racial terms. Having conquered the indigenous peoples and deprived them of much of their land, Whites were obliging them to provide cheap labor for their homes, their farms, and their industries. The same core mythology legitimized the structure of the European empires in Africa, Asia, and the Caribbean. It also legitimized general discrimination against black people in the United States of America. However, scholars had begun to dismantle the racist paradigm during the colonial era, and after the Second World War the reaction against racism gradually penetrated the popular consciousness in Europe and America, in conjunction with the termination of European colonialism and the growth of black power in the United States.

4

THE STRANGE CAREER
OF SLAGTERSNEK

I

The subject of the previous chapter, the concept that human "races" are unassimilable, is at the heart of the Afrikaner nationalist mythology, and of the political economy that it endorses. This chapter deals with a different phenomenon: a specific political myth. The myth of Slagtersnek is a tale about a particular historical episode, which is interpreted as illustrating both elements in the core mythology—the ethnic element and the racial element.

The episode occurred in 1815 and 1816 on the eastern frontier of the Cape Colony, which already had a history of social and political instability. Throughout the first three quarters of the eighteenth century, Afrikaner pastoralists, who became known as *trekboers* or simply as *Boers* (farmers), had been carrying the colonial frontier farther and farther eastward from the Cape peninsula, grazing their sheep and cattle on vast tracts of arid land.[1] Unable to stop them, the Khoikhoi inhabitants lost control of the sparse springs and streams of the area and with them their capacity to survive as independent communities. Instead, they became shepherds, cattleherds, and general servants for Boers. The Dutch East India Company paid little attention to these events; its interest in South Africa was confined to the harbors in the Cape peninsula and the products of the adjacent arable lands. Consequently, the Boers were able to deal with their Khoikhoi dependents as they wished. In practice, treatment varied with the personality of the individual Boer and his family and ranged from benevolent paternalism to callous brutality.[2]

During the 1770s the easternmost Boers began to impinge on the territory of Bantu-speaking African farmers in the vicinity of the Fish River, five hundred miles from Cape Town. In the frontier conflicts that followed, the Boers relied on the colonial government for military assistance, as well as for supplies of arms and ammunition. As the Dutch East India Company officials became involved in the defense of the Boers, they inevitably began to take cognizance of the social relations that had developed in the frontier region; and so did their successors, the British officials who ruled the colony from 1795 to 1803. Becoming aware that some of the Boers were abusing their power over their Khoikhoi serfs, they tentatively tried to stop the worst abuses. Some of the frontier Boers, reacting against what they regarded as unwonted interference in their affairs, rebelled against the Dutch Company regime in 1795 and against the British regime in 1799. In turn, during the latter rising some of the Khoikhoi seized the opportunity to abscond from their Boer masters and collaborate with hostile Africans.[3]

After wresting the Cape from the Dutch for the second time in 1806, the British colonial officials made a deliberate effort to bring a measure of law and order to the eastern districts, but without threatening the basic racial structure of colonial society. In 1809 the governor issued a proclamation that legalized the serflike status of the Khoikhoi ("Hottentots"), requiring them to have a fixed place of abode from which they were not to move without a pass signed by their employer or by an official. On the other hand, the proclamation also provided them with some protection by prohibiting such abuses as deductions from wages and by requiring all contracts for periods of a month or more to be registered before an official.[4]

Second, extending a practice that had been started by the Dutch regime of 1803–06, the British divided the colony into a larger number of districts and subdistricts, thus bringing the administration closer to the people. Nevertheless, the British preserved the old Dutch system of local administration. The central government appointed one full-time, salaried career officer known as a *landdrost* to each district, but a *landdrost* was dependent on the cooperation of the leading Boers of a district: *heemraden*, who were fellow members of the district court, commandants, who led the district militia, and field cornets, who were responsible for keeping the peace in each ward or subdivision of the district. The Boers had a say in the appointments of these part-time officials, as the government in Cape Town selected them from double lists supplied by the outgoing officeholders. Moreover, many of the *landdrosts* were men who had served the Dutch government and stayed on in South Africa after the British conquest. For example, Andries Stockenström, *landdrost* of Graaff-Reinet, who would play a major role in the Slagtersnek episode, was born in South Africa, the son of a Swede who had entered the service of the Dutch East India Company and been killed by Africans during the war of 1811–12. The other *landdrost* who became involved in the affair, Jacob Glen Cuyler, was a New Yorker of Dutch descent who had left America as a Loyalist during the Revolution.[5]

Third, from 1811 onward commissions of the colonial court made annual circuits of the colony, hearing criminal cases in each district headquarters. The circuit court of 1812 heard several cases brought by members of the London Missionary Society, which had begun operations in South Africa at the end of the eighteenth century, charging Boers with ill-treating Khoikhoi servants. Although most of the Boers were found not guilty, the fact that they had been brought to court to answer such charges was an innovation that made a strong impression. The circuit of 1812 became known as the Black Circuit.[6]

Fourth, an 1813 proclamation changed the system of land-ownership. Previously, Boers could easily acquire de facto ownership of large "loan farms" by paying small annual "recognition fees" to the government; and in practice most frontier Boers who occupied land were in arrears or had never paid the annual tax at all. The new law put pressure on the Boers to have their tenure converted into perpetual quitrent, on conditions that limited the size of farms and led to the land being surveyed for the first time.[7]

Fifth, in 1811 and 1812 a mixed force of British regulars, local Boers, and Khoikhoi troops drove all Africans beyond the colonial boundary, which ran along the lower Fish River and a line to the east of the upper Fish River. The government also constructed a line of forts along the banks of that river, with garrisons to defend the frontier and to enforce a policy of strict separation between the colony and the Xhosa farming communities.[8] The principal military force that was stationed on the frontier was the Cape Regiment, consisting of white officers and Khoikhoi and Coloured other ranks. The Dutch Company had started the practice of using such people in the army in 1793, and from then until 1870 all Cape colonial governments made use of them.[9]

By 1815, the year in which the peace settlement at the end of the Napoleonic Wars confirmed the British in their possession of the Cape Colony, the colonial government's innovations were creating an unprecedented measure of control over the turbulent frontier zone. The episode that became known as the Slagtersnek rebellion would put them to the test.

II

In April 1813 a Khoikhoi, whose name appears as Booy in the records, traveled thirty-five miles from his employer's farm to make a complaint at the office of the assistant *landdrost* at the new frontier post named Cradock. His employer, a fifty-three-year-old man named Cornelis Frederik Bezuidenhout, known as Freek Bezuidenhout, occupied land in the valley of Baviaan's River, near the eastern boundary of the Cape Colony. Booy claimed that Freek was holding back part of his pay and would not allow him to leave with his cattle, although his contract had expired. That was the first link in a chain of events that led to the death of Freek, of his brother Johannes Jurgen Bezuidenhout, known as Hans, of five other frontier Boers, and of one Coloured soldier.[10]

During the next two years, Freek repeatedly refused to leave his land to respond to Booy's complaints. Meanwhile, Booy left Freek's employment. In May 1814 he returned to the farm to claim his cattle, but Freek refused and drove him off with a stick. Later that year, another Khoikhoi caught Booy making love to his wife and killed him in the vicinity of Freek's homestead. Freek's knowledge of Booy's death may have stiffened his resolve to ignore the official summonses, for fear that he might be charged with the murder.

In October 1815 the Circuit Court of two colonial judges visited Graaff-Reinet, where the young *landdrost,* Andries Stockenström, placed the case of the absent Freek Bezuidenhout on the charge sheet. The judges were not aware of the death of Booy, but they had to deal with Freek's persistent refusal to respond to the summonses. They found him guilty of contempt of court and sentenced him in absentia to one month's imprisonment.

The undersheriff charged with arresting Freek found that the local field cornet was not willing to participate, because he knew Freek to be a dangerous man who had already threatened to resist any attempt to arrest him. Indeed, Freek and his kinsmen were marginal people in Boer society. They ignored its religious and social norms. Freek himself had never been through a marriage ceremony but had fathered at least three children, none of whom had been baptized. In 1815 he was living with a Coloured woman, and his household also included a young Coloured man, who was his son by an earlier liaison.[11]

Since the civilian officials refused to help, the undersheriff obtained assistance from the detachment of the Cape Regiment that was stationed at the nearest military post. On the morning of 10 October 1815, the undersheriff, two white officers, and sixteen Coloured soldiers reached Freek's farm. Seeing them approach, Freek and his son fired warning shots in their direction, then fled from the vicinity of the house and took refuge in a cave on a hillside. The undersheriff tried repeatedly to persuade Freek to surrender. After three or four hours of verbal stalemate, the officer in command ordered his men to surround and enter the cave to carry out the arrest. The Coloured sergeant led the way to the entrance to the cave and, seeing that Freek was standing up with his gun at his shoulder, apparently about to fire at him, he shot him dead.[12]

A couple of days later, twenty or thirty people, including three of Freek's brothers and some of their children, attended Freek's funeral, which was conducted by an itinerant Dutch teacher. Afterward, at a rowdy party at the homestead, Freek's brother Hans Bezuidenhout swore vengeance on the three white people he regarded as having caused his brother's death at the hand of a Hottentot: Landdrost Stockenström, the field cornet of Freek's ward, and the officer in command of the sergeant who fired the shot.

Hans Bezuidenhout then began to organize a conspiracy. His principal accomplices were men who had personal reasons to wish to defy the authorities, such as Hendrik Frederik Prinsloo, who was nicknamed Kasteel because his father had been imprisoned in the castle in Cape Town as a leader of the 1799 rebellion in the Graaff-Reinet district; Stephanus Bothma, who had been convicted of forgery in 1800 and banished from the colony for five years; and Cornelis Faber, Hans Bezuidenhout's brother-in-law, who had lived among the Xhosa for several years to avoid punishment for taking part in the 1799 rebellion.[13]

Their goal was to oust the British regime and the hated Cape Regiment. To achieve this, the conspirators tried to mobilize two distinct forces: the frontier Boers and the neighboring Xhosa. By visiting likely households and circulating inflammatory letters, they managed to gather some support from fellow white frontiersmen, especially from members of families who, like themselves, lived on the fringes of organized society, moving from place to place and occupying land without paying the prescribed "recognition fees." They played on the grievances of such people, who regretted the passing of the time when the Dutch East India Company had treated them with benign neglect. As one sixteen-year-old put it when he was eventually charged with treason: "I am a young man who does not yet know what a Government is, as I was never near one."[14] Several of the men they enlisted were members of families that had risen against the Dutch government in 1795 and against the British government in 1799. They especially resented the recent innovations, such as the 1809 proclamation concerning the Khoikhoi, and the proceedings of the Black Circuit of 1812. They loathed the Cape Regiment, manned as it was by Coloured people. They also disliked the new land regulations, which increased the cost of the annual occupation licenses at a time when it was no longer easy to acquire fresh land to the east, where they were impinging on the territory of the Xhosa chiefdoms. However, in addition to harping on such grievances, Hans Bezuidenhout and his closest fellow conspirators intimidated Boers into joining them with the threat that Xhosa allies would murder them if they did not cooperate. On this basis, Hans Bezuidenhout managed to gather a hundred or more men. Most of them did not know very much about the situation they were becoming involved in; and some of them were terrified at the thought of a Xhosa invasion.

The conspirators did indeed try to obtain Xhosa assistance. Cornelis Faber led two expeditions eastward to the homestead of Ngqika, the principal chief of the Rarabe Xhosa, to invite him to invade the colony. If he would help them to drive away the Cape Regiment, eject the British officials, and allow the Boers to occupy the Kat River valley, Ngqika's people could regain the area west of the lower Fish River known as the Zuurveld, from which British troops and colonial commandos had ejected them in 1812. They could also keep the cattle they looted from the Cape Regiment. According to the Khoikhoi who interpreted for Ngqika, Faber told the Xhosa chief that "the whole of the Baviaans River were united and all the people through Graaff-Reinet as far as the Cape, and that there were six hundred Hollanders who were also ready, and that there was but a handful of English here."[15]

News of the conspiracy soon reached the local officials. Rebels blabbed in the presence of neighbors, who informed the authorities. On 10 November, an emotional letter soliciting support for the rebellion fell into official hands. It was signed by Hendrik Frederik Prinsloo and read:

> Dear and much esteemed Cousin, Jacobus Krugel, I wish you the most necessary for Soul and Body. Cousin,

I write to you in the Name of the Burghers of the whole of Bruintjes Hoogte, Zuurveld and Tarka to represent the Business to your District, and especially the Field Cornet, Van der Walt, that we have unanimously resolved, according to our Oath, which we took to our Mother Country, to remain as Protectors to remove the God forgotten Tyrants and Villains, as every one, let him be who he may, is convinced with God, how shocking, and how God forgotten it goes with our Country, which we took an Oath for, for everyone is convinced, whether or not they shall be present at the appointed date; and to you I trust the Business to bring it under the people's eyes as speedily as possible, whether they will or not, and I send you the letter in the hands of the Burgher, Christiaan Muller, and request an answer with the Bearer what the people say; the consequences speak for themselves, I trust to you to bring it under the people's eyes. And this letter I recommend into your hands to burn; you see my great confidence in you, the letter serves you all. I therefore hope you will burn it directly you bring it under the people's eyes verbally. Now I trust in you, and am, with esteem and greetings to you, your Cousin.[16]

Most of the substantial Boers in the eastern frontier districts, including nearly all the local officials—the *heemraden,* the field cornets, and the commandants—stood by the government; and in cooperation with Landdrost Andries Stockenström of Graaff-Reinet, Landdrost Cuyler of Uitenhage, the Cape Regiment, and the British frontier dragoons they rapidly organized to suppress the uprising with as little bloodshed as possible. On 13 November, Kasteel Prinsloo was arrested and taken to the military post known as Vanaardtspos on the Fish River. The next day, learning of the arrest, Hans Bezuidenhout led about two hundred armed men to Vanaardtspos and demanded his release. When that was refused, he persuaded some of his followers to swear an oath that they would remain faithful. During the next few days Bezuidenhout's followers began to melt away, but about sixty men moved northward with him. On 18 November they were about twelve miles north of Vanaardtspos, at the bottom of a hill on the side of a mountain pass that was known as Slagtersnek. The word means Butchers' Neck and had been applied to it because it was a place where butchers' agents from Cape Town came to buy cattle from the Boers.[17]

There, on the eighteenth, a loyalist force of fellow Boers and British dragoons caught up with them. The Boer officials tried repeatedly to persuade Hans's people to lay down their arms, but he managed to constrain most of them until, apparently by chance, Cornelis Faber and his party arrived on the scene on their return from their second mission to the Xhosa. They brought the news that Ngqika would do nothing to help, which broke Hans's hold over most of his remaining followers. Eighteen or twenty of them surrendered and the rest dispersed. Most returned to their homes, but Hans Bezuidenhout and his family, Cornelis Faber, Stephanus Bothma, and several others fled northward into Xhosa country. On 29 November twenty-two Boers and a hundred members of the Cape Regiment caught up with them beyond the Winterberg Mountains, nearly fifty miles northeast of Slagtersnek. Faber, Bothma, and the rest surrendered; but Hans Bezuidenhout, his wife Martha (who was Faber's sister), and their twelve-year-old son resisted fiercely. While Martha reloaded his guns, Hans fired several times, killing one of the Coloured soldiers. The soldiers returned the fire, wounding and capturing all three Bezuidenhouts. Hans died the same day, but Martha and their son recovered from their wounds.[18]

Soon afterward, forty-seven prisoners were tried at Uitenhage. The Circuit Court started taking evidence and then handed the case over to a special commission of the colonial High Court. The proceedings were thorough. Indeed, when the relevant documents were collated and published in 1902, they ran to nearly a thousand printed pages, which constitute a rich documentation for early nineteenth-century frontier society.[19] Trying to identify the ringleaders, the court interrogated numerous witnesses and every one of the accused, some of them as many as four times. Eventually, confronted with compromising evidence, most of the accused admitted the facts as related by Landdrost Cuyler, who served as prosecutor, but almost every one of them claimed that he had acted involuntarily, under pressure from Hans Bezuidenhout, who, being dead, could not respond. On 22 January 1816 the judges, both of whom were Dutch, delivered their verdict. Thirty-eight of the accused were to be taken to the vicinity of Vanaardtspos, where some of them had sworn the oath on 14 November, and there six of them were to be hanged: Hendrik Prinsloo, Cornelis Faber, Abraham Bothma, Theunis de Klerk, Stephanus Bothma, and Willem Krugel. The other thirty-two, after witnessing the hangings, were to undergo various punishments, ranging from banishment for life to imprisonment for one month or a fine of fifty rix dollars.[20]

Lord Charles Somerset, governor of the Cape Colony, commuted the death sentence on Krugel and reduced many of the other sentences. The five death sentences were carried out at Vanaardtspos, twelve miles south of Slagtersnek, on 9 March 1816 in the presence of about three hundred soldiers as well as Landdrosts Cuyler and Stockenström, the *heem-*

raden and field cornets of the districts of Uitenhage and
Graaff-Reinet, and T. J. Herold, the Dutch Reformed clergyman from George, as well as the other convicted rebels.
No other civilians were obliged to be present, but some
friends and relatives of the condemned men were there.

The executions were bungled. The government in Cape
Town had sent written instructions to the hangman, who
lived two hundred miles to the west at George, but the letter
implied that only one person was to be hanged. Consequently, he brought only one rope with him. On reaching
Uitenhage and discovering that there were five condemned
men, he obtained four more ropes—but these were rotten,
with the result that when the trap was removed only the
sound rope held; the others broke and four live men fell to
the ground. They pleaded to Landdrost Cuyler for mercy;
but he lacked the authority to comply. In the words of Landdrost Cuyler, who was in charge: "They, all four, got up,
one attempted to leave the spot and rush towards the place
where the College of Landdrosts and Heemraden were. They
all four spoke, and at this moment some of the spectators
ran to me soliciting pardon for them, fancying it was in my
power to grant it."[21] Eventually, all four were hanged in
succession from the sound rope. Cuyler's report continued,
"I cannot describe the distressed countenances of the inhabitants . . . who were sentenced to witness the execution."[22]

The Reverend C. I. Latrobe, an English Moravian who was
visiting South Africa, reached George a week after the cul-
mination of these events. In the account of his journey,
which was first published in 1818, he wrote:

After dinner [on Sunday 17 March 1816], the reverend
Mr. Herold, minister of George, having returned from
Uitenhagen, called on the landdrost, to make a report
of his attendance on the five rebellious boors, who were

executed last Saturday in that district. He gave a most melancholy account of that event. The hangman was a black. The halters were too weak, or rather, as some suspected, intentionally cut; but no sooner had the delinquents been turned off, and the platform removed, than four of the five fell from the gallows. Having unfortunately been persuaded to believe, that by English custom, a man thus falling down is free, the poor wretches cried for mercy, and one, addressing the by-standers, exclaimed, that by this accident it was made manifest, that God would not permit them to be put to death. The landdrost, Colonel Cuyler, was, however, obliged to let justice take its course, and other halters being procured, they were launched into eternity. The clergyman described them all as well prepared to die, acknowledging the justice of their sentence, and appearing truly penitent. Not many spectators attended; but their wives and relatives were present, which is hardly to be explained by the standard of English feeling. No disturbance whatever took place, a party of dragoons and the Cape regiment keeping guard. This is said to be the first time, that any African's [sic] descendants from Europeans, have suffered death for crimes deemed capital in Europe. Government has often extended mercy to such as deserved condign punishment, but it seems only to have had that effect, that the rebels believed no Government to have the courage to take away their lives, for crimes committed against the state. It was, therefore, necessary to make an example, and out of twenty-four condemned to die, five of the most notorious offenders had been selected for the purpose. The rest were punished with imprisonment, forfeiture, or banishment. The reverend Mr. Herold seemed greatly agitated, and declared, that the impression, made on his mind by so dreadful a catastrophe, would not be soon effaced.[23]

In September 1816, Governor Somerset received two official reports on the events. W. D. Jennings and F. R. Bresler, the members of the Circuit Court that had been in the area at the time of the rebellion and had started the interrogation of the prisoners at Uitenhage, wrote that they had

> much satisfaction . . . in asserting that the cause of the rebellion may be clearly traced to a few discontented inhabitants of the neighbourhood of the Baviaans River, the relatives and friends of F. C. Bezuidenhout, whose uniform disobedience to the laws for years past, and at last, violent resistance to them, led to his own destruction. That those who joined them were deceived by misrepresentation, and compelled by threats, but that the most respectable, and by far the most numerous class of the inhabitants of the outer districts beheld with indignation the resistance of a part of their fellow subjects to the wise and efficacious regulations of your Excellency's Government.[24]

P. Diemel and W. Hiddingh, the members of the Special Commission that had conducted the trial of the rebels, came to much the same conclusion. They reported that the ringleaders were not landowners but lived with others or had no fixed residence. Those who claimed to be acting to avenge the death of Frederik Bezuidenhout were using it as a pretext for their long cherished criminal intentions. Above all, Diemel and Hiddingh assured Lord Charles Somerset, "The well-to-do farmers are animated with a good spirit."[25]

The events of 1815 and 1816 were, indeed, of some significance. For the first time in the history of the Cape Colony, white colonists who had been tried and convicted of high treason had actually been executed. The substantial Boers, including nearly all the *heemraden* and field cornets, had cooperated. The episode marked the coming of law and order to a previously anarchic frontier zone.

III

These events did not have widespread repercussions at the time. In April 1816 the government published a brief account of the episode, based on Cuyler's brief for the prosecution, and copies were sent to the *landdrosts* for distribution.[26] When Governor Somerset toured the frontier districts in 1817, he received a cordial reception. Moreover, according to Andries Stockenström, after the hangings at Vanaardtspos there was no opposition when Boers were prosecuted and executed for murdering Coloured people:

> Some years later a poor miserable Hottentot was murdered by a member of a very respectable Burgher family. It became a most painful duty to prosecute him; great sensation prevailed; but he was taken and conducted to prison by Boer field-cornets, found guilty upon Boer testimony, and executed in the midst of a Boer armed force under my orders, when there was not a single soldier or bayonet within one hundred miles, without my ever having received a single cross look from those who were bewailing the tragedy in tears, whilst they joined in the general admission that justice had been done.[27]

The rebellion did, inevitably, leave a deep impression on the surviving participants, and their friends and neighbors. In 1816 the Reverend Latrobe traveled eastward after meeting the Reverend Herold at George and visited the farm occupied by the sixty-seven-year-old Marthinus Prinsloo, who had been a leader of the rebellions in 1795–96 and

1799 and whose son, Kasteel, had recently been hanged. Latrobe found that old Prinsloo had no compunction in showing that he hated the English for administering the law more efficiently than their Dutch predecessors.[28]

In 1820, Thomas Pringle was the leader of a party of twenty-four Scottish immigrants who settled in the Baviaan's River valley on land that had been expropriated from the convicted rebels. In his widely read *Narrative of a Residence in South Africa*, which was published in 1835, Pringle gave an account of the rebellion, based on the official report and on his personal knowledge of his Boer neighbors and several of the officials who had been involved in the events. He described the rebels as "inexperienced hot-headed young men" and wrote that their friends and relatives "had . . . received a lesson not likely to be soon forgotten; and we found them very submissive subjects to the Government, and inoffensive neighbors, so far as *we* were concerned."[29] Pringle was, however, extremely critical of the racial attitudes of the Boers, including the *heemraden* and field cornets:

The fact is, that even the very best of these men have been trained from their childhood to regard Bushmen and Caffers with nearly the same feelings as they regard beasts of prey—only with far more rancorous animosity; so that they can scarcely be brought to view even the treacherous slaughter of them as a crime. But while this circumstance may be allowed to palliate the guilt of such untutored men, it casts a darker shade over the conduct of those in authority, who knowing well the habits and prejudices of those semi-barbarous back-settlers, yet intrust them with a perilous discretion towards the natives, which, from the very nature of things, cannot fail to be often grossly abused.

Pringle was not a typical representative of the British settlers. He went on to say:

> Nor would it be just to represent those feelings towards the natives as confined solely to the Dutch-African population. Some of the British settlers, I grieve and blush to say, and those not exclusively of the lower orders, appear to have imbibed, in their full extent, the same inhuman prejudices towards the natives of the soil, and have even had the hardihood to avow such sentiments in print.[30]

In most other works published before the 1870s, the events in the Baviaan's River valley in 1815 faded into oblivion. George Thompson, who wrote an account of his extensive travels in southern Africa, published in 1827, merely referred in passing to "that foolish and criminal insurrection."[31] William Burchell, who wrote exceptionally fine travel literature, published in two volumes in 1822 and 1824, did not mention it at all. Nor did John Philip, the superintendent of the London Missionary Society in South Africa, in his 1828 *Researches in South Africa,* although he might have interpreted the rebellion as material to serve his purpose, which was to influence the British public to have the government intervene in the Cape Colony on behalf of the Khoikhoi.[32] Similarly, I have found no reference to the uprising in the numerous polemics that were published on both sides of a heated debate about the rights of Africans during the 1830s and early 1840s.[33]

Furthermore, there do not seem to have been any substantial links between the 1815 rebellion and the decision of many of the frontier Boers to leave the Cape Colony in the late 1830s. J. A. Heese has shown that nearly all the rebels' families did not take part in what later became known as the Great Trek, while many of the families of the Boer officials who suppressed the rebellion did participate.[34] Among the surviving writings of *voortrekkers*, many of which include lists of grievances against the British and colonial governments, there are scarcely any references to the rebellion. Indeed, law and order was a primary consideration for the people who undertook the task of founding independent Boer polities. For them, the Bezuidenhouts and Prinsloos of Slagtersnek cannot have been attractive models. On 2 February 1837, for example, the *Grahamstown Journal* published a statement from the man who would become the first leader to be recognized by the majority of the emigrants: Piet Retief's "manifesto," which became the classic statement of "the causes of the Great Trek," made no mention of the rebellion.[35] Similarly there is nothing about it in the narratives written in later life by a cousin of Freek and Hans Bezuidenhout and by a niece of Piet Retief.[36] In 1892, a Dutch Reformed clergyman who knew some of the *voortrekkers*, declared: "We have never heard it from the mouth of a single Voortrekker that he has named it [the rebellion] as one of the causes of the Trek."[37]

There was one exception to this trend. In the 1850s Henry Cloete, a Cape colonial official of Afrikaner descent who had played a leading part in the British annexation of Natal and was the first judge in the new colony, gave a series of five lectures in Pietermaritzburg on the Boer migration. Soon afterward, these speeches were published in Pietermaritzburg and Cape Town. Cloete called his opening lecture "The First Boer Rebellion." After summarizing the events of 1815 and 1816, he said:

> In fact, I know, from personal interviews with several of the descendants of those who were then executed, that these events which I have now detailed, have left in their minds a far more indelible impression than even

their losses by the Kafir wars, or the abolition of slavery. When here as Her Majesty's Commissioner, in 1843 and 1844, I endeavoured frequently, in converse with many influential farmers, to soothe down the feelings of hostility which they openly avowed against Her Majesty's Government; and when I had frequently (I hoped) succeeded in convincing them of the mistaken views which they had imbibed as to the principles and objects of Government in public matters, and proved to them satisfactorily, that (as regarded their future prospects) an entire new system had been laid down, and was now carrying on, to give them the enjoyment of the utmost share of rational liberty in all their political institutions; when I had succeeded so far in convincing their minds, I have more than once felt a pang to hear the embodiment of their inmost feelings expressed in the words— "We can never forget Slachters Nek!"[38]

In fact, the only Boers in Natal in 1843 and 1844 who were closely related to any of the executed rebels were the widow and some of the descendants of Theunis de Klerk.[39] It was natural that they should have been bitter. Cloete had met some of them in Natal and was generalizing from their particular case. The balance of the evidence is against his suggestion that the events of 1815 and 1816 were in the minds of many of the other Boers as they left the Cape Colony twenty years after the rebellion. Cloete may have made much of the rebellion in his first lecture for the simple reason that he knew a lot about it, having been the secretary to the Circuit Court that imposed the sentence of a year's imprisonment on Freek Bezuidenhout in October 1815 and that also took initial cognizance of the rebellion later that year, before the special commissioners arrived to try the prisoners. Moreover, by the time he gave those lectures in

" We can never forget Slachters Nek! "

the 1850s, his recollections of the events of 1815 were not completely accurate. His summary of the episode included several palpable errors. For example, he said that the oath (14 November 1815) and the executions (9 March 1816) occurred at a place called "the 'Slachters Nek,' "[40] whereas in fact the mountain pass of that name was twelve miles to the north of the site of the oath and the executions. However, Cloete's lucid lecture and the official summary that was published in 1816 were the only substantial primary sources that were available to the people who resurrected the episode and used it for political purposes later on. Then, Cloete's dictum was endlessly repeated: "We can never forget Slachters Nek!"

key — of the creation of a myth.

Cloete's error in locating the hangings at Slagtersnek—the place where butchers' agents from Cape Town came to buy cattle from the frontier Boers—was to have serious consequences. I have found no evidence that the name had previously been applied to the hangings or to the rebellion as a whole. The colonial government had not done so, nor had Thomas Pringle in his memoir of his time in South Africa. Cloete set an example that was followed by others. The very name *Slagtersnek* had a strong emotional impact because the application of the Afrikaans word *slagter,* meaning a butcher, to the place where the rebels were hanged conjured up visions of a slaughter or massacre.[41]

The history textbooks that were used in the Cape colonial schools in the second half of the nineteenth century included brief accounts of the episode and called it the Slagtersnek rebellion. A typical textbook of the period devoted two pages to the subject, derived from the official report of 1816 and Cloete's lectures, with embellishments from Pringle's account. It was a straightforward narrative that reflected the official British colonial point of view, vindicating the sentences while deploring the "fact" that the *scaffold* broke down. The conclusion cited Cloete and echoed his statement: "Its effect, however, was to raise up a bitter feeling against the British, and to frequently give rise to the expression, 'We can never forget Slachter's Nek.' "[42]

Most of the books that were written in English and published in the Cape Colony or England in the later nineteenth century and that referred to the uprising did so in similar terms, endorsing the actions taken by the officials and repeating Cloete's assertion about its effects. For example, a textbook published in 1877 said:

> This affair arose out of the passionate and revengeful feelings of a few individuals. . . . This was the first instance of any colonists suffering death for crimes deemed capital in Europe. The friends of the condemned men hoped to the last that the utmost severity of the law would not be enforced; and the abhorrent circumstances connected with the execution created an excitement and an ill-feeling which rankled in the minds of the old border colonists for many years after.[43]

A book published in 1885 made a particularly strong casual connection between Slagtersnek and the entire *voortrekker* movement: "The Boers never forgot Slagter's Nek, and it was one of the causes which led to the 'great trek' or emigration of Boers from Cape Colony, which resulted in the settlement of the Transvaal and the Orange Free State."[44]

At the end of the century, as the tensions mounted between Great Britain and the Boer republics, these British writings became more strongly anti-Boer, while remaining anti-Black. The Liberal imperialist James Bryce stereotyped the frontier Boers as "ignorant, prejudiced, strongly attached to old habits, impatient of any control" but called the affair a "deplorable incident," which "produced wide-spread and bitter resentment."[45] Similarly, W. Basil Worsfold, a British

New Myth: Slagteris Nek leads to great Trek.

journalist, devoted 6 pages in a book of 190 pages to Slagtersnek, and reiterated Cloete's cliché.[46]

IV

Toward the end of the nineteenth century, when people
began to compose an Afrikaner nationalist historiography in
response to the new British imperialism, they highlighted
the Slagtersnek episode. The process can be traced back to
1868, the year in which Great Britain annexed Lesotho (Basutoland) at the request of the aging Chief Moshoeshoe to
prevent the Orange Free State from exacting exceptionally
onerous terms after winning a long and hard-fought war.[47]
In that year a play about Slagtersnek was performed in Cape
Town, and a correspondent advised readers of a Bloemfontein paper to "Think of Slagtersnek."[48]

The place of Slagtersnek in the Afrikaner mythology became quite firmly established in 1877, the year of the British
annexation of the Transvaal,[49] when the Reverend S. J. du
Toit of Paarl published his pioneering history of South Africa
in the Afrikaans language, interpreted from a deeply committed pro-Afrikaner, anti-imperialist point of view.[50] He
devoted 6 pages out of 235 to the "Uprising of Bezuidenhout." In addition to using the published sources that were
then available, notably Cloete's lectures, du Toit had gathered recollections and traditions about the episode from a
considerable number of Afrikaner families. Most of his account was a description of the events; but he made a drastic
transformation of the judgments that were current in the
official colonial historiography. The issue in 1815 and 1816
was not law and order, but tyranny. The British government
was a great Oppressor. The Boer officials who took part in
suppressing the rebellion were Traitors. The rebels were Heroes. The uprising and its denouement were a major cause
of the Great Trek, the central saga in Afrikaner history. They

Brit. govt. turned into great Oppressor.

made a vital contribution to the formation of an Afrikaner national spirit. The passage concludes with a peroration:

> Weep Afrikaners!
> —Here lies your flesh and blood!
> —martyred in the most brutal fashion.
> Wrong it was to rise up against their government:
> yet they did it not without reason!
> Wrong it was to take up weapons;
> only because they were too weak!
> They were guilty, says the earthly judge;
> but what will the Heavenly Judge have to say?
> . . . But come! It grows darker!
> —If we sit here too long we shall be regarded as
>   conspirators!
> —come, another day will dawn,
> —then we shall perhaps see the grave in another
>   light!
> —come, let us go home with a quiet sigh![51]

In 1880 another Dutch Reformed clergyman, the Reverend J. D. Kestell, wrote a monograph on Slagtersnek in much the same vein.[52] In the following year, using the pseudonym Leinad, Kestell also tried to bring the subject to the attention of English readers. A London firm published his play, *The Struggle for Freedom; or the Rebellion of Slagters Nek; a Tragedy in Five Acts.* Kestell, too, had read the documents that were available before 1902, when H. C. V. Leibbrandt published the trial documents. Writing in the manner of Shakespeare, Kestell portrayed the loyal officials as traitors "to thy people's sacred rights," the judges as "mean adventurers of English blood." In act 1, scene 2, Freek Bezuidenhout soliloquizes in blank verse:

> These English courts proclaim
> The white and black in law have equal rights! . . .

Shall I yield unto rule so tyrannous,
That taketh from us our most sacred rights,
That giveth unto Hottentots and slaves
The honours which their present ignorance
Cannot appreciate, but doth abuse?
No, never, never! Henceforth will I live
For ancient rights; henceforth I give my life
To free my country from the tyranny
'Neath which it groans. Therefore, my heart, be
   strong
And I will stand, though I do stand alone,
Though I do wield alone, alone the sword.[53]

Apparently Kestell's attempt to penetrate the English and Anglo–South African markets was a failure. We are told that the sales were so poor that he buried almost the entire edition in a garden in Stellenbosch.[54]

C. P. Bezuidenhout's book on the history of the Afrikaner people was published in Bloemfontein in 1883. Whether or not the author was related to the Bezuidenhouts of the Baviaan's River valley, he claimed to have been told about that "devilish deed" by contemporary witnesses. He did not provide a summary of the entire episode, omitting the activities and death of Freek Bezuidenhout. Instead, he wrote purple passages about two particular events. The first was the death of Hans Bezuidenhout, whose "name remains in honor among posterity." The second was the "barbarous" execution: "The bloodhound was insatiable in his thirst for blood, and that was the cause that the gallows broke when they were half dead." He also introduced a new detail, which may have formed part of the oral traditions that were current from the beginning among some of the affected families: no sooner had the executions been completed than a messenger arrived from the Cape with a pardon for the five victims.[55]

By the end of the century an Afrikaner nationalist myth of Slagtersnek was becoming crystallized in the literature that was written by authors sympathetic to the Boer republics in their resistance to British imperialism. Both J. W. G. van Oordt, a Dutch immigrant (1826–1904), and his son J. F. van Oordt (1856–1918) wrote monographs on the episode.[56] The Transvaal government had commissioned the elder van Oordt to research the history of the Cape Colony for relevant material. His book, written in Dutch, was published in Amsterdam and Pretoria in 1897, the year after the surrender of the members of Dr. Leander Starr Jameson's filibustering expedition, when Great Britain and the Transvaal were set on a collision course.[57] Despite its title, *Slagtersnek: Een Bladzijde uit de voorgeschiedenis der Zuid Afrikaansche Republiek* (Slagtersnek: A page out of the prehistory of the South African Republic), his monograph was a history of the eastern districts of the Cape Colony throughout the decade starting in 1806, when the British won the colony from the Dutch for the second time. Only the last four chapters focused on the Slagtersnek episode. Besides using the established sources, van Oordt had access to some of the unpublished material that H. C. V. Leibbrandt was beginning to assemble for his 1902 publication. His conclusions were a synthesis of the two thrusts in the growing Afrikaner mythology: anti-British and anti-Black. Although the rebels were wrong to seek an alliance with Africans against the colonial government, "Englishmen" were not qualified to criticize them on that account, because they themselves had repeatedly sided with Blacks against Whites, as in the annexation of Basutoland and in giving the franchise to black men in the Cape Colony.[58] Moreover, there were extenuating circumstances. Freek Bezuidenhout's reason for refusing to answer the charges brought against him by Booy was that the colonial courts made no distinction between innate superiors and inferiors; and his brother Hans sought to avenge his death because he could not reconcile himself to the fact that Freek had been killed for such reasoning. The rebellion was not just a foolish failure. The Bezuidenhouts were rising against a government that was applying its "unnatural and stupid policy of equalizing born masters and born servants." The elder van Oordt also drew contemporary lessons from the episode. In the growing crisis of the 1890s, the question again arose "whether the wretched ideas that have prevailed in Europe since the eighteenth century may doom the colonists in South Africa, clearly called to be the aristocracy and the salt of the earth, to dependence on the mass, and that even a black mass."[59]

Besides writing his own monograph on Slagtersnek, the younger van Oordt, in a book on Paul Kruger and the rise of the Transvaal republic, laid great stress on its effects on the minds of Afrikaners: "Year after year must pass before the Afrikaans and especially the Transvaal folk will forget Slachtersnek. . . . can anyone have any difficulty in understanding that after the events of 1799 to 1816, the Boers in the Eastern frontier had a hatred, a deep inveterate hatred against the English?"[60]

On the eve of the Anglo-Boer War, in another effort to reach English readers, C. N. J. du Plessis provided a heartrending description of the execution of the five ringleaders. Like van Oordt senior, he drew a contemporary lesson from that episode. He compared President Kruger's "nobleminded, Christian, humane, forgiving disposition," as shown in his commuting the death sentences that the Transvaal court had imposed on the gold-mining industrialists who had led a revolt in Johannesburg in conjunction with the Jameson Raid, with the failure of Governor Somerset to pardon the Slagtersnek rebels. 'Yes, . . . this example, compared with that of your Governor in 1816, has put the English nation to shame!'"[61]

In the same fateful year 1899, J. C. Voigt, a Cape colonial doctor, included a 28-page chapter on Slagtersnek in *Fifty Years of the Republic of South Africa 1795–1845*. He embellished his account with reflections on the thoughts of the participants: "Perhaps, as he [Freek Bezuidenhout] took his station at the entrance to the cave, he dreamed of the future, when, through his death, his people would be brought to rise in arms against those whom he regarded as tyrants and oppressors."[62] Like the elder van Oordt, Voigt took pains to reconcile his racial attitude with the attempts the rebels had made to get help from the Xhosa:

Is it strange, is it unnatural, that men about to engage in a struggle for life and death against one of the most powerful of European empires, finding that civilised Power did not scruple to enlist the Hottentot under its banners, should look to Native Chiefs for aid? . . . Gaika's Kaffirs were barbarians, it is true, but "noble savages" compared to those who served under the flag of England. . . . Still, the mission to Gaika, though from a humanitarian point of view defensible as perfectly justifiable under the circumstances, was a mistake when regarded from its political aspect. It is known that Hendrik Prinsloo himself did not approve of any alliance whatsoever with the Kaffirs, and many of his followers, no doubt, thought with him. A peculiarly characteristic feature of the white inhabitants of South Africa, and especially of the older Colonists and their descendants, has always been their pride of race—their belief in the dominant power of the white race. The very cause of the insurrection was dissatisfaction with England for invading the rights and privileges of the white inhabitants, and for employing native soldiery in the execution of the civil law against a free white burgher. The heinousness of this offence in the eyes of the people should have deterred the leaders from seeking any assistance, or even the semblance of assistance, from the Kaffirs or from any other Native race.[63]

Voigt also imputes bad faith to the judges: "The rebellion was at an end: now followed the 'justice' of the government of Lord Charles Somerset and of King George. The result of the trial was a foregone conclusion. The officials of the day knew what was expected of them—no half measures."[64] Finally, after an emotional account of the executions, Voigt declaims: "Memories of Slachtersnek have done more to give birth to the [Transvaal] Republic, and, in after days, to consolidate it, than perhaps anything else in the history of South Africa. They have made England's dominion over all South Africa impossible. The spirit of Hendrik Prinsloo did not die."[65]

Soon after the Anglo-Boer War eventually broke out, the government of the South African [Transvaal] Republic published a tract that made much of the Slagtersnek episode. As in most of the propaganda from both sides in that war, the authors assumed that every potential sympathizer shared their racist paradigm:

Notwithstanding the wild surroundings and the innumerable savage tribes in the background, the young Afrikander nation had been welded into a white aristocracy, proudly conscious of having maintained its superiority notwithstanding arduous struggles. It was this sentiment of just pride which the British Government well understood how to wound in its most sensitive part by favoring the Natives as against the Afrikanders. So, for example, the Afrikander Boers were forced to look with pained eyes on the scenes of their farms and property devastated by the Natives without being in the position of defending themselves, because the British Government had even deprived them of their ammunition. In the same way the liberty-loving Afrikander burgher was coerced by a police composed of Hottentots, the lowest and most despicable class of the aborigines, whom the Afrikanders justly placed on a far lower social level than that of their own Malay slaves. No wonder that in 1815 a number of the Boers were driven into rebellion, a rebellion which found an awful ending in the horrible occurrence on the 9th of March, 1816, where six of the Boers were half hung up in the most inhuman way, and in the compulsory presence of their wives and children. Their death was truly horrible, for the gallows broke down before the end came; but they were again hoisted up in the agony of dying, and strangled to death in the murderous tragedy of Slachter's Nek. Whatever opinions may have been formed of this occurrence in other respects, it was at Slachter's Nek that the first bloodstained beacon was erected which marks the boundary between Boer and Briton in South Africa, and the eyes of posterity still glance back shuddering through the long vista of years at that tragedy of horror.[66]

V

During the first half of the twentieth century most professional historians, including textbook writers, continued to treat Slagtersnek as an important episode in South African history. However, they laid less stress on those aspects of the story that cast an unfavorable light on the behavior of the white participants, both official and rebel. A relatively bland interpretation emerged, consonant with the goal of reducing ethnic conflict among Whites in South Africans.

As we have seen, it was the Canadian-born historian George McCall Theal who provided the basis for virtually all the textbooks that were used in South Africa during the first half of the twentieth century.[67] Imbued with the ideal of white solidarity, Theal steered a deft course between the Scylla of British imperialism and the Charybdis of Afrikaner nationalism; and he did this, inexorably, at the expense of the black population. In his short book published in the popular *Story of the Nations* series in 1899, his account of Slagtersnek says nothing about the rebels seeking help from the Xhosa, nor does it mention the fact that the executions were bungled.[68] In the relevant part of his eleven-volume *History of South Africa,* the first edition of which appeared in 1892, he wrote an elaborate account of the episode. His narrative was quite sound, but he injected romantic sentiment into his conclusions in extenuation of the behavior of the rebels. The frontier Boers, wrote Theal, were "engaged almost constantly in defending their herds from the depredations of their barbarous neighbors," but they were "quite uneducated from books, turbulent, and averse to restraint in any form." They were reputed to be "excessively harsh in their treatment of coloured servants . . . though such occurrences did not deter Hottentots from taking service with them as cattle herds." Freek Bezuidenhout is introduced as a person who "lived on his secluded farm with only his wife [actually an unmarried Coloured woman], his little daughter, a half-breed servant [actually his son], and a youth . . . who assisted in herding his cattle."[69] Theal describes the death of Hans in the following terms:

> He was an illiterate frontier farmer, whose usual residence was a wattle and daub structure hardly deserving the name of a house, and who knew nothing of refinement after the English town pattern. His code of honour, too, was in some respects different from that of modern Englishmen, but it contained at least one principle common to the noblest minds in all sections of the race to

which he belonged: to die rather than to do that which is degrading. And for him it would have been utterly degrading to have surrendered to the pandours [Coloured soldiers]. Instead of doing so he fired at them. His wife, Martha Faber, a true South Africa countrywoman, in this extremity showed that the Batavian blood had not degenerated by change of clime. She stepped to the side of her husband, and as he discharged one gun loaded another for his use. His son Gerrit Pieter, too, a boy not quite twelve years of age, took an active part in the skirmish. One Hottentot soldier was killed. Then Bezuidenhout received two severe wounds, from which he died in a few hours, and both his wife and his son were disabled and seized. Ten guns and about eighteen kilogrammes of powder were found in the waggons.[70]

Theal continues: "The sentences were in accordance with the letter of the law," but "banishment would have been equally effective as a warning to others," and "the burghers who aided the government . . . were afterwards horrified at the thought that they had helped to pursue their deluded countrymen to death."[71] Finally, he quotes Cloete's oft-repeated dictum, they "could never forget Slachter's Nek!" and asserts:

In public discussions during eighty years it was constantly referred to as a cruel and unjustifiable stretch of power, and more than any other single occurrence it kept alive a feeling of hostility to British rule. The descendants of those who supported the government felt as strongly on the subject as the descendants and relatives of those who were punished, and maintained that if such a result could have been foreseen very few indeed would have aided the authorities.[72]

Because, in his customary manner, Theal cited no sources, we cannot verify claims such as those made in the last quotation.

In the first decade of the twentieth century, an Englishman, George Cory, did some original research on the Slagtersnek episode. Cory was professor of chemistry at Rhodes University College in Grahamstown, the heart of the area that had been occupied by the British settlers of 1820, and less than fifty miles from the Baviaan's River valley. He toured the area on foot and bicycle, collecting the historical traditions of the British settlers. After working through the official records of the trial of the Slagtersnek prisoners that had been published by H. C. W. Leibbrandt in 1902, he included a forty-six-page chapter on Slagtersnek in the first volume of *The Rise of South Africa,* which was published in 1910. His conclusions were similar to Theal's. Both the British imperialist and the Afrikaner nationalist interpretations were false—"imperfect and even mythical," whether as being representative of "the character of the eastern Boer" or as a symbol of British tyranny.[73]

Authors of the school textbooks that were current during the period between the end of the Anglo-Boer War in 1902 and the electoral victory of the Afrikaner National Party in 1948 were constrained by the fact that success depended on the adoption of their works by the public bodies that were responsible for the school syllabuses and examinations; and those bodies included both Afrikaans-speaking and English-speaking white South Africans. Consequently, a white South African consensus emerged, based largely on Theal and, to a lesser extent, on Cory. It included considerable concessions to the Afrikaner nationalist interpretation of history where that did not conflict with the ethnic emotions of the bulk of the members of the English-speaking white community. The textbooks presented the rebels as simple, courageous people.

They were vindicated for resenting the government's use of Coloured soldiers to arrest a white man. They were criticized for seeking Xhosa aid. The government was legally justified in allowing the death sentences to be carried out but was regarded as politically inept for not having commuted them. And the uprising was said to have created a legacy of perpetual hatred for the British government, as distinct from the British people in South Africa. The consensus was also significant in what it omitted. It failed to explain that the life style of the Bezuidenhouts and many of their allies did not correspond with the twentieth-century Afrikaner norms of religious observance and racial purity; it played down the facts that most of the frontier Boers would have nothing to do with the rebellion and that local Boer officials had been largely responsible for repressing it.

Typically, a senior school textbook that was first published in the early 1920s called it "a great fault" to send "Hottentots" to arrest Freek Bezuidenhout "because no frontier Boer would allow himself to be arrested by Hottentots." Also, Lord Charles Somerset committed "a great fault" in allowing the executions to be carried out, "since the people regarded this tragic death of the victims as the fatal result of the struggle against the policy of equality between whites and non-whites."[74]

Similar conclusions were drawn by C. de K. Fowler and G. J. J. Smit in their highly successful senior school textbooks that were published in both Afrikaans and English and used in South Africa from the early 1930s to the middle of the 1950s. "The sending of Hottentots to arrest a white man was a grave mistake." Moreover, in having the death sentences carried out,

Somerset evidently hoped that . . . he would inculcate implicit obedience to the authority of the government.

But it was a serious mistake, for the insurgents did not realize that resistance to the government was a grave offence, as they had been accustomed to lax administration on the frontier. The victims were regarded by a large section of the frontiersmen as martyrs who had died in the cause of the white man against the government and its Hottentot friends.[75]

Some authors of textbooks were palpably confused about how to handle the episode. For example, an Afrikaans history in its 1930 edition devoted two chapters to it. The author started by saying: "It is a great event in the history, which had very important consequences." But when he had reached the end of his narrative, he reversed himself: "The so called Slagtersnek rebellion was actually an affair of little meaning. . . . The 1815 rebellion was, in a word, the deed of a little group of fools, and if ever there was a case where the law should be respected it was here." Nevertheless, the text proceeded to claim that "precisely through Slagtersnek were the boers a thorn in the side of England for a hundred years."[76]

Despite the emergence in the textbooks of a sanitized white consensus interpretation, derived from Theal, the nationalist myth of Slagtersnek lived on in the minds of many people. C. J. Langenhoven, one of the most popular of all Afrikaans writers, gave a tremendous fillip to the use of the uprising as a symbol of Afrikaner nationalism. His collection of verse entitled *Die Pad van Suid-Afrika* (The path of South Africa) was first published in 1921 and was republished many times. Here is his poem on the Bezuidenhout brothers:

> I summon you, Freedrik Bezuidenhout—come out
>   of your cave and surrender:
> I summon you in the name of the law on the au-
>   thority of King George;

Rebellion as a symbol of Afrikaner nationalism.

Once, twice, three times—I summon you to come
  out of the cave—
And now for the last time: Freedrik Bezuidenhout,
  come!

What should the answer have been? One man
  against the British Empire?
Against the majesty of the law? Against every principle of justice?
And what would his death help? Would anyone
  benefit from it?
Look, Freek, you're a fool. Shall a worm resist a
  cliff?
Surrender, man, and live and serve your land with
  your life.
Or die like a villain and a fool.

Silence. So still that the step of the seconds sounds
  audibly.
Tense, the future listens. Here's a man who with
  open eye
Must choose his death or his life. And he does not
  choose for himself—
He chooses for a nation that doesn't yet exist, a
  nation that he won't see.
Tick . . . Tick . . . Tick . . . South Africa waits.
What will the choice be?

Hear, King George, in the report of the deathshot
  the doom of your dominion:
The sighing mother's love sought and found love.
Through the cave, through the blood of a fool,
Goes the Path of South Africa.

Again there sounds a summons to surrender and
  one man stands,

Surrounded, alone, Bezuidenhout, Jan
   Bezuidenhout—
Your dead brother with his foolish resistance is an
   example for you. We summon you, surrender!
Yes, truly, my dead brother is an example for me.
For me and for generations
*That will come. Are you summoning me? you renegades
   and hirelings?*
*In my land, that will inherit my nation? Look, here it
   is I who summon here.*
*And I summon on a higher authority, the authority of
   South Africa.*
*I summon you—draw off your gangs or put up with
   my bullet,*
And the bullets that will come from my nation,
That will come, until the dominion over South Africa
Shall belong to her children alone.
*The bullets that will come? No, stronger forces than
   weaponry*
*Will fight for our freedom from tyranny. Do you see
   who is loading my gun?*
*It is my wife and my child, the dearest treasures of my
   heart.*
*Once, twice, three times . . . traitors—give way or I
   shoot . . .*
*Load, dear wife, load quickly—they are coming on in a
   crowd. And here,*
*Here's one man who must stand alone today on the
   side of South Africa.*

*Farewell, dear wife, farewell child. I die on the path
   that doesn't branch off or give way—*
*The path marked off for the journey of my nation to
   be—*
The Path of South Africa. [77]

This poem was accompanied by a drawing of the cave and the corpse of Freek Bezuidenhout. It was followed by an equally sentimental poem on the executions, with a drawing of the gallows.[78]

Members of the Afrikaner National Party that General J. B. M. Hertzog founded in 1914 soon recognized that the myth of Slagtersnek was a powerful ideological weapon. On 9 March 1916, a thousand people gathered at the site of the hangings, near the early nineteenth-century British military base of Vanaardtspos, for the unveiling of a monument to the rebels. Hertzog sent his good wishes, and so did General Christiaan de Wet, who was in jail for leading a rebellion against the government of the Union of South Africa for its decision to participate in the First World War on the Allied side.[79] The students of Victoria College, the future Stellenbosch University, sent a telegram saying: "Young South Africa wishes to uphold the lessons transmitted by Slagtersnek to posterity." Daniel F. Malan, who would lead a later National Party to victory in 1948, was the principal speaker. He sympathized with the rebels of 1815. However, said Malan, they were not true folk heroes because they had invoked African aid; but Christiaan de Wet was such a hero.[80] Twenty-two years later, one of the wagons traveling through South Africa to celebrate the centenary of the Great Trek came to the monument and more speeches were made. That Christmas, people sent cards to one another bearing the words which Langenhoven had used at the end of his poem on the hangings: "On Slagtersnek there stands an arch of honor that casts a dark shadow:/Over the Path of South Africa."[81]

During the Second World War, when anti-British passions reached a new peak among some Afrikaners, an enthusiast located what may well have been the actual beam that was used for the hangings and sent it to Pretoria amid a flurry of publicity, but his wish to place it on public exhibition was not granted. It remains there in the cellars of the South African archives.[82]

All this had a profound effect on the young Afrikaner mind. J. A. Heese says: "My contemporaries will still remember how we were inspired by Langenhoven's *Die Pad van Suid-Afrika*. One of my most unforgettable moments was when I as a schoolboy listened to how Tommie Beckley, a lecturer of my school days, recited from it. Freek Bezuidenhout was the hero of my adolescent school years."[83]

VI

The tale of Slagtersnek, as related in Afrikaner nationalist mythology, is a typical myth. Although it is firmly rooted in an actual historical episode, it has deviated from the facts, for example, in appropriating the gruesome name Slagtersnek. Despite the contradictions in the behavior of the leading rebels, the myth rests on the racist assumptions that were common in Western science in the nineteenth century and the early part of the twentieth century, and thus endorses the racist facet of Afrikaner nationalism. Its major effect, however, was to contribute to the resistance of a colonial people to British cultural and political imperialism.

Like dramatic episodes in the history of other societies, such as the career of Joan of Arc in France, the 1815 rebellion on the frontier of the Cape Colony was appropriated by different people and used for different purposes at different times. During the nineteenth century, British historians and publicists used it to bolster the stereotype of Afrikaners as brutal, stupid, ignorant, and lawless; whereas toward the end of that century Afrikaner intellectuals began to use it as part of their portrait of British oppression.

Like other myths, the Afrikaner nationalist myth of Slagtersnek is itself a historical phenomenon. It originated as a

key component of a liberatory ideology. So long as Great
Britain seemed to be a serious threat to their group interests,
Afrikaner poets, journalists, politicians, teachers, and historians made it penetrate deep into the minds of their people.
Since then, however, historians have reworked the evidence
and revealed the factual inaccuracies in the myth, scientists
have rejected its racist assumptions, and, with the waning
of British power, Afrikaner nationalists themselves have
ceased to find relevance in the anti-British thrust of the myth.
The fate of the Slagtersnek myth in the circumstances of the
late twentieth century is discussed in chapter 6.

Slagtersnek – a key component of liberatory
ideology.

Historians made it penetrate deep into the minds
of their people.

5

THE COVENANT

I

The sixteenth of December is a public holiday in South Africa. It is the anniversary of events that took place in 1838, when four hundred and sixty-eight Afrikaners, with their Coloured and African servants and about sixty African allies, formed a *laager* with their wagons and repulsed repeated attacks by a vast Zulu army, thus paving the way for white hegemony in Natal. Formerly, it was known officially as Dingaan's Day, after the name of the Zulu king, but in 1952 the name was changed to the Day of the Covenant and in 1980 to the Day of the Vow.[1] This refers to a pledge made several days before the battle by Afrikaner members of the commando that if God granted them a victory in the coming struggle they would build a memorial church and they and their posterity would always celebrate the anniversary of the victory, to the honor of God.

During the twentieth century it has become customary for Afrikaner nationalists to organize ceremonies on this anniversary, when leading politicians indulge in emotional rhetoric, relating the events of 1838 to contemporary politics. In monopolizing the centenary celebrations in 1938, the Malanites took a vital step toward wresting control of the Afrikaner political movement from the Hertzogites, and in the 1980s Andries Treurnicht and his fellow conservatives have been trying to repeat the process at the expense of the party

of P. W. Botha. For example, on 16 December 1983 Treurnicht, who was opposing the government's decision to give
a limited say in the central South African political system to
Coloured and Asian people (as distinct from Africans), declared that they "must stop making concessions" to "the
liberalists and Marxists." He continued: "A surrounded and
threatened people, in its hour of utmost need, in a struggle
for life and death, placed its dependence in belief in God,
and He saved them. . . . Today our people are again a surrounded people."[2]

No historian has rigorously examined all the evidence concerning the origin and growth of the official tradition of the
Covenant. Until recently, to do so was taboo in South Africa.
Indeed, in March 1979, when a leading Afrikaner historian
did question some of the aspects of the tradition, conservative
opinion was so outraged that a band of white toughs broke
into an academic meeting and, quite literally, tarred and
feathered him in the presence of more than forty astonished
scholars.[3]

In this chapter, I shall review the evidence afresh: first the
evidence concerning the events in the commando that Andries Pretorius led against the Zulu in December 1838; second, the evidence concerning the commemoration of those
events; and third, the evidence concerning the function of
the commemoration of those events in the history of white
supremacy and Afrikaner nationalism. We shall find that we
cannot be sure precisely what actually happened concerning
the taking of the covenant or vow in the commando in 1838;
that once they had defeated the Zulu and sacked their headquarters, nearly all the members of the commando proceeded
to forget all about any such vow or covenant; that in the
last quarter of the nineteenth century a number of clergy,
politicians, and intellectuals in the Transvaal and Orange
Free State republics began to resurrect, embellish, codify,

and celebrate a version of the events of December 1838 for the purpose of promoting pride and self-confidence among Afrikaners in the face of British imperial aggression; and that their successors have modified the story during the twentieth century as British imperialism has waned and African nationalism has replaced it as the principal threat to Afrikaner nationalism.

Here, as with the story of Slagtersnek, are all the hallmarks of a classic political myth: its partial concordance with historical reality, its delayed codification followed by rapid development and fervent deployment for political purposes, and its adaptation to changing circumstances. However, the myth of the covenant differs substantially from the myth of Slagtersnek. Its discrepancies from historical reality, though considerable, are less extreme. It conveys a message that has continued to serve the Afrikaner nationalist cause. And, whereas the 1815 uprising was a transitory and exclusively secular episode, the covenant portrays the religious behavior of Afrikaners in the central saga of the nationalist version of their history. Consequently, we shall find that the Slagtersnek myth has been sloughed off from the nationalist mythology, while the myth of the covenant has continued to be crucial to it but the subject of intense debate as to precisely how it should be interpreted in the domestic and global context of the late twentieth century.

II

Whereas during 1815 the vast majority of the frontier farmers had at least acquiesced in the British colonial regime, by 1836 disaffection was widespread. Afrikaners of substance and prestige had come to the conclusion that the government was failing to provide for their security and was threatening their way of life. A series of events had shaken their confidence. The government had abolished the office of *heemraad,* and with it the long-established participation of leading white farmers in district administration. It had also replaced the old high court of the colony, whose judges were not necessarily trained lawyers, with a supreme court manned by lawyers who had been admitted to the bar in England or Scotland. At the same time, it had made English the only official language in the courts.[4] In 1828 it had promulgated an ordinance abolishing the legal distinctions between the white population and the Khoikhoi, and in 1833 the British parliament had passed an act providing for the emancipation of the slaves in the British Empire after four years of "apprenticeship." The emancipation act provided compensation for slaveowners, but the sum voted fell far short of the value of the slaves; moreover, compensation had to be collected in England, so that colonial slaveowners had to deal with agents who charged for their services. In effect, Afrikaner slaveowners, who included some of the more prosperous Boers in the eastern districts, received no more than a fraction of the market value of their former property.[5]

These changes did not deprive Afrikaner farmers of their landholdings, nor in the long run did they enable many of the black inhabitants to dispense with the necessity of working for white people for survival. Nevertheless, as their former serfs and slaves tried to give expression to their legal freedom in the immediate aftermath of legal emancipation, Boers experienced labor shortages and uncertainties and an unprecedented amount of pilfering. Frontier Boers were also experiencing land shortage. The period of an open frontier for settlement by young and restless men had ended early in the nineteenth century, when the relatively dense populations of Xhosa farmers blocked further Boer expansion to the east.[6]

Events in the eastern frontier zone were the final straw that undermined the confidence of many of the Afrikaner inhabitants of the eastern districts in the colonial regime. At the end of 1834, masses of Xhosa invaded the colony in a desperate attempt to recover land they had lost in earlier wars. The governor, Lieutenant-General Sir Benjamin D'Urban, a veteran of the Napoleonic Wars, supervised an overwhelming response. Using British regular troops as well as Afrikaner commandos, the Cape Regiment, and African allies, he organized raids far beyond the boundary line, destroying villages, burning crops, and capturing cattle, and he issued a proclamation annexing still more Xhosa territory to the British Empire. However, accepting the argument of radical British missionaries that the Xhosa had been justified in their efforts to regain their land, the government in London sent D'Urban a stiff reprimand; whereupon he felt obliged to disannex the newly conquered territory.[7]

Several prestigious Afrikaners then planned to lead their kinsmen, their friends, and their coloured clients away from the Cape Colony, with the intention of establishing independent states beyond the colonial borders, where they would recreate their customary mode of life. Piet Retief summed up his reasons for emigrating in his letter to the editors of Dutch and English colonial newspapers. He deplored "the turbulent and dishonest conduct of vagrants," the "severe losses which we have been forced to sustain by the emancipation of our slaves," and "the continual system of plunder which we have endured from the Caffres and other coloured classes, and particularly by the last invasion of the colony." He complained of "the unjustified odium which has been cast upon us by interested and dishonest persons, under the cloak of religion, whose testimony is believed in England." And he declared that "we will uphold the just principles of liberty; but, whilst we will take care that no one shall be held in a state of slavery, it is our determination to maintain such regulations as may suppress crime, and preserve proper relations between master and servant."[8]

Among the emigrants was Retief's niece, Anna Steenkamp, who summed up her feelings in a private letter she sent from Natal in 1843 to relatives who had remained in the Cape Colony:

> The reasons for which we abandoned our lands and homesteads, our country and kindred, were the following:—1. The continual depredations and robberies of the Kafirs, and their arrogance and overbearing conduct: and the fact that, in spite of the fine promises made to us by our Government, we nevertheless received no compensation for the property of which we were despoiled. 2. The shameful and unjust proceedings with reference to the freedom of our slaves: and yet it is not so much their freedom that drove us to such lengths, as their being placed on an equal footing with Christians, contrary to the laws of God and the natural distinction of race and religion, so that it was intolerable for any decent Christian to bow down beneath such a yoke; wherefore we rather withdrew in order thus to preserve our doctrines in purity.[9]

By 1838 some four thousand men, women, and children, including members of all classes of Afrikaner frontiers people—patrons and clients, rich and poor—had trekked northeastward in their wagons, with their coloured servants, their cattle, their sheep, and their movable property.[10] They were fortunate in the timing of their migration. They were moving into two fertile regions that had recently become sparsely populated as a result of devastating wars among the African inhabitants: the interior plateau on either side of the Vaal

River, which was dominated by Mzilikazi's Ndebele people, and the coastal lowlands south of the Tugela River, which were dominated by the Zulu kingdom under Dingane, the assassin and successor of his half-brother Shaka.[11]

During 1837 the emigrants drove Mzilikazi and his people northward across the Limpopo River, where they carved out a new kingdom in the southwestern part of modern Zimbabwe. However, most of the emigrants preferred to settle below the mountain escarpment rather than on the interior plateau. With their better rainfall, the lowlands were far more lush and promised an easier life. Moreover, they included a potential harbor at Port Natal, through which the emigrants hoped to open up economic and diplomatic relations with the Netherlands and other states in continental Europe, and thus terminate their dependence on Britain. To this end, in November 1837 Piet Retief, whom most of the emigrants accepted as their leader, led a party of horsemen to Dingane's Zulu headquarters, seeking his approval for them to settle in the region south of the Tugela River. Dingane signified his consent, on condition that they would show their goodwill by restoring some of his cattle, which he said had been raided by Africans who lived across the mountains on the plateau. Retief did as requested by tricking the African chief deemed to be responsible for the thefts into handing over the cattle. In February 1838 he returned to Dingane's headquarters at the head of a cavalcade of seventy Afrikaners and thirty of their Coloured servants.

Retief had sent Dingane a message boasting of the Boers' military victory over Mzilikazi's people in the Transvaal; and men, women, and children were already trekking across the Drakensberg Mountains with their wagons and their livestock and settling in the fringe of Zulu territory. Pondering these events, the Zulu king and his councillors had come to the conclusion that the Boers were threatening their vital interests. Accordingly, they decided to resort to force in the

Murder of
Piet Retief

hope of putting a stop to white settlement in their vicinity. After Dingane had put his mark to a treaty and entertained his visitors, his warriors murdered Retief's party and attacked the Boer encampments around the sources of the Tugela River, where they killed another 281 white men, women, and children, and some two hundred of their Coloured servants, at what became known as Weenen—the place of weeping.[12]

In December 1838, having received reinforcements from the Cape Colony, the emigrants mustered a powerful commando against the Zulu. Led by Andries Pretorius, it trekked with fifty-seven wagons toward the heart of the Zulu kingdom. Every white member of the commando possessed at least one gun, and the expedition also had two small cannons. As they advanced, they formed a defensive fortress— a *laager*—at night by lashing their wagons together. On the night of 15 December they laagered on the bank of the Ncome River. At dawn the next day, a vast Zulu army— perhaps ten thousand strong—launched the first of a series of attacks. Handling their firearms skillfully from their defensive position, the emigrants repulsed repeated onslaughts by Zulu warriors armed with their customary assagais and stabbing spears. When the Zulu survivors eventually retreated, they left about three thousand dead around the *laager*. The commando had not lost a single member. The victors named it the Battle of Blood River, from the staining of the adjacent stream with Zulu blood. It was perhaps the most decisive military encounter between Black and White that has taken place in South Africa. The Wenkommando (Victory Commando), as the emigrants called it, then proceeded to the Zulu headquarters, where it buried the corpses of Retief and his party. In further operations it captured 3,600 head of cattle before returning westward and disbanding.[13]

Andries Pretorius himself wrote quite brief reports of these events on 23 and 31 December and 3 and 9 January.[14] Soon

Battle of
Blood River

3000 Zulu
killed.

after the commando disbanded, a far more detailed report was written by Jan Bantjes.[15] His services were in great demand because he was handier with a pen than most of the other emigrants. He had served as secretary to the Volksraad (People's Council) they had elected when they were on the plateau and was secretary to their Volksraad in Natal when Pretorius selected him to be his amanuensis on the commando.[16] Bantjes wrote that he had joined the commando for the express purpose of making a record of its proceedings.[17] His status was secretary to Pretorius and there can be no doubt that his account accorded with the wishes of his commanding officer.

These documents are the only firsthand evidence that we have of the proceedings in the Wenkommando. Pretorius and Bantjes composed them for the public record as well as for the information of the Volksraad. The Pretorius reports dated 23 December and 9 January were published in supplements to the *Zuid Afrikaan,* a sympathetic Cape Town newspaper, on 16 February 1839; the Bantjes report on 14 June 1839.[18]

According to these reports, the commando was inspired by profound religious fervor. All the elders were extremely solicitous for the favor of God. They held prayer meetings every day. Sometimes Sarel Cilliers, who had been a church elder in the colony, conducted them for the entire commando; usually the three or four senior officers held separate prayer meetings for their own followers.

The crucial religious events appear to have occurred on Sunday, 9 December, when they were encamped at a stream they named the Wasbank because they washed their clothes there. According to Bantjes:

> That Sunday morning, before the service began, the
> chief Commandant called together the men who would

conduct the service, and told them to suggest to the congregation that they should all pray to God fervently in spirit and in truth for his help and assistance in the struggle with the enemy; [he said] that he wanted to make a vow to the Almighty, (if they were all willing), that "should the Lord give us the victory, we would raise a House to the memory of his Great Name, wherever it shall please Him;" and that they should also invoke the aid and assistance of God to enable them to fulfill this vow; and that we should note the day of the victory in a book, to make it known even to our latest posterity, so that it might be celebrated to the Honor of God.[19]

The Bantjes report continued:

Messrs. Cilliers, Landman and Joubert were glad to hear it. They consulted their congregations about it and obtained their general consent. After that, when divine worship began separately, Mr. Cilliers conducted the one that took place in the tent of the Head Commandant, where he started with the singing of Psalm 38 verses 12 to 16, then delivered a prayer, and preached about the first 24 verses of chapter 6 of the Book of Judges; and then followed with the Prayer in which the aforementioned vow was made to God, with a fervent supplication for God's help and assistance in its fulfillment. The 12th and 21st verses of the said 38th Psalm were again sung, and he ended the service with the singing of Psalm 134.[20]

The rest of Bantjes's report included only one further remark about religion. Having described the battle at Blood River, he noted: "Prayers and thanksgiving were offered to God, and after divine service had been performed, the chief commandant again sent a strong party to pursue the Zulus as far as they could."[21]

The documents signed by Pretorius, too, included several religious invocations. The first paragraph of his report dated 23 December included the following statement: "The undertaking was great and our force small, as it consisted of only 460 men; therefore we could entertain no other confidence than in the justness of our cause and in the God of our Fathers; and the result thus far has also shown that— He who trusts in the good God/Has surely not built on sand." Pretorius's report of 23 December also stated: "The Almighty, who had given us the victory, was pleased to grant it without the loss of lives." The same report ended with a statement about the vow:

> I also wish to inform you that we have here decided among ourselves *to make known* the day of our victory, being *Sunday, the 16th of this month of December, among our entire community,* and that we shall consecrate it to the Lord, and celebrate it with thanksgivings, since, before we fought against the enemy, we *promised in a public prayer* that should we manage to win the victory, we would build a house to the Lord in memory of his name, wherever He shall indicate it; which vow we now also hope to honor, with the help of the Lord, now that He has blessed us and heard our prayers.[22]

III

Soon after the Victory Commando completed its mission, the emigrants named their principal encampment Pietermaritzburg after Piet Retief and Gert Maritz, another deceased leader, and made it the capital of their Republic of Natal. Initially, they held religious services in a rough con-

struction of wood and reeds. By May 1839, their Volksraad
was organizing a collection of funds in the Cape Colony as
well as among the emigrants who were scattered throughout
Natal and the highveld on either side of the Vaal River for
the erection of a permanent building. Pretorius and other
local people took part in the building work, and during 1841
a modest barnlike structure was completed.[23]

No record seems to have survived to demonstrate that
Pretorius or any other emigrant ever explicitly referred to
that church as a fulfillment of their vow. Moreover, that
building ceased to be used for worship in 1861, when the
Dutch Reformed congregation in Pietermaritzburg moved
to a new church on a different site. The old building was
then sold, and for the next forty-seven years it was used for
commercial purposes. We are told: "It was in turn a wagon-
maker's shop, a mineral water factory, a tea room, a black-
smith's workshop, a school, and the Government considered
using it for the Supreme Court but decided not to do so. It
had become a wool shed in 1908 when the Council of the
Dutch Reformed Church decided to convert it into the Voortrekkers' Museum."[24]

Pretorius's modern biographer comments that "the explanation for this apparently lies in the rapid oblivion into which
the vow fell."[25] Indeed, the other ingredient in the vow—
the annual celebration of the battle in thanksgiving to God—
was never observed at all by the vast majority of the people
who are said to have made it. On 16 December 1839, the
first anniversary of the battle, some people celebrated it in
Pietermaritzburg with prayer and thanksgiving.[26] After that,
it was apparently ignored for a quarter of a century by all
but a tiny number of exceptionally religious individuals.
Sarel Cilliers, who died in 1871, is reputed to have celebrated
it piously throughout his life.[27] Erasmus Smit, an emigrant
who was a former member of the London Missionary Society

(but had not accompanied the Victory Commando), is said to have invited interested people to come to his house in Pietermaritzburg on Sunday 15 December 1844, and to have preached a commemorative sermon; and thereafter he is reputed to have celebrated the anniversary each year until he died in 1863.[28] However, these were private, not official, events, and there is no evidence that they involved more than a handful of people. The Volksraad did nothing to commemorate the vow, and—remarkably—Pretorius himself, according to his modern biographer, is not recorded as ever having referred to it after he had made his reports on the Victory Commando.[29] Writing in 1919, the biographer of Cilliers, who, as we shall see, was a principal propagator of the myth of the covenant, admitted: "In the first year after Blood River the day was only observed in a limited circle." He also noted that Cilliers claimed to have rebuked Pretorius for failing to fulfill his vow.[30]

These facts raise serious questions about the covenant. How reliable are the religious components of the only contemporary eyewitness accounts of the Victory Commando? What were the actual events that were to become known as the vow or the covenant?

One possibility is that Andries Pretorius, the commanding officer, and Jan Bantjes, his secretary, exaggerated the religious behavior of the commando, to counteract evangelical domestic pressures on the British government to annex Natal and reestablish control over its emigrant subjects. The emigrants were certainly obliged to take cognizance of the British factor. While their commando was in the field, a British military detachment controlled the emigrants' only independent access to the outside world at Port Natal (Durban), and pressure groups were urging the British government to follow up its migrant subjects and annex Natal. On 6 December 1838, acting in the spirit of his instructions from

Cape Town, Major Samuel Charters, in command at Port Natal, issued a proclamation annexing the port and wrote a letter to Pretorius demanding that he should "desist from all offensive measures against the Zulu chief or any of the native tribes of these regions." Charters added a threat couched in typical evangelical terms:

> You must be well aware Sir of the unvarying perse-
> verance with which the British Government has for
> many years past protected to the utmost of its power,
> the Native tribes of Africa; of the sacrifices which the
> nation has made to accomplish so great an object, and
> of its determination to triumph in so noble a cause—
> be assured therefore that Her Britannic Majesty will
> never submit to be thwarted in her measures by a hand-
> ful of Her own Subjects, who taking the law into their
> own hands and passing the land boundary of the Colony
> carry bloodshed and desolation amongst tribes and na-
> tions, not only at peace with Her Majesty but which
> have every claim to Her Majesty's protection; assure
> yourself therefore that if you persevere in your present
> course misfortune and ruin sooner or later await you.[31]

This communication from Major Charters did not reach Pretorius before his commando had completed its operations against the Zulu.[32] Nevertheless, the emigrants knew that the evangelical lobby was a powerful influence in British politics. Missionaries, they realized, had been largely re-sponsible for the removal of the restrictions on the move-ments of the Khoikhoi in the Cape Colony, and also for the reversal of the frontier policy of Sir Benjamin D'Urban. As we have seen, in Retief's public letter explaining his decision to leave the Cape Colony, he had shown that he and his fellow emigrants resented what he called "the unjustified odium which has been cast upon us by interested and dishonest persons, under the cloak of religion, whose testimony is believed in England."[33] Consequently, in penning reports that were likely to be published, as those reports were, Pretorius and his secretary had an incentive to highlight, even to exaggerate, their Christian convictions and the religious exercises performed by the commando.

However, the propaganda factor does not take us very far toward understanding what happened in the Victory Commando. It is necessary to attempt to consider the religious ideas and customs of the emigrants, and to relate them to the specific circumstances of the commando.

The evidence about early nineteenth-century Boer religion is spotty and contradictory. Churches and clergy were few and far between in the Cape Colony. As we have seen, the Reverend Herold had to ride all the way from George to the Fish River valley—a distance of more than two hundred miles—to attend the executions of the five rebels in 1816.[34] Indeed, Uitenhage did not receive its first resident clergyman until 1817.[35] Nevertheless, many frontier people took the trouble to go all the way to the nearest district headquarters to have their marriages legalized, and to the nearest church for the baptism of their children and for quarterly communion services. Religion on a daily basis was therefore a household matter. European travelers found that some Boer households assembled for prayers at least once a day. For example, Henry Lichtenstein, a German doctor who held an appointment under the Dutch government at the Cape between 1803 and 1806, described the routine in a substantial household in the northern part of the colony:

> Much time was also passed in the services of devotion, at which I regularly attended; although it must be acknowledged, that for the most part I found them very tiresome. The day was begun regularly with a psalm

being sung, and a chapter from the Bible being read.
Not only the children, but all the slaves and Hottentots,
were required to attend. . . . [In the evening] the whole
collective body of people belonging to the house were
again assembled. In the first place came a female Hottentot, with a large tub full of water, in which the feet
of every individual in the family, from the father to the
smallest infant, were washed. A table was next set out,
at which all the christians seated themselves; the slaves
and Hottentots squatting, as in the morning, round the
room. The father then read some extracts from his old
sermons, which was followed by the whole company
singing a psalm. The ceremony was concluded by the
evening blessing. Besides this, on the Sunday morning
a solemn service was performed; at which a long sermon
was read. . . . [T]here were no other books in the house
but the sermons and the Bible.[36]

Lichtenstein also regarded many of the Boers as being ignorant and naive, and liable to be duped by cranky immigrant clergy from Europe.[37]

One cannot determine how general such religious practices were, or how deeply Christian belief penetrated the
various regional and class sections of the Boer population,
or what was the theological content of their Christianity.
Two foreigners who actually resided among the emigrants
in Natal recorded their impressions. One was a Frenchman
named Adulphe Delegorgue, who arrived in Natal about six
months after the Victory Commando had disbanded and who
lived there for four years. After returning to France, he published an account of his experiences. He depicted the emigrants as religious in the sense that they frequently indulged
in the singing of psalms—but he considered that they did so
mainly for want of other forms of entertainment. In writing

about the Victory Commando, he made no reference to the covenant; and he described Pretorius, whom he claimed he had come to know quite well, as a coward and even a traitor, on account of his failure to exert effective leadership when the British made their final invasion of Natal.[38]

Perhaps one should discount the judgment of Delegorgue. An anticlerical Frenchman, he may have been inherently unsympathetic to the emigrants. That charge cannot be laid against Daniel Lindley, an American Presbyterian clergyman. Lindley arrived in South Africa in 1835 in the service of the American Board of Commissioners for Foreign Missions. Two years later his first assignment in South Africa foundered when an emigrant commando attacked the people among whom he was working in the Transvaal—the Ndebele of Mzilikazi. Lindley then withdrew southward from the Transvaal with the commando. Later that year he founded a mission station at Umlazi in Natal. Piet Retief and his party spent a night there on their first journey to the Zulu headquarters. On 1 December 1837 Lindley made some stringent comments in a letter to the United States:

> I now wish to ask help from some quarter for the Boers. They are, in truth, as much objects of Christian charity as the people to whom we have come. They have no minister, no teacher for their children, almost no books and almost nothing to keep them from sinking into the depths of heathenism. They express a strong wish to be supplied with books and teachers such as they need. As a body they are ignorant and wicked. There are among them some orderly, well-behaved persons, a *few* of whom may be pious. . . . The Boers are all matter-of-course members of the Reformed Church to which they have a bigoted, rather than intelligent, attachment. . . . The first faithful man who shall labour among them will

find more trials than we among the heathen. The greatest difficulties will arise out of the fact that they already regard themselves as good *Christen menschen*. They are about as good Christians as the Nestorians.[39]

In 1839, after visiting twelve of their encampments in Natal, he made a further comment:

The Boers, *as a body,* are an exceedingly illiterate people. . . . In most of their houses you will find a Bible, for which they have a hereditary reverence. But this good book is, with a *few* exceptions, little read and less understood by them.[40]

It is possible that Lindley's account of the emigrants may have been influenced by a touch of intellectual elitism, or by his evangelical theology. Be that as it may, in 1841 the Natal Volksraad, having failed to persuade any *predikant* of the Dutch Reformed Church in the Cape Colony to come and serve them, invited Lindley to become their official minister, and he accepted. He gave them devoted service for the next six years, during which, as their only pastor, he made annual tours throughout the vast region where they were establishing their settlements, stretching from the Natal coast to the northern Transvaal, preaching, catechizing, confirming, marrying, baptizing, and dispensing communion. He earned their affection and gratitude, and in due course they named a village in the Orange Free State for him. Nevertheless, though he grew to respect them and understand their problems, his biographer has apparently found no evidence that he changed his mind about their behavior or the shallowness of their religious convictions.[41]

As to the content of the religious beliefs of early nineteenth-century Boers, a series of historians has claimed that they were rigid Calvinists, in the sense that they regarded themselves as constituting a Chosen People with a Divine Mission.[42] It is true that they often took comfort in texts from the Old Testament that emphasized the history of the Israelites, since they too were stockfarmers and they too faced serious challenges. Nevertheless, André du Toit has demonstrated that before the second half of the nineteenth century the Boers made no claim to be a Chosen People. In a careful investigation of the sources, he has found only one assertion that Boers made such a claim, and it came not directly from Boers themselves but was attributed to them by Adulphe Delegorgue.[43]

We come closer to understanding the origins of the vow or covenant that was taken by members of the Victory Commando when we consider certain precedents in the history of Afrikaner frontier people. In 1796 the leaders of the Graaff-Reinet rebellion persuaded some of their followers to swear to be true to them and their cause.[44] The practice was repeated in 1815, when a local Boer official, who under pressure from Hans Bezuidenhout had been coerced into joining the uprising described in the previous chapter, had people swear to be true to him and the cause. The judges of the special court that conducted the trial included the following perceptive passage in their final report to the governor:

A third subject to which we believe we may take the liberty to draw your Excellency's attention, is the weight which in this trial appeared to be attached by the residents to an oath. This Johannes Bezuidenhout knew so well, that . . . he . . . deemed it necessary to bind the collected multitude with an oath to remain together, as he otherwise foresaw that the failure of this first attempt [to release Kasteel Prinsloo] might easily have the effect that the multitude would have dispersed. . . . He therefore had a circle formed, and an oath of fidelity sworn, more particularly by the provisional Field-Cornet W. F. Krugel abovementioned, making the others repeat it with the understanding that this oath, sworn by the said W. F. Krugel, would be binding for all his men because they had come together by his orders. Some accordingly expressly repeated that oath, others gave their adhesion to it by taking off their hats, or by other signs, and others again conducted themselves merely passively, so that on the arrival of Landdrost Cuyler at Slachters Nek with his Commando, this oath was for a long time a hindrance, in consequence of which he had much trouble to bring them to subjection. However much this oath, demanded and taken for a criminal purpose, may therefore not be considered binding, it has nevertheless appeared to us not improbable that a binding power *was* ascribed to it in accordance with the conception of simple but deluded country people, which caused conscientious scruples in them; and from this supposition we believe we may draw this conclusion that this pledge on oath was considered sacred by them, and had it been demanded and given in a lawful manner, would have run no danger of being violated.[45]

We also know that there was a precedent for oath-taking among the emigrant body. At a gathering of emigrants on the highveld in June 1837, when Piet Retief had been sworn in as their governor, they had adopted nine articles of association, the first of which obliged every member of the community to take a solemn oath to have no connection with the London Missionary Society, whose South African superintendent, John Philip, was a formidable critic of Afrikaner racism.[46]

As the commando trekked into KwaZulu in December 1838, its leaders must have been profoundly anxious about the outcome of their enterprise. On the face of it, they were being extremely foolhardy. They were invading a country which possessed a vast army and which had won a spectacular series of victories. The Zulu monarchy had already demonstrated its determination to ward off white encroachment by murdering Piet Retief and his party, by wiping out many of the emigrants, including women and children, in the surprise attack at Weenen, by repulsing several subsequent probes by groups of Boers, and by annihilating a force of rival Africans led by British traders. In their dangerous plight, the leaders of the commando were bound to apply every idea that might conceivably contribute to success, including the invocation of divine aid. That naturally reminded them of an established custom: to bolster the morale of the Boer members of the commando, to inspire them with faith in their cause, and to bind them together into a cohesive unit, they would use the powerful sanction of an oath.

We can have no precise knowledge of what transpired in the Victory Commando. However, when one considers what is known of the religious culture of nineteenth-century Afrikaners, including their resort to oathing in times of crisis, as well as the interest that Pretorius had in placing their conduct in a favorable light in the eyes of a British government that was subject to evangelical pressures, one is cautious about accepting the assertions of religious enthusiasm and conformity as set out in the reports of Pretorius and Bantjes. Indeed, those reports include a number of undoubted internal contradictions. In particular, if, as reported by Bantjes, Cilliers included the vow in a prayer during a service in Pretorius's tent, two conclusions follow. First, the majority of the 468 Afrikaner members of the commando could not possibly have been present in the tent; and second, those who were present could not have taken the vow individually. It therefore seems doubtful that the vow or covenant was as central to the proceedings of the commando as Bantjes and Pretorius reported, and that the average member of the commando paid much attention to it. Perhaps, as in 1815, some of those who were present when oathing occurred in the Victory Commando "expressly repeated the oath, others gave their adhesion to it by taking off their hats, or by other signs, and others again conducted themselves merely passively." Skepticism is always warranted about a literal reading of an official report written for public consumption in a time of crisis; and in this case skepticism is vindicated by the nature of the evidence.

Furthermore, there is no doubt whatever that for many years the covenant was ignored by the officials in the Afrikaner republics. Indeed, almost everyone involved seems to have forgotten all about it. Here, too, the 1815 precedent seems to be relevant. After the suppression of that frontier uprising, the people concerned seem to have forgotten about the oath that had been imposed by Hans Bezuidenhout. Moreover, the early Cape colonial promoters of Afrikaner nationalism, who would certainly have been able to make good use of it, do not seem to have known that any members of the commando made a vow or covenant. S. J. du Toit, in his consciousness-raising book *The History of Our Land in the Language of Our People,* which was published in 1877, mentioned the Battle of Blood River but said nothing about a vow; nor did G. M. Theal mention it in his early writings, which appeared in the same decade. Modern Afrikaner scholars recognize the existence of this lacuna in the tradition. B. J. Liebenberg says that the vow was quickly forgotten; and Floris van Jaarsveld writes: "We know that until 1864 the covenant was not observed at all."[47]

IV

The first signs of public interest in the achievements of the Victory Commando came in 1864, when P. Huet and F. Lion

Cachet, two Dutch Reformed clergy who had been born in
the Netherlands, persuaded the general assembly of the
Dutch Reformed Church in Natal that "the 16th of December
should be celebrated religiously as a day of thanks."[48] Three
years later, Cachet organized a celebration on the site of the
Blood River *laager*. People arrived with forty or fifty wagons
and erected a memorial pile of stones.[49] However, these
events made very little impact on the general Afrikaner population. Moreover, there is no evidence that in commemo-
rating the victory over the Zulu, Cachet and his associates
focused attention specifically on the vow or covenant.

In 1876, H. J. Hofstede published the first history of the
Orange Free State, the Afrikaner republic that Great Britain
had recognized as independent in 1854.[50] The Free State
government subsidized the publication of the book, and a
member of its Volksraad praised it for telling the world "of
the many grievances of the Afrikaner nation, and especially
those of the Free Staters."[51] It included a "Journaal" (Journal) by Sarel Cilliers, who had died on his farm in the Orange
Free State in 1871. Hofstede introduced the passage by saying
that Cilliers had written it on his deathbed, and that he
himself had put it in order with the help of three other
people.[52]

This deathbed statement by Cilliers, as edited and published by Hofstede, was to become the principal source for
the myth of the Covenant. It focused on the piety of the
Victory Commando, and especially on Cilliers's own role as
its religious leader in the absence of an ordained minister.
Cilliers and his fellows, awed by the immense numerical
disparity between themselves and the Zulu, were sure that
"if the good God was not with us, there was little hope of
victory."[53] He and Pretorius decided that, as with the Jews
of the Old Testament, "we, too, were bound to make a
promise to the Lord, that if He gave us the victory over our

enemy, we would consecrate that day, and keep it holy as a Sabbath in each year."[54] Pretorius wanted them to make the promise collectively, and the other officers agreed:

It was on 7th December. I complied to the best of my weak capacity with the wish of all the officers, and I knew that the majority of the burghers concurred in the wish. I took my place on a gun-carriage. The 407 men of the force were assembled around me. I made the promise in a simple manner, as solemnly as the Lord enabled me to do. As nearly as I can remember, my words were these: "My brethren and fellow-country-men, at this moment we stand before the holy God of heaven and earth, to make a promise, if He will be with us and protect us, and deliver the enemy into our hands so that we may triumph over him, that we shall observe the day and the date as an anniversary in each year, and a day of thanksgiving like the Sabbath, in His hon-our; and that we shall enjoin our children that they must take part with us in this, for a remembrance even for our posterity; and if anyone sees a difficulty in this, let him retire from the place. For the honour of His name will be joyfully exalted, and to Him the fame and the honour of the victory must be given."[55]

Cilliers added that "we confirmed this in our prayers each evening, as well as on the next Sabbath."[56] He then described the battle at the Blood River. The victory was due to God. "That evening we had a thanksgiving for the great help and deliverance granted to us." However, the people were boast-ing about their prowess. "I upbraided them with this. . . . Let us not say that our hands and our courage have secured the victory."[57]

This version of the events differed in two significant re-spects from the contemporary reports of Pretorius and

Bantjes. In Cilliers's deathbed version, he himself enunciated a vow in the open air in the presence and in the name of the entire commando, whereas Bantjes had reported that the members of the commando held separate religious meetings in the tents of their respective leaders, and that Cilliers included a vow in a prayer in a meeting he conducted in Pretorius's tent, which could not have accommodated more than a fraction of the 468 commando members. Second, in Cilliers's version the vow itself contained only one commitment: an annual day of thanksgiving. It said nothing about building a memorial church.

Cilliers's version of the vow made little impact at the time. C. P. Bezuidenhout, who wrote the next patriotic history of the Orange Free State, which was published in Bloemfontein in 1883, included no specific mention of a vow, though he was steeped in religious piety and attributed the victory at Blood River to the hand of God.[58]

The initiative in using the emerging myth of the vow for political purposes was not taken in the Orange Free State but in its more powerful neighbor, the Transvaal. The first Afrikaner settlers in the Transvaal paid very little attention to the achievements of the Victory Commando because they had purposely dissociated themselves from the emigrants who had settled below the mountains in Natal. However, during the decade after the British government annexed Natal in 1843 most of the emigrants returned northward to settle in the Transvaal or the Orange Free State. Eventually, in 1865 the Transvaal government proclaimed 16 December a public holiday, "to commemorate that by God's grace the immigrants were freed from the yoke of Dingane,"[59] but there was no mention of a vow or covenant, and there were no official ceremonies to mark the holiday.

Conditions were transformed in 1877. Theophilus Shepstone led a small British force to Pretoria at a time when

Afrikaner morale in the Transvaal was extremely low. The republican government was virtually bankrupt, and its commandos had failed to conquer the Pedi people who occupied mountainous terrain 160 miles northeast of Pretoria. After desultory negotiations, there was no physical resistance when Shepstone proclaimed the territory to be a British colony on 12 April.[60] Three years later, however, the Transvalers rose in revolt and incorporated the emerging myth of the vow in their patriotic consciousness-raising symbolism. Hostilities commenced in December 1880, when, in the words of a modern historian, "the covenant was 'renewed' at Paardekraal by piling a cairn of stones, symbolizing both past and future: the past because the covenant had freed them from Black domination, and the future because they saw it as a sign that they would continue fighting until they regained their independence from the British imperialists."[61] The Transvaal commandos soon won a series of brilliant victories against poorly led British forces, and in 1881 the Gladstone government came to terms, granting the Transvaal a qualified independence. Thereafter, in 1881 and every fifth year, the government organized great patriotic festivals on Dingaan's Day.[62]

Previously, although the world view of Afrikaner frontiersmen had always borne the imprint of the Bible, their most common reading material, and the emigrants had found obvious parallels between their own lives and those of the Israelites as recorded in the Old Testament, scarcely any of them had claimed that they constituted a Chosen People in the theological sense.[63] By the 1880s, however, several Transvaal clergy were asserting such a claim. It is possible that it originated in allegations by foreign critics, such as David Livingstone, the British missionary-explorer who had clashed with the Transvaal government in the 1850s and to whom the proposition was scandalously heretical.[64] Be that as it may, it did become incorporated in the doctrines of the most conservative of the three Dutch Reformed churches in the region, the Gereformeerde Kerk. The Gereformeerdes, or Doppers as they were called, had broken away from the Nederduitse Gereformeerde Kerk of the Cape Colony in 1859, largely because they objected to the singing of hymns in church. They were influenced by the reaction against theological liberalism and pietism in the Netherlands, where, later in the nineteenth century, it was led by Abraham Kuyper, an influential Dutch theologian and politician, and the Free University of Amsterdam.[65]

Paul Kruger, the indomitable president of the Transvaal from 1881 on, was himself a Dopper and he lent his immense prestige to the new concept. His view of the world was rooted in the Bible, particularly the Old Testament. God was for him the absolute sovereign over mankind; events were under His direct control. The victory at Blood River was a miracle that demonstrated that God had selected the Afrikaners to be His Chosen People of modern times. Their setbacks—from the British annexation of Natal in 1843 to the British annexation of the Transvaal in 1877—were God's chastisements for their failure to honor their vow. Nevertheless, the achievements of the Victory Commando were never dominant in Kruger's mind. In 1838 he had been a lad of fourteen, and he and his family had been on the highveld among the followers of Hendrik Potgieter, who had later become Pretorius's rival for the leadership of the emigrants in the Transvaal. Events that he had personally experienced always dominated Kruger's historical perspective. In celebrating the sixteenth of December, he was mainly concerned with the renewal of the vow at Paardekraal in 1880, leading to victory in the War of Freedom in 1881, which reaffirmed God's selection. Moreover, for Kruger, God's modern Chosen Peo-

Paul Kruger [handwritten marginal note]

ple were the Afrikaner people of his republic, rather than the wider Afrikaner population. Even as British pressures on the Transvaal increased again after the discovery of the gold reef on the Witwatersrand in 1886, he continued to maintain that if they held fast to the Law and the Covenant, things would go well; if they fell away again, chastisement would follow.[66]

The five-yearly festivals at Paardekraal were great social occasions, attended by Afrikaners from all parts of the republic. In 1881 the people in the crowd, estimated to number between twelve and fifteen thousand, were exhilarated by their victories and their regained independence. On the first day, 13 December, there were patriotic speeches by President Kruger and others; the next day featured a shooting contest and a great feast when many toasts were drunk, and in the evening a fireworks display; on 15 December, entertainments on horseback and athletic contests, such as tugs-of-war, sack races, footraces, and long jumps were held; and the climax came on 16 December, when a clergyman explained the reasons for the festival. However, in all the patriotic speeches that year no mention was made of the Victory Commando or the original vow.[67]

At the celebrations in 1891 the connection with the events of 1838 was made more explicit. The Cilliers version of the vow was printed in the program and, unveiling a monument over the historic heap of stones, the president spoke about the Battle of Blood River, warning the people that 16 December should not be corrupted into a worldly feast. Otherwise, "God will no longer live among us." Even so, as Paul Kruger's speeches combined the politics of freedom with the theology of a People specially elected to receive the favor and chastisement of an omnipotent and omnipresent God, his references to the vow were general rather than specific, and his audiences always knew that his mind was on Paardekraal in 1880 rather than the Victory Commando and 1838.[68]

In December 1895 Transvaal clergy and officials organized a ceremony near Weenen in Natal, where the bones of the victims of the 1838 massacre were collected and buried in a casket in the foundation of what was to be a memorial monument. Sir John Robinson, prime minister of Natal, was present, and in his memoirs published during the South African War he described the ceremony:

A movement, carefully fostered and directed by the Dutch ministers of the districts—those Predikants whose influence over the minds and hearts of their flocks has contributed so greatly to present events—was set afoot for the solemn burial of these remains and for the erection over them of a suitable commemorative monument. . . . Families and visitors from far and near responded to the call. . . . About 1200 visitors—mostly family parties—had encamped close to the Blaauwkrantz River. . . . In front . . . stood the great square "casket" or box, draped in black, in which had been deposited all that could be found of the murdered Voortrekkers. The rest of the tent was filled with the Dutch visitors, a large proportion of whom were women and children. Of the service itself little need be said. . . . There were depths of suppressed passion in the extemporised prayers uttered over those crumbling bones, and the written sermon was listened to with profound and unbroken attention. It was a powerful appeal for the unity and brotherhood of the Africander race, and there was, no doubt, in its glowing words a deeper significance than was suspected then.[69]

1895

Burial of sacred bones of victims of 1895 massacre (Piet Retief) buried at site of future National monument voortrekkers = pioneers.

Indeed, by the 1890s Afrikaner clergy and intellectuals in various parts of southern Africa were responding to the pressures of British imperialism and mining capitalism by propagating knowledge of the historical achievements of their people and the virtues of their culture. Before the 1870s, the Afrikaners who left the Cape Colony in the 1830s and 1840s had usually been referred to as "emigrante" (emigrants), sometimes as "verhuisers," "uitgewekeners," or "weggetrokkeners," (migrants, refugees, leavers), though some people used the word "voortrekkers" (pioneers) to describe the first Afrikaners to arrive in a given locality. During the late 1860s, however, a few individuals were beginning to apply the word "voortrekkers" to all the Afrikaners who had trekked out of the Cape Colony in the spirit of Piet Retief between 1836 and 1854, and by the end of the century virtually all who regarded themselves as Afrikaners were using it in that sense. Self-conscious Afrikaners were also treating the movement itself as a great central saga in South African history, and calling it the Great Trek. Even some English-speaking South Africans were beginning to adopt that usage.[70]

During the last quarter of the nineteenth century, Afrikaner editors were glad to publish the recollections of aged, surviving *voortrekkers;* and after 1881 the Transvaal government appointed a Dutch teacher to seek out survivors and record their memoirs.[71] Several editors of English-medium publications, too, published documents by emigrants; notably John Bird, a Natal government official, who produced two massive volumes of *Annals of Natal,* which included a considerable amount of emigrant material in English translation, such as the reports on the Victory Commando by Pretorius, Bantjes, and Cilliers.[72] The numerous general histories of South Africa that poured from the British presses as the South African crisis moved to its climax in the Anglo-

Boer War of 1899–1902 also contained accounts of the movement.[73]

The late-life memoirs of members of the Victory Commando vary greatly in their handling of the religious factor. Several of the statements—such as those by Willem Jurgen Pretorius, Paulus van Gass, and Daniel Bezuidenhout—contain nothing at all about a vow or covenant.[74] Others refer briefly and vaguely to such an event but say that it took place either on a different day or at a different place from 9 December and Wasbank as indicated by Bantjes, a far more credible witness.[75] Indeed, as one would expect, these memoirs, produced between forty and sixty years after the event, are unreliable. Moreover, several of them seem to have been affected by feedback from the previously published memoirs of Cilliers, which themselves were, as we have seen, a late-life statement that enhanced the role of the author and introduced several palpable inaccuracies for dramatic effect, for example, by having Cilliers standing on a gun-carriage while he read out the oath to the entire commando. Thus, Isak Breytenbach, who was fourteen years old in 1838, had the vow taken at the wrong place and Cilliers standing on a wagon.[76] On the other hand, J. H. Hatting, whose statement is regarded by some historians as relatively accurate, made no more than an oblique reference to a vow, and said that it took place in the *laager* at Blood River on 15 December.[77]

There are similar problems with all the other late-life statements by members of the Victory Commando. For example, Izak de Jager, W. G. Nel, and P. J. Coetser all said that the vow was made when they were in *laager* at a place they called Danskraal rather than on a later occasion at Wasbank.[78] Other evidence that came to light in the late nineteenth century is no more convincing about the vow. For example, Anna Elizabeth Steenkamp did not mention the vow in the letter that she wrote from Natal to her relatives in the Cape Colony in 1843 and that was published in the *Cape Monthly Magazine* in 1876;[79] nor did Erasmus Smit, the pious former missionary who was among the *voortrekkers* in Natal, mention the vow in his diary, though he did write frequently about the events of the period.[80]

The publication of all this new and previously unpublished material reflected the rise of national consciousness among Afrikaners toward the end of the nineteenth century. Much of it laid great stress on the religious intensity of the commando; but it did little to indicate what actually happened in the matter of the vow or covenant. Indeed, on balance it tended to divert attention from the best sources in favor of the version that Sarel Cilliers had created on his deathbed in 1871. For example, F. Lion Cachet's history of the Transvaal Afrikaners (1882) included an exact duplication of the words of Cilliers.[81]

Some of the accounts that were written from an Afrikaner nationalist point of view after the publication of Bird's *Annals of Natal* in 1885 were derived from Bantjes and Pretorius as well as Cilliers, and they too emphasized the religious character of the Victory Commando. For example, J. C. Voigt's pro-Boer history published in London in 1899 included the following:

Firmly believing in the justice of their cause, and confident that Providence would assist them in their struggle to avenge the death of the unfortunate victims of the great massacre, the Voortrekker warriors were sincere and fervent in their religious devotions. Many of their leaders set them that example of unfeigned piety which strengthened and encouraged them in the fray. Religious observances were never omitted at the evening encampments. There was much fervent praying,

and the psalms and hymns of the Dutch Reformed
Church service were frequently sung at these meetings. . . . It was the unanimous opinion of all the Emigrants that the campaign could not be successful
without the help of Heaven.[82]

Of the covenant itself, all Voigt said in his long chapter
on the campaign was:

It was resolved that the entire army should take a vow
to God, that, if he granted them victory, they would
build a Church and set aside a thanksgiving day to commemorate the event. Cilliers says in his Diary [sic] that
Andries Pretorius first spoke to him about this solemn
vow, and asked him at Danskraal to address the commando on the subject. This he did. It was then decided
to advance. . . . On that Sunday morning, Andries Pretorius called . . . Landman and the aged P. Joubert, with
Sarel Cilliers, to his tent, in order to take their opinion
on the subject of the ceremonies to be observed in connection with the ratifying and confirmation of the vow
to God. Religious services were then performed in three
tents set apart for the purpose.[83]

On the other hand, some pro-Boer writings of the period
ignored the vow completely. This was even true of the passionate propaganda pamphlet, *A Century of Wrong,* that J. C.
Smuts and others produced on the outbreak of war to bring
the republican cause to the attention of Europeans and
Americans.[84]

By that time, the religious intensity of the Victory Commando and, in some cases, the taking of a vow or covenant,
had also found their way into the writings of British and
Anglo-colonial authors. George McCall Theal, who sympathized with Afrikaners but had said nothing about a vow

in his early historical writings,[85] included a highly roman-
ticized version in the South African volume of the popular
British *Story of the Nations* series, the fifth edition of which
was published in 1899:

> The commando resembled an itinerant prayer meeting
> rather than a modern army, for the men were imbued
> with the same spirit as the Ironsides of Cromwell, and
> spoke and acted in pretty much the same manner. There
> was no song, no jest heard in that camp, but prayers
> were poured forth and psalms were sung at every halt-
> ing-place. The army made a vow that if God would give
> them the victory over the cruel heathen, they would
> build a church and set apart a thanksgiving day in every
> year to commemorate it. The church in Pietermaritzburg
> and the annual celebration of Dingan's day bear witness
> that they kept their pledge.[86]

It is notable that in this purple passage Theal ignored two
crucial facts: first, at the time when he was writing, the
"church" in Pietermaritzburg was being used as a commercial building, as it had been since 1861; and second, most
of the men who took the vow never did anything to honor
it.

Other writings by Cape colonists of British descent took a
simple racial line in describing the Blood River campaign.
For example, Alexander Wilmot, a member of the Cape parliament and a copious author on South African historical
themes, made no mention of the vow and explained that
after the Zulu had killed Retief's party and many of the
emigrant women and children, "it was . . . evident that the
cruel Zulu power must be crushed, or the white man could
not live in South-East Africa."[87]

On the eve of the South African War, British imperialist
authors tended to justify their aggression against the Trans-

vaal republic by describing its Afrikaner inhabitants as religious bigots, but in their accounts of the activities of the *voortrekkers* in Natal they, too, did not mention the vow. C. P. Lucas, in his volume in a series of historical geographies of the British colonies published by the Clarendon Press in Oxford in 1897, wrote that "South Africa became the home of Protestants of an unbending type, slow to modify their thoughts and ways, modelled on the Old Testament rather than the New."[88] James Bryce, in his influential *Impressions of South Africa* (1897), wrote that the emigrants "deemed themselves, like many another religious people at a like crisis of their fortunes, to be under the special protection of Heaven, as was Israel when it went out of Egypt. . . . Escaping from a sway which they compared to that of the Egyptian king, they probably expected to be stopped or turned back." Although Bryce, too, did not mention the vow, he did say that 16 December was "still celebrated by the people of the Transvaal"—thereby implying that the Transvalers had always celebrated it.[89] Elsewhere in his book, Bryce included religion in his patronizing stereotype of the Afrikaner people: "They are strangely ignorant and backward in their ideas. They have no literature and very few newspapers. Their religion is the Dutch and Huguenot Calvinism of the seventeenth century, rigid and stern, hostile to all new light, imbued with the spirit of the Old Testament rather than of the New. They dislike and despise the Kafirs. . . . They hate the English also."[90]

During the South African War, several of the Boer officers made use of the symbolic significance of the anniversary. In 1899, 16 December fell on the day after a great Boer victory over the British on the Natal front at Colenso, and it was an occasion for jubilant celebrations. On the next two anniversaries, when they were waging guerrilla warfare with hit and run raids on British forces and lines of communication, commando leaders such as C. F. Beyers and J. H. de la Rey used the occasion to bolster the spirit of their men; and some of the women whom the British had removed from their homes and placed in concentration camps remembered the day in their own way. "We celebrated Dingaan's Day, not in a festive style but each one in her room," recorded one such woman in 1901.[91] The British officers, too, were aware of the significance of the day as a symbol of Afrikaner resistance; they destroyed the symbolic heap of stones that the Boers had erected at Paardekraal.[92]

Thus, after several decades of incubation during which nearly all the participants did nothing about the vow, Afrikaner religious and political leaders in the Transvaal incorporated a reference to it in their periodic national festivals, which they organized for the purpose of raising the political consciousness of their people in the face of British imperialism. By the turn of the century, interest in the history of the emigrants, now becoming known as *voortrekkers*, plus, in some cases, information about the emerging myth, was beginning to spread beyond the Transvaal. The Orange Free State, which entered the war on the side of the Transvaal, had made 16 December a public holiday in 1894; and although the day was not celebrated officially in the Cape Colony or Natal, imperialist as well as pro-Boer journalists and historians were writing about the history of the Afrikaner emigrants in Natal. Some of them included a statement about the vow, but the version that they adopted followed the deathbed account of Sarel Cilliers rather than the more reliable participant accounts of Pretorius and his secretary. Moreover, Afrikaner history and culture were being interpreted in the context of the existing tensions between Boer and Briton, rather than the past conflict between Black and White. Among republican Boers and their sympathizers, the emerging myth formed part of a nationalist, anti-imperialist

ideology; while among British imperialists and their sympathizers the Transvaal president was being taken to exemplify the anachronism and dispensability of the Boer
republics.

V

The Great Trek was the central theme in the Afrikaner nationalist mythology that came to maturity in the first half of
the twentieth century.[93] And at the very core of the story
was the Covenant, which gradually became crystallized in
the version that Sarel Cilliers had formulated when he was
near death in 1871, thirty-three years after the event.

The most prolific contributor to historical writing about
the Great Trek, and in many respects the most influential,
was Gustav S. Preller. His biography of Piet Retief ran
through ten printings and sold more than 25,000 copies by
1930; while his six volumes of edited *voortrekker* reminiscences, his edition of the diary of the early *voortrekker* Louis
Trichardt, and his biography of Andries Pretorius were also
well received.[94] In *Andries Pretorius,* Preller's account of the
Victory Commando included extensive paraphrases of the
reports by Bantjes and Pretorius as well as of Cilliers's statement, but he made scarcely any attempt to analyze them or
place the events in context. Typically, he published quotations from all three sources about the vow, without any
suggestion as to which was to be given greater credence.[95]
Preller wrote in colorful, romantic prose, using *voortrekker*
history to inspire his Afrikaner contemporaries with pride in
their past. His methods were rough and ready; his judgments
were wholly partisan; and by 1938 he was being influenced
by German National Socialism. Almost the entire *voortrekker*
community, including Retief and Pretorius, were heroes

larger than life; the motives and actions of their British and African adversaries received no consideration at all. This was the historical corpus that molded the historical consciousness of many Afrikaners. The Great Trek was "a national movement," its purpose "freedom from the oppressor."[96]

Another trend setter was J. H. Malan, whose *Boer and Barbarian*, first published in 1911, was successful enough to warrant a second edition in 1918. Malan had a keen sense of the power of history: "If posterity does not shun it; if, what is still worse, posterity deviates from the quality of decency, the dignified propriety, the ironstone character, and the piety of our pioneers, it will plant its footsteps on only one path. That path leads eventually to ruin and destruction."[97] *Boer and Barbarian* includes an elaborate account of the Victory Commando. Following Cilliers, it says that the vow was made on Sunday 9 December at Danskraal and that Cilliers uttered it standing on a wagon, "with his hands spread out towards heaven." It then gives the substance of the vow in the precise words that Cilliers had used in his 1871 "Journal," but whereas Cilliers had introduced them by saying, "As nearly as I can remember, my words were these," Malan's book declares that those were "the actual words used by him."[98]

In 1919 G. B. A. Gerdener produced a biography of Sarel Cilliers, whom he elevated to the same level as Piet Retief and Andries Pretorius in the growing body of *voortrekker* hagiography: "Pieter Retief, the Martyr of the Great Trek, Andries Pretorius, the Warrior of the Great Trek, and Sarel Cilliers, the Prophet of the Great Trek."[99] This book, too, is written in an intensely sentimental, religious, and nationalist vein; and its account of the Victory Commando, too, comes essentially from Cilliers's narrative and includes Cilliers's version of the wording of the vow. An appendix reproduces Cilliers's description of the commando from Hofstede's 1876

Piet Retief : martyr of the Great Trek
Pretorius : warrior of the Great Trek
Cilliers : prophet of the Great Trek.

history of the Orange Free State; but Gerdener provides yet
another tilt toward the legitimation of this version by labeling
this late-life document "The *Journal* of Sarel Cilliers," without explaining its origin.[100]

As the centenary approached, the harvest increased. It
included a collection of *voortrekker* documents from the
Transvaal and Natal archives; an account of the ways in
which Dingaan's Day had been celebrated in the past; a
biography of Hendrik Potgieter, who had been Pretorius's
principal rival for the leadership of the emigrants in the
Transvaal in the 1840s; still more *voortrekker* reminiscences;
and a collection of essays dealing with the history of the
voortrekkers in Natal by E. G. Jansen, who would become
minister of native affairs in D. F. Malan's government in
1948 and governor-general of the Union of South Africa in
1951.[101]

The emphasis on the Great Trek and the stereotype of
voortrekkers as an ultrareligious community were reinforced
in the schools. This was largely because of the enduring
influence of George McCall Theal, whose multivolume *History of South Africa* was reprinted without amendment
throughout the decade following his death in 1919. According to the fourth edition of volume 3, which was published in 1927, the *voortrekkers*.

came to regard themselves as God's peculiar people and
to consider all education beyond that of the bible as
superfluous, and all that was not in accord with its
science dangerous and sinful. These views did not indeed originate with the emigrants. Such opinions had
been gathering strength in secluded parts of South Africa
for five or six generations, but they reached their highest
point of development with those who grew up in the
wandering.[102]

The account of the Blood River campaign in the fifth edition of the second volume of Theal's *History,* which was published in 1926, was a slightly expanded version of what he had written in 1899 in the *Story of the Nations* series. It summarized the oath and, without referring to the commercial vicissitudes of the building, it asserted: "The church—now, since the erection of a better building as a place of worship, the Voortrekkers' museum—in Pietermaritzburg and the annual celebration of Dingan's day bear witness that they kept their pledge."[103]

Writers of school textbooks in both English and Afrikaans, relying on Theal's interpretations as well as his data, transmitted his stereotype of a homogeneous, godly people to the next generation. The first edition of the highly successful senior textbook by C. de K. Fowler and G. J. J. Smit, which was published in both English and Afrikaans versions in 1932, described the Blood River campaign without specifically mentioning the oath but included it in later editions.[104] A 1920s Afrikaans textbook by D. J. J. de Villiers and others said that the commando "solemnly promised God that if he should give them the victory, then they would build a house in honor of His Name, always celebrate the day as a Sunday, and tell their children that they must honor it also, for remembrance for the upcoming generations."[105] An Afrikaans textbook by W. Fouché included a close paraphrase of Theal's sentimental ascription of religious fervor to the Victory Commando and declared that "the whole army stood and made this holy vow."[106]

In chapter 2, I described the enthusiasm that was evoked by the celebration of the centenary of the Great Trek in 1938.[107] In December of that year, eight ox-wagons, bearing names such as *Piet Retief, Andries Pretorius,* and *Sarel Cilliers,* having trekked throughout South Africa from different starting points, converged on a hill overlooking Pretoria, where a crowd estimated at 100,000 people—nearly all of them Afrikaners—participated in three days of ethnic ceremonies, culminating in the laying of the foundation stone of a memorial to the *voortrekkers*. [108]

The vow was at the very heart of this outpouring of nostalgia. Hendrik Klopper, who had had a hand in founding the Afrikaner Broederbond and was one of the principal planners of the centenary celebrations, set the tone. On 8 August, he addressed a crowd that had gathered at the foot of the statue of Jan van Riebeeck in Cape Town to see the ox-wagon *Piet Retief* start its long, slow journey to Pretoria:

> On this solemn occasion, at this spot where almost three centuries ago Jan van Riebeeck stepped ashore, it is fitting, in view of the great ethnic deed [*volksdaad*] which we now begin to celebrate, that we should remember the vow of Sarel Cilliers: "Brothers and fellow-countrymen, we stand here before the Holy God of Heaven and Earth to make a vow that, if He will be with us and protect us and give the foe into our hands, we shall ever celebrate the day and date as a Day of Thanksgiving like the Sabbath in His honor. We shall enjoin our children that they must take part with us in this, for a remembrance even for our posterity. For the honor of God shall herein be glorified, and to Him shall be given the fame and the honor of the victory." . . . We bring praise to those who won for us a land and a future and we give honor to the Almighty, in the firm belief that He will make us a powerful People before His countenance. [109]

Predikants, politicians, and professors dominated the ceremonies on the hill outside Pretoria. Their sermons and speeches were rooted in the contemporary context of 1938, when poverty was widespread among Afrikaners and many of them were first-generation migrants from the rural areas to the industrial towns—a wholly new environment where they were liable to lose their Afrikaner identity. The orators painted the *voortrekkers* in heroic hues, giving them all the qualities that they deemed necessary to promote the nationalist cause. The *voortrekkers* were profoundly and uniformly religious. They were adamantly opposed to the mixing of the races. They stood for Afrikaner freedom and solidarity in the face of alien Western influences—this last being a disguised attack on the ruling United Party, with its appeal to white South Africans of British as well as Afrikaner descent. As expressed by the Reverend L. N. Botha, "The solemn covenant [*verbond*] locks the Voortrekkers with God. They take the Vow [*Gelofte*] in the name of the *volk* of South Africa."[110] F. Postma, rektor of Potchefstroom University College, spoke for an ancient wagon that was present and was said to have actually been with the Victory Commando. "I was witness of the birth of the Afrikaans Volk under the direction of God."[111] In a long historical survey, G. F. Combrink called the Great Trek "the Central Event in the History of South Africa. . . . Blood River made the Afrikaner volk a Covenanted volk [*Verbondsvolk*]." Combrink added: "Afrikaners, after you have again considered anew the heritage of your Fathers, what right have you before the God of the Voortrekkers to stay divided any longer? The oxwagons and Blood River call you to come all together in a mighty Afrikaner laager with a circular wall of Spiritual Voortrekker wagons around you."[112] The Reverend T. F. Dreyer stressed the racial factor: "God created the color line. . . . So if we efface God's lines of separation, we destroy his handiwork. If we go and mix with Indians, Coloureds, and Natives, our descendants will be mules who will not be able to hide their long ears, the sign of their bastardization. It is a heritage from our forefathers, which must be beautiful for us and which we must honor and value. God has willed that we must be a separate, independent volk."[113]

D. F. Malan came to the rostrum toward the end of the proceedings on 16 December. He started with a tribute to the *voortrekkers*. They had done the right thing in their time.

> Behind you lie the tracks of the Voortrekkers' Oxwa-gons, deeply and ineradicably imprinted across the wide high plains and over the sneering dragon-like mountain areas [Drakensberg = Dragons' Mountains] of South African history. They heard the voice of South Africa. They received their task from God's Hand. They gave their answer. They made their sacrifices. There is still a white race. There is a new volk. There is our own language. There is an undying urge for freedom.[114]

However, continued Malan, we now stand at the dividing line between two centuries, and there are profoundly serious questions ahead.

> You and your children will make history. Will South Africa still be a white man's country at the end of this new century? Will there then still be a poor white problem which this rich land of ours will face with weary eyes as a heavy reproach?[115]

Malan then proceeded to deliver a straight political oration, describing the urbanization process, the impoverishment of Afrikaners, and the dangers flowing from black competition in the cities, and ending with a call for all Afrikaners to unite to preserve their identity and their culture.

In subsequent years, every 16 December was an occasion for Afrikaner nationalists to use the mystique of the *voortrekkers* to endorse their policies. A second great festival came in 1949, when the Voortrekker Monument was officially unveiled.[116] Whereas in 1938 the Nationalists had been a minority splinter group to the right of the ruling United Party, in 1949 they ruled South Africa, having won a bare majority of parliamentary seats in the general election of May 1948. This time, the proceedings were supported by the government of the country, and E. G. Jansen, now governor-general of South Africa, was chairman of the organizing committee. In a modification of the 1938 Ox-wagon Trek, dispatch riders rode on horseback to Pretoria from fifteen starting points, and celebrations were held at more than four hundred places. Once again there was a plenitude of ethnic symbolism. While young boys and girls wore the uniforms of the *voortrekker* movement—the Afrikaner breakaway from the Boy Scouts—adults in traditional *voortrekker* costume sang ethnic songs and performed ethnic dances. There were no fewer than twenty-four speeches. D. F. Malan, now prime minister of South Africa, reiterated the linkage between the *voortrekkers* and the present generation, before he gave the nod for the opening of the front door of the monument.[117]

The Voortrekker Monument is a squarish granite building in a commanding position overlooking the capital city. It has two special features. In the center of the basement there is a granite cenotaph, placed so that a sun ray falls onto it through an aperture in the dome of the building at precisely twelve o'clock every 16 December. In his speech Malan explained that this was "a symbol of that godly truth, so saliently affirmed by the Voortrekkers, that no great ideal can be achieved without its sacrifices, that it is along the way of the cross that victory is won, and that it is the dead from whom life appears."[118] The second special feature is a marble bas-relief frieze surrounding the Hall of Heroes above the basement. The frieze, which is 320 feet long by 7 feet, 6 inches high, comprises 27 panels depicting the history of the

voortrekkers. Panel number 20 shows Sarel Cilliers enunci-
ating the oath. He stands on a gun carriage with his arms
outstretched to heaven, and seven *voortrekkers* gaze at him
in admiring expectation.[119] In the words of the official guide
to the monument: "Sarel Cilliers has mounted Old Grietjie,
the Voortrekker gun, and repeats the Vow that if the Lord
gave them the victory over their enemy, they would consecrate that day and keep it holy as a Sabbath in each year
and that they would build a church to the glory of God."[120]
In this crystallized form the myth of the Covenant lives on
in the Afrikaner historical consciousness.

6

ADAPTATION AND EROSION OF THE AFRIKANER NATIONALIST MYTHOLOGY

I

As a result of the victory of the National Party in the general election of May 1948, the Afrikaner nationalist mythology became an exclusively conservative mythology; it provided legitimacy for the regime. This occurred in a period of rapid changes in the global and domestic contexts—changes that led to fundamental differences between South Africa and the rest of the world.[1]

In 1948, all South Africa's neighbors were European colonies, racial segregation was the norm in the United States, and the Western powers dominated the infant United Nations and its agencies. By the mid-1980s the external environment was radically different. The European empires were dismantled. Lesotho, Botswana, and Swaziland had become independent from Great Britain in the 1960s, and, after long guerrilla wars, African nationalist movements in Angola and Mozambique had won their independence from Portugal in 1975–76 and in Zimbabwe (the former Rhodesia) from the local white minority in 1980. Third World and Communist countries commanded a large majority in the United Nations, which had created an Anti-Apartheid Unit and banned the sale of arms to South Africa. Although the

Soviet Union was not committing major resources to the region, it was providing black South African revolutionaries with diplomatic support and modest material aid. Moreover, the civil rights movement had made substantial gains in the United States, where overt racism was no longer conducive to political success, as was illustrated by the volte-face of George Wallace, who had tried to stop the University of Alabama from being desegregated in the 1960s but was re-elected governor on a nonracial platform in the 1970s.

During this very period when white hegemony was diminishing and statutory racial discrimination was being jettisoned in the rest of the world—although those processes were gradual, erratic, and subject to setbacks—South Africa was moving decisively in the opposite direction. Race was the bedrock of the policy of *apartheid* that was professed by the Afrikaner National Party that came into power in 1948. South Africa's four "races"—White, African, Coloured, and Asian—were unassimilable; each had its own character, its own potential, its own destiny. It was the duty of the Whites, constituting the civilized, Christian race, to use their control of the state to prevent racial friction and racial bastardization by ensuring that the races would be separated from one another. So far as practicable, each race should develop along "its own lines" in "its own area." Significantly, however, the politicians tolerated a fundamental deviation from the ideal of absolute separation: Africans, Coloured people, and Asians would continue to provide labor for Whites, at least for the foreseeable future.

In practice, *apartheid* involved systematization of the existing racial features and the elimination of the contradictory tendencies in South African society. As the essential prerequisite for the fulfillment of the *apartheid* goal, the Nationalist-dominated parliament passed the Population Registration Act in 1950, which prescribed a racial identity for every

South African. The government was then able to enact laws banning interracial marriage and interracial sex; dividing the towns and cities into uniracial residential and business zones; and generally enforcing racial separation with discrimination in every social setting, except in the workplace, where customary and legal color bars ensured white superiority and black subordination. Consequently, whereas before 1948 South African society had been constituted on the same racial principle as society in the colonial empires and North America, the South African parliamentary election in that year was followed by a parting of the ways: elsewhere, the beginning of a process of deracialization; in South Africa, an unprecedentedly radical, doctrinaire enforcement of racism. By the 1980s, indeed, South Africa was a unique phenomenon: a pigmentocratic industrialized state.[2]

Meanwhile, the South African economy was growing at an exceptionally rapid rate and accelerating structural changes in South African society. In 1948, the historic ethnic division was still the main cleavage among white South Africans. Though outnumbered by Afrikaners, English-speaking white South Africans still controlled the bulk of the wealth and dominated the commercial, industrial, and financial sectors of the economy. Already, however, some of the ethnic associations that had been founded by the Broederbond were promoting the growth of Afrikaner economic power and its concentration in the hands of a rising class of urban entrepreneurs. Since then, assisted by a government that channeled official business in their direction, Afrikaners have acquired substantial stakes in all sectors of the economy. By the 1980s, Afrikaans- and English-speaking capitalists shared many common interests and were beginning to merge into a single dominant social class. This process created acute strains in the National Party. As Afrikaner businesspeople became more numerous and more successful, they became committed to the market economy, and consequently less dependent on political patronage and less tied to the rigid racial ideology of the past.[3]

The structure of black South African society was also changing. Despite the government's attempts to stop it, the African population was becoming increasingly urban. As in other developing countries, economic pressures were pushing black South Africans out of their rural areas, where the economy was stagnant, and drawing them to the cities, where the economy was expanding. There, they came face to face with the contrast between their own living conditions and those of white people: for example, between "white" Johannesburg, where most of them worked, and its "black" satellite township of Soweto, where they lived. Exhilarated by the news of the changes outside South Africa, culminating in the independence of Mozambique and Zimbabwe, and spurred on by their own experiences of racial discrimination and, often, of callous treatment at the hands of petty white officials, a new generation of Africans, many of them born and bred in the towns, was highly receptive to the ideology of "black consciousness." The generational shift was marked by a change in the demeanor of Africans toward Whites: a change from deference to defiance. Two major explosions marked the transition. The first was in 1960, when the police opened fire on unarmed Africans protesting the pass system and killed 67 and wounded 186 at Sharpeville in the Transvaal. Soon afterward, the government banned the African National Congress (ANC) and its offshoot, the Pan-Africanist Congress (PAC), with the result that their leaders came to the conclusion that they should abandon their reliance on nonviolent methods; armed struggle, they concluded, was the only way to liberate their people from a regime that lived by violence. The second explosion came in 1976. It started in Soweto, where police fired on African schoolchildren who were protesting against the compulsory use of Afrikaans as a medium of instruction in the schools. The violence spread to other urban areas and eventually, according to a government report, at least 575 people were killed: 494 Africans, 75 Coloureds, 5 Whites, and 1 Indian. The government then banned seventeen anti-apartheid movements and arrested hundreds of people under laws that denied them a fair trial and exposed them to solitary confinement, torture, and, in several cases, including that of a popular leader named Steve Biko, death.[4]

By the early 1980s, there was a sense of crisis in South Africa. The regime itself seemed to be in jeopardy. New resistance movements, involving members of all three subordinate "races," were springing up to replace those that were banned. The "Homeland" strategy, according to which Africans were to forfeit their South African citizenship by becoming citizens of their ten separate ethnic territories, was stalled. The leaders of the Zulu, the most populous African group, with a proud military tradition, declined to accept "independence" on the government's terms, and so did the leaders of five of the other "homelands." Furthermore, independent Mozambique and Angola were providing military bases for the ANC and for the South West African Peoples Organization (SWAPO), the potential successor to the South African regime in Namibia. Since the 1976 disturbances, thousands of young Africans, burning with a desire for revenge, had fled from South Africa to find refuge in the neighboring countries. In the early 1980s some of these refugees, having received military training in tropical Africa or the Soviet Union, were managing to reenter South Africa, link up with the domestic underground, and commit sabotage against key targets, including nuclear installations, plants that converted coal into oil, and, most spectacularly, government offices in the heart of Pretoria and Johannesburg.[5]

The South African government claimed that this "Total Onslaught" was being orchestrated by the Soviet Union. To cope with it, Prime Minister Pieter Botha and Minister of Defense General Magnus Malan devised a "Total Strategy." ARMSCOR, a state corporation and the third largest industrial enterprise in the country, expanded to produce a high proportion of the regime's military matériel, and armaments that were still not being manufactured locally were imported from Europe, Israel, or North America, despite a ban imposed by the United Nations. Thus equipped, the Defense Force, with 40,000 regulars, 60,000 national servicemen (every white man being subject to two years service), and 380,000 reserves, was the most powerful military machine in Africa. The security apparatus and the military bore down ruthlessly against domestic opposition and intimidated South Africa's neighbors—assassinating leading refugees, making periodic sweeps deep into Angola, launching air and commando raids against targets in Lesotho and Mozambique, and providing military, technical, and economic support for African factions that were challenging the governments in both former Portuguese territories.[6] In March 1984 these tactics paid off. In return for reciprocal commitments by South Africa, the Mozambique government undertook not to assist South African revolutionaries and it expelled the ANC military cadres and many ANC civilians from its territory.

By then, too, the South African government was making a series of changes in the racial laws in an attempt to appease foreign critics and to intensify the cleavages among the black inhabitants. It opened up some of the more expensive hotels and restaurants to black customers who could afford to patronize them; it recognized and gave limited rights to black trade unions; and it allowed a small proportion of the African population, who met stringent qualifications, to acquire quasi-permanent rights of domicile in the urban areas. In

1984 the government also introduced a new constitution, which replaced the all-white parliament with a legislature of three houses, one each for Whites, Coloureds, and Asians; but the constitution ensured that the existing *apartheid* laws remained in force and that Whites had the final say in all important matters. Moreover, it did nothing for the African majority.[7] Indeed, the government was continuing a series of brutal actions to remove hundreds of thousands of Africans from their homes in areas it had zoned for white occupation and where, in many cases, they had lived for generations.[8]

The changes in the racial laws did not defuse resistance to the regime. Most Coloured and Asian people boycotted the elections for the new legislative bodies, and during the second half of 1984 there were widespread strikes by African workers as well as renewed protests by African schoolchildren. This time the government deployed soldiers as well as police. For example, starting at two o'clock in the morning on 23 October, seven thousand men began a systematic house-to-house search of Sharpeville and two other townships in the southern Transvaal; by the end of the day they had arrested 350 Africans.

As a result of these developments, the National Party was attracting increasing support from the English-speaking white electorate, swollen by refugees from Zimbabwe, but losing the support of right-wing Afrikaners—small farmers and urban workers for whom the overriding identifications were still racial and ethnic, and who regarded the new constitution as the thin end of a wedge that would ultimately submerge them under black domination and destroy their way of life. Far-right organizations were founded to accommodate such people: the Conservative Party led by Andries Treurnicht, an ordained *predikant* and former member of Botha's cabinet, the still more radical Herstigte Nasionale

Party (Reestablished National Party), and an extraparlia-
mentary neofascist movement, the Afrikaner Weerstandbeweging (Afrikaner Resistance Movement).[9]

These changes in the domestic and foreign environment
posed serious problems for Afrikaner intellectuals and politicians—the classes whose predecessors had been responsible for formulating, crystallizing, and propagating the
nationalist mythology and adapting it to changing circumstances. The following sections explore the ways in which
they handled the mythology in the light of these changes.

II

As I have indicated in chapter 1, by the 1980s mainstream
scientists in Europe and North America had abandoned the
racial paradigm that had dominated professional minds since
the Renaissance. Leading members of the historical profession had followed suit, although with somewhat less assur-
ance and conviction. However, the general public in Europe
and North America was still finding it difficult to accept and
internalize the new scientific perspectives on human populations. This was partly because the racist paradigm, dividing the human species into relatively stable, bounded
entities, each with distinctive cultural as well as physical
characteristics, is quite easy to understand; whereas its successor, fluid populations defined genetically and statistically,
and subject to continuous cultural and even physical change
by processes of adaptation to environmental conditions,
which are themselves subject to change, is a much more
complex model. In addition, the racial paradigm satisfied the
European and white American sense of identity, self-esteem,
and self-interest.

It is not surprising that white South Africans should be
still more tightly wedded to the racist paradigm since, in
addition to the features mentioned above, it corresponded

with the ongoing structure of their own society and, indeed, it was an essential psychological instrument for justifying the status quo from which they derived their power and wealth and, they were wont to believe, their security. With their deep-rooted conviction that *races* and *nations* and *tribes* are the crucial human categories, most white South Africans persisted in rejecting the concept of flexible, variable populations, without any endemic correlation between physical and cultural characteristics.

Their persistence was encouraged by the state. Previous South African statutory bodies had not shown much concern with historical details. For example, the reports of the Native Economic Commission in 1932 and the Native Laws Commission in 1948, and those produced during and immediately after the war by the Social and Economic Planning Council, paid no attention to the chronology of African migration to South Africa and very little attention to the ethnic divisions among Africans.[10] Very different were the commissions appointed by the Nationalist government. In 1955 a commission chaired by F. R. Tomlinson produced a massive report, *The Socio-Economic Development of the Bantu Areas,* which became the basis for the "Homeland" policy.[11] The Tomlinson report relied on racial theory in an extreme organicist form, likening races to organisms that have distinctive cultural as well as physical properties and characteristic courses of development: "Racial differences—and here we mean inherited biological characteristics which cannot be explained away, and also spiritual characteristics whatever their origin—are undoubtedly peculiar to particular social organisms."[12] The report made much of the differences between Whites and Blacks: "Europeans and Bantu . . . are culturally and racially alien to each other."[13] It also stated that Europeans were superior to Bantu: the "European national organism" had "a form of Western Civilisation as its vital basis." This constituted a "higher cultural content" than

Bantu culture possessed.[14] Relying on the racial categories established by Theal, Seligman, and others, the report made the Bantu people "the product of intermingling of Negroes of Africa with Hamitic invaders from the North East," and had them moving southward from central Africa "in various successive waves." Although it did not offer a date for the first crossing of the Limpopo River, it said that the spearhead did not reach the Orange Free State or the Transkei south of the Umtamvuna River before the seventeenth century.[15]

Tomlinson and his colleagues also stressed the divisions among the Bantu, while claiming that white South Africans constituted a single organic unit. This was a new and significant assertion:

> Alongside this growing European organism, there is a number of Bantu national organisms falling ethnically into various main groups and which have come or are still coming into contact with the European at different levels of intensity. Wherever, therefore, we speak of the alteration of the life of the Bantu, the reference is not to the alteration in the Bantu as a homogeneous people, but to changes in the organic-cultural life of the various Bantu national organisms and of individuals belonging to those organisms.[16]

A similar trend toward the use of historical statements to justify official policies may be found in the official South African *Yearbooks*. Those published before the Second World War contain nothing about the history of South Africa before the European impact. Typically, the historical chapter in the volume published in 1923 started with a quotation about European colonization from C. P. Lucas, the author of the Clarendon Press textbook on South Africa (see pages 94–95), followed by the statement "The Cape of Good Hope was discovered in 1487 by the Portuguese navigator, Bartholomew Diaz . . . ," and two pages later there is a Table of Notable Events, starting with the same event.[17] The 1941 edition of the *Yearbook* excludes the historical narrative but has the same initial entry in its Table of Notable Events.[18]

After 1948, however, the *Yearbooks* contained elaborate chapters on "The Peoples of South Africa" and on the emerging Homelands policy of the government. Firmly grounded in organicist assumptions, these *Yearbooks* laid great stress on the internal divisions in South Africa, with its "disparate and incompatible ethnic and racial groups."[19] The "self-confident and virile" white population "ranks among the top dozen most advanced nations in the world,"[20] whereas the other groups are far behind, in some cases by as much as "2,000 years in development."[21] Moreover, the Afrikaner and British elements in the white population, despite earlier differences, have now amalgamated "to form a single nation."[22] The Africans, on the other hand, constitute nine (later changed to ten) "separate ethnic groups, each with its own language, legal system, life-style, values and socio-political identity," and the South African government is therefore treating them as "embryonic nations."[23] Furthermore, the Africans have no greater historical claim to the land than the Whites because "the Blacks started settling in the northern part of the country more or less at the same time as the first White people began settling at the southern tip of the country during the 17th century."[24]

The same ideas have become disseminated in numerous other propaganda ventures of the South African government. For example, an Information Newsletter supplement to the widely distributed weekly *South African Digest* of 25 July 1980 declared:

Many centuries ago the forebears of the Black peoples of South Africa struck south in three streams from their ancestral homes around the great lakes of Central Africa. The vanguard of two of these migrations reached and crossed the northern frontiers of what is today South Africa at about the same period in history as the Dutch pioneers landed in Table Bay (1652). The subsequent Black settlements in South Africa were not purposive or permanent in the Western sense. All tribes relied heavily on hunting and their cattle, practising a kind of subsistence agriculture to tide them over from one season to the next. They selected the best-watered regions for their cattle, and as soon as one parcel of cultivated land was exhausted they moved on in search of virgin soil.[25]

After the Second World War, scholars incorporated similar themes in textbooks for use in South African schools and colleges. In 1969, C. F. J. Muller edited *Five Hundred Years: A History of South Africa,* which summed up Afrikaner scholarship of the quarter century since the war. This book maintained the custom of starting with the European discovery and settlement at the Cape of Good Hope. However, it included an appendix by D. Ziervogel, a professor of Bantu languages, on "The Natives of South Africa." Like his predecessors, Ziervogel relied on migration as the principal historical process, but he added material emphasizing the divisions among the Africans and claiming that they had arrived quite recently in South Africa. Of migration, he wrote as follows: "There are many indications that successive waves of peoples came down from the north of Africa. We can only surmise how one primitive culture was overrun by the next more advanced one."[26] He emphasized African divisions by devoting the bulk of the appendix to a "tribe" by "tribe" treatment. On chronology, he wrote: "At the beginning of the 16th century the Black peoples—the Bushmen and Hottentots had much lighter skins—who later became known as the Bantu began moving towards the south of Africa."[27]

Most school textbooks moved in the same direction as *Five Hundred Years*. All the many editions of the highly successful high school textbooks by Fowler and Smit were firmly fixed in the racial paradigm; but before the Second World War they said nothing about the origins of the African population, whereas the postwar editions, which continued to be produced until 1969, stressed the differences among the African "tribes." They did, however, have Africans entering South Africa before the time of van Riebeeck, with the first Sotho people entering the Transvaal from Botswana "during the sixteenth century" and the first Nguni people entering South Africa "at a comparatively late stage" and crossing the Drakensberg in the fifteenth century.[28] By the 1980s the South African history syllabuses included a section on precolonial African history in standard 8 (equivalent to the American tenth grade), but not later standards, and textbooks were being produced for each standard separately. A typical standard 8 text by M. C. E. van Schoor and others declared that, "as concerns physique, culture and language," Africans were "divided into numerous nations which themselves comprise a variety of tribes, each with its own characteristic group or tribal name, e.g. Xhosas, Zulus, Tswanas, etc. There is therefore a great degree of splintering or fragmentation among the Bantu." The text proceeded to describe African migration to South Africa: "It is not known precisely when the van of this migration reached South Africa, but there is considerable evidence to suggest that it occurred shortly before or during the 15th century." There is also a migration map, with great arrows coming down from the north.[29] On the other hand, social studies texts prescribed for use in African farm schools in the Orange Free State in the early 1980s contained nothing at all about the precolonial history of the ancestors of the children for whom they were prescribed.[30]

Nevertheless, the official racial mythology had ceased to be acceptable to scholars outside the Afrikaner nationalist milieu long before the 1980s. As early as the 1920s William Miller Macmillan had used the papers of John Philip of the London Missionary Society to rebut the racist interpretations of the history of social relations in the Cape Colony and of the colony's frontier conflicts with the Xhosa during the first half of the nineteenth century; in the 1930s Macmillan's student, Cornelis de Kiewiet, had applied a similar perspective to British policy toward the Afrikaner republics, and in 1941 de Kiewiet had published a masterly, nonracist survey of the history of South Africa since the beginning of white settlement.[31]

After the Second World War, historians and anthropologists added a new dimension: the precolonial history of the African societies in the region. In 1969—the year of the publication of Muller's *Five Hundred Years*—the editors' preface to the first volume of *The Oxford History of South Africa* criticized "misleading assumptions that have shaped writing about South African history": that it began with the Portuguese "discoveries"; that precolonial African societies were static; that physical type, language, and economy are necessarily correlated; and that South Africa contained several "pure races."[32]

Since then, fresh research and fresh thinking, including work in a Marxist perspective, have probed every element in the mythology surrounding the South African racist paradigm and found it wanting.[33] In later sections of this chapter we shall see that the Slagtersnek myth has been demolished and edged out of the lexicon, and although the myth of the Covenant cannot be completely abandoned because it has played a crucial ideological role in the triumph of Afrikaner

nationalism, it has become the object of criticism by professional historians and of passionate controversy among
Afrikaner clergy and politicians.

Research has also punctured the myth of the vacant land,
the unassimilable cultures, and the ten black nations, which
is at the core of the official policy of separate development.
Richard Elphick has demonstrated beyond all reasonable
doubt that the previously established account of the precolonial history of the western two-thirds of southern Africa
is wrong. He rebuts the contention that there were two distinct physical and cultural types in the region—"Bushmen"
(San) hunter-collectors and "Hottentot" (Khoikhoi) pastoralists—and that the latter were quite recent invaders. Instead,
Elphick shows that all the people whom the Dutch encountered in the region were members of the same basic genetic
population; that most of their ancestors were hunting and
collecting people who had lived there for many millennia;
and that in the early Christian era some of them acquired
sheep and cattle from neighbors to the north (probably Bantu
speakers), after which pastoralism spread fairly rapidly wherever conditions favored it but with reversions to the hunting
and collecting mode of life in bad times.[34]

The previously established version of the precolonial history of the Bantu-speaking farming people of southern
Africa, like that of the Khoikhoi, relies heavily on the
assumption that migration is the single most important process involved, and a sufficient explanatory concept. David
William Cohen, Robert W. Harms, and other historians of
tropical Africa have replaced the migration model with plu-
ralistic models. Although large-scale and rapid migrations
did sometimes occur, movement more often took the form
of gradual infiltration into fresh land by small family groups,
with cultural differentiation developing as people adapted
to different environments.[35] In southern Africa the principal

process in the pre-Shakan history of the Bantu-speaking farming people, who were the ancestors of 72 percent of the present inhabitants of the Republic of South Africa and its satellite homelands, is best delineated as such a process of gradual infiltration by family groups moving out beyond their natal villages and building up settlements where their culture adapted to the different environments of the region. Jeff Guy has provided an illustration of this in the case of the Zulu, and William Beinart in the case of the Mpondo.[36]

The official stress on racial or national differences among precolonial Africans is also misleading. Precolonial Africans, like members of other preindustrial and preliterate societies, identified with different levels of social organization for different purposes. It is true that the scale of overt political organization was usually quite small; but people identified with others beyond the political boundaries and readily incorporated strangers into their own polities.[37] African linguistic communities were very extensive. Virtually all the inhabitants of the region on the coastal side of the mountain escarpment that runs from what is now KwaZulu to what is now the Ciskei spoke one of several mutually intelligible dialects of the Nguni language; and most of the farming inhabitants of the interior plateau spoke a dialect of Sotho. More than that. All the southern Bantu languages are similar in vocabulary and syntax, so that a Sotho-speaker can quite easily understand, and even acquire fluency in, Nguni, and vice versa. Indeed, the cultural distances among the African farming peoples of the region were less great than those that have existed between Afrikaners and white South Africans of British descent until very recently. Nowadays, despite the separatist devices of the government, the Bantu-speaking Africans of the entire region are becoming more rather than less conscious of having a common identity, since they all experience the powerful impact of the South African state

and the capitalist system and are drawn into similar conditions of wage labor and deprivation. If, then, it is appropriate to speak of one white South African nation, it is no
less appropriate to refer to a single black South African
nation.[38]

Most white South Africans have been able to ignore many
of these new intellectual findings and interpretations, because they have represented changes from relatively simple
to relatively complex explanations of human taxonomy and
historical processes. However, since the Second World War,
applied science has also produced one category of evidence
that was more difficult to ignore, because it demolished the
chronology of the vacant land myth in simple numerical
terms. The dating of organic materials by measuring their
carbon-14 content, which deteriorates at a standard rate,
began to be applied to materials recovered by archaeologists
from sites in South Africa soon after the Second World War.
By 1960 it was apparent that people who possessed the
material culture of the nineteenth-century African populations of the region—owning sheep and cattle, growing crops,
and working iron—were present in some localities in South
Africa by the middle of the first millennium A.D. As the
postwar years progressed, the archaeologists' maps of the
region became studded with more and more such sites, and
by the 1980s archaeologists had sufficient evidence to describe basic processes in its precolonial history, distinguishing
the settlement patterns and the pottery types of an "early
iron age," starting before A.D. 300, from those of a "later
iron age," starting in about A.D. 1000. At Phalaborwa in the
northeastern Transvaal modern mining has exposed strata
indicating continuous occupation by farming peoples for
many of these centuries. In the light of this mass of evidence,
one is either ignorant or obtuse to deny that ancestors of
the modern Bantu-speaking Africans have been settling in

South Africa since at least the third century A.D., that is to say, some fourteen hundred years before the Dutch East India Company founded the first white settlement at the Cape of Good Hope.[39] Consequently, the persistent reiteration by South African propagandists and educationalists that Bantu-speaking Africans began to arrive in South Africa only at about the same time as Whites exposes them to ridicule.[40]

This is merely the clearest of the many indications that since the end of the Second World War a vast gap has opened up between the official South African mythology, insofar as it remains tied to the racial paradigm, and the nonracial perspectives that have become increasingly dominant in the rest of the world.

III

In chapter 4 we have seen that the Slagtersnek uprising of 1815 formed the basis for a typical political myth. There was the usual time lag of more than a generation between those events and their first translation into myth. Then, during the following half-century or so, Afrikaner cultural entrepreneurs fashioned sentimental accounts of those events in poetic as well as prose forms. They invested the events with vast significance, repeating the cliché "We shall never forget Slagtersnek." They also manipulated the details of the events, omitting or making light of elements that were inconvenient—the sexual behavior of the protagonists, their search for African assistance against the colonial government, and the neutrality or outright opposition of most of the frontier Boers, especially those who were relatively prosperous. Indeed, they created a romantic image of preindustrial Afrikaner society, painting it as far more religious, cohesive, and biologically stable than it was.

The career of the myth corresponded closely with the changing interests of the population it served. In origin, it was an anti-imperialist myth, born as part of the Afrikaner reaction against the new British imperialism of the late nineteenth century: the annexation of Basutoland in 1868, the diamond fields in 1871, and the Transvaal in 1877. It flourished so long as Afrikaner nationalists regarded Great Britain as the principal threat to their interests—the period covering the Anglo-Boer wars, Lord Milner's reconstruction program, the Botha–Smuts conciliation policy, and South Africa's participation in two world wars as an ally of Great Britain. It started to decline soon after the Second World War, when the last symbols of British overrule were removed and the African, Coloured, and Asian inhabitants began to mount a serious challenge to white hegemony, making it clear that black South Africans rather than Great Britain and British South Africans constituted the principal threat to Afrikaner power, wealth, and cultural identity. The Slagtersnek myth had served the cause well so long as Great Britain was perceived to be the principal threat to Afrikaner interests; it became irrelevant, perhaps even counterproductive, by the time of Verwoerd, Vorster, and Botha, when Afrikaner nationalists came to the conclusion that white unity was essential in the face of a rising tide of black resistance.

Slagtersnek has virtually disappeared from the South African school textbooks since the mid-1950s, when the syllabuses were altered to omit any aspects of the history of the region before the Great Trek.[41] Nevertheless, Afrikaans surveys of South African history that were written for college students and general readers continued for many years to provide variations on the settler synthesis of the story, with Afrikaner nationalist nuances. In 1951 senior Afrikaner scholars produced a two-volume work that ranked as the major Afrikaans synthesis for more than a decade. It gave a romantic pen-portrait of Freek Bezuidenhout, said the use of Coloured soldiers to arrest a white man was "not sensible," quoted the cliché about not forgetting Slagtersnek, and concluded that "even after the Great Trek Slagtersnek had not disappeared into oblivion." [42]

In 1969, by which time much of the historiography in the English language was breaking loose from the racist settler tradition, the substantial survey edited by C. F. J. Muller continued to focus on the white section of the population. Ten of the eleven contributors were Afrikaners, but the book was published in both official languages. It contained a fresh slant on Slagtersnek, consonant with the new nationalist emphasis on the black rather than the British menace. The episode was still regarded as an important expression of "seething discontent among the farmers," but several of the ringleaders were shown to have been far from heroic figures. "They had spent most of their lives among the Bantu and had degenerated sufficiently to attempt to obtain help from Gaika [Ngqika]. . . . They had to some extent succumbed to the influence of a primitive environment."[43] This interpretation was followed in the article on Slagtersnek in the semi-official *Standard Encyclopaedia of Southern Africa,* which was published in 1973.[44]

In that same year, however, J. A. Heese published his careful study of *Slagtersnek en sy Mense* (Slagtersnek and its people), based on a dissertation that Muller had supervised. In the foreword, Muller himself wrote:

> Renewed research on the myths in our people's past is urgently necessary. Only then can greater clarity be obtained about what really happened. Myths, too, are historically important, but then they must be recognized as myths. True history cannot be written if illusions are treated as realities. The sequence of events that is known

as the Slagtersnek uprising was—as Dr. J. A. Heese con-
vincingly demonstrates in this work—falsely interpreted
for more than a century and a half. Heroes were seen
where there were no heroes.[45]

Heese's major conclusions were as follows:

The Slagtersnek uprising was no expression of the Afrikaner's striving for independence—it was rather a false
note in the development of the Afrikaner nationality.
Savage people like the gloomy Bezuidenhouts, Faber,
and some of the Prinsloos were violators of the traditional values of the Afrikaner, such as his sense of race
purity and his respect for church sacraments. It was the
turbulence of Freek Bezuidenhout, the lust for vengeance of Hans Bezuidenhout and the personal rancor
of S. C. Bothma and H. F. Prinsloo that caused the rising.
The conservative and orderly Afrikaner of 1815 wanted
to have nothing to do with people who colluded with
the hostile blacks.[46]

Heese's meticulous research has exposed many of the
weaknesses of the mythical interpretation of the Slagtersnek
episode. Nevertheless, he himself wrote within an Afrikaner
nationalist paradigm. He called it "a false note in our nation's
history."[47] To him, the Bezuidenhouts, Prinsloos, and Both-
mas were unsuitable symbols of Afrikaner heroism because
of their unconventional living arrangements and their attempts to obtain aid from the Xhosa. He agreed with them
in disapproving of the use of the Cape Regiment, with its
Coloured soldiers, to arrest Freek; and he claimed that the
courts of the time were applying "the equalization of whites
and blacks,"[48] whereas in fact they were giving effect to a
proclamation that sanctioned the subordination and im-
mobilization of the "Hottentots," while providing for the

registration of their contracts of service and minimal conditions of employment. He also implied that several earlier rebellions by frontier Boers were justified on the ground that the leaders were more substantial Boers and above all because they did not make alliances with Africans: "In the previous uprisings there were no important efforts to collude with the blacks against their fellow burghers; the leaders of 1815 brought inexcusable shame on their necks by calling in the enemies of the frontier boers against their own people."[49]

It was left to Hermann Giliomee to place Slagtersnek in a broader perspective, instead of trying to adapt it to the ongoing needs of Afrikaner nationalism.[50] He has shown that the 1815 uprising, like previous disturbances in 1795 and 1801, was the product of strains created in a local white society by the transition from a "pioneering frontier" to a "closing frontier." In the pioneering stage, Boers had easily been able to maintain an extensive, near-subsistence mode of life by acquiring fresh land to take up their population increase, and the Dutch East India Company had not attempted to control their relations with their Khoikhoi serfs, whose land they were occupying. By the end of the eighteenth century, however, the Boers were no longer able to continue their expansive movement to the east, because it was blocked by the Xhosa people, so that they were experiencing land shortage. Furthermore, by 1815 the British colonial government was taking active steps to close the frontier. It was collecting the land tax more efficiently and making it more difficult for the Boers to acquire legal rights to land (1813); it was prescribing conditions for the employment of Coloured servants (1809, 1812); it was sending judges on annual circuits from Cape Town to administer the law at the district headquarters, where they took unwonted cognizance of relations between Boers and their Coloured servants (1811 ff.); and it stationed along the frontier zone not only British military detachments but also the Cape Regiment, with its white officers and Khoikhoi other ranks. In addition, British and continental European missionaries were beginning to work among Khoikhoi and Xhosa communities; they were expounding different norms from those of the Boers, and some of them were drawing the government's attention to abuses of power by Boers over their Coloured dependents.

Giliomee has also used the data provided by Heese to show that there was a distinct class factor in the Slagtersnek episode. The rebels were, for the most part, the new, landless, propertyless class of Boers, and the Boer officials who stood by the government were members of the landed class who had accommodated to the British regime, which at that time was quite congenial to the interests of the landowners. The collaborative relationship would collapse in the 1830s, when the government had removed the legal restrictions on the Khoikhoi, emancipated the slaves, and persistently failed to use its authority to establish security of life and property for Whites as well as Blacks in the frontier zone, with the result that substantial Boers like Piet Retief and Gert Maritz became leaders of the exodus from the colony.

It is, indeed, evident that the dominant culture among the frontier Boers of the early nineteenth century was not the inflexible racism of the myth of Slagtersnek. Giliomee says: "Predominant in the Afrikaner frontiersmen's perception was cultural chauvinism rather than an immutable belief in their biological superiority."[51] Moreover, they were pragmatic. How else can one explain the fact that it was not only the failures among white frontier society who made alliances across the color line? In the 1790s, for example, the leading frontier Boers cooperated with Ngqika to drive people whom he regarded as his subjects eastward across the Fish River.

The early nineteenth-century Boers were more concerned with personal, regional, and class interests than with rigid racial categorizations. *Apartheid* was not the issue in 1815.

By the 1980s the Slagtersnek was no longer functional for Afrikaner nationalism. Although the myth rested on racist assumptions (e.g., the impropriety of using Coloured personnel to arrest white people), it was primarily an anglophobic myth. It had served a useful purpose so long as Great Britain and British South Africans posed the major threat to Afrikaner interests; but that time was past. Afrikaner nationalist interests now required the cooperation of English-speaking white South Africans and the sympathy of the peoples and governments of America and Europe, including the United Kingdom. In these circumstances, the Slagtersnek myth was best forgotten. Moreover, not only were scholars chipping away at the historical events from which the myth was derived, but also it was a secular myth in which the Afrikaans churches had no stake, and it had no place in the official South African calendar. Consequently, by the 1980s Slagtersnek was being eased out of the Afrikaner lexicon. For those older people who had been reared on it, it was still a powerful symbol; but it had ceased to form a vital part of the Afrikaner political mythology, or of the historical consciousness of the new generation of Afrikaners. The myth of the Covenant, as we shall see, was a very different story.

IV

The Covenant has been by far the most influential element in the Afrikaner political mythology ever since the birth of the nationalist movement in the late nineteenth century. One of the first Acts of the Union Parliament in 1910 was to make the anniversary of the Battle of Blood River an official public holiday, and the 1938 festival culminating in the laying of the foundation stone of the Voortrekker Monument ensured that 16 December would continue to be a great ethnic event in the Afrikaner calendar. The Covenant was the prime symbol of Afrikaner Christian culture, the exemplary vindication of Afrikaner hegemony in South Africa. Whereas it was possible to play down the Slagtersnek episode, the mythology could not dispense with the Covenant.

The material changes that took place in South Africa after 1948, including changes in the Afrikaner class structure and Afrikaner political affiliations, precipitated intense disputes over the significance and the meaning of the Covenant. Professional historians began, somewhat cautiously, to reappraise the events of 1838. In March 1979 the University of South Africa convened a conference on "Problems in the Interpretation of History with Possible Reference to Examples from South African History Such as the Battle of Blood River."[52] The star performer was to have been Floris van Jaarsveld, a prolific historian who had made major contributions to Afrikaner cultural nationalism. By the time the conference met, however, it was known that van Jaarsveld's paper would treat the history of the Covenant in a secular spirit and would question some of the elements in the established myth. When he went to the podium,

> a gang of about 40 burly men burst into the hall, surrounded historian Floris van Jaarsveld, emptied a tin of tar over him and plastered him with feathers. During the assault, a man who identified himself as Eugene Terreblanche, of the *Afrikaanse Weerstandbeweging* (Afrikaans Resistance Movement) seized the microphone and swung the tail of a sjambok through the air. Standing behind the Vierkleur flag of the South African Boer Republic, he said: "We as young Afrikaners are

tired of seeing spiritual traditions and everything that is sacred to the Afrikaner desecrated and degraded by liberal politicians, dissipated academics and false prophets who hide under the mantle of learning and a false faith—just as Professor Floors van Jaarsveld now, at this symposium, attacks the sanctity of the Afrikaner in his deepest essence. . . . this standpoint draws a line through the significance of the Afrikaner's history and is blasphemous."[53]

After the intruders withdrew, the conference continued, and in the following year the University of South Africa published a report with a dedication to van Jaarsveld. His own paper was the most substantial part of that report. It went some way to demythologizing the Covenant. It showed that there was no way of knowing the exact wording of the Vow and that it was not observed at all before 1864. It also pointed out that Afrikaners were by no means the only people who have believed that God was on their side.[54]

The debate about the Covenant among Afrikaner clergy has had far more serious political effects than the debate among historians. Unlike Slagtersnek, the Covenant has profound religious connotations. In South Africa, more than in any other Protestant country, the clergy—specifically, the *predikants* of the white Dutch Reformed churches—are still a major force in politics.[55] Since nearly all the members of their congregations are Afrikaners, and most Afrikaners are members of their congregations, the *predikants* preside over solidly ethnic institutions. Foreigners tend to underestimate their power and influence. *Predikants* made vital contributions to the triumph of Afrikaner nationalism. They inspired resistance to British cultural hegemony; they became deeply involved in the Broederbond; and, as we have seen, they fostered and propagated the myth of the Covenant and

played leading roles in the great ethnic festivals at the Voortrekker Monument outside Pretoria. Moreover, during the
first half of the twentieth century many of them interpreted
the myth as meaning that Afrikaners are a Chosen People
with a God-given mission to rule South Africa. *Predikants*
also became intimately connected with the National Party.
Prime Minister Daniel François Malan, who led the party to
victory on the *apartheid* platform in 1948, was a *predikant;*
so was an influential and thoroughly racist brother of Prime
Minister Balthazar Johannes Vorster; and so is Andries
Treurnicht, who presided over the Conservative breakaway
from the National Party in 1982. The Afrikaans press has
always given immense prominence to religion, printing numerous biblical quotations, editorials, special articles, and
letters to the editor on religious themes on the leader page.
Indeed, despite the inroads of urbanization and capitalism,
religion continues to be a determining influence over the personal   beliefs,   the   corporate   behavior,   and   the   self-
justifications of Afrikaners. In 1984 the Afrikaans press explained the massive incursions into Angola by the South
African army in religious terms.[56]

The principal Dutch Reformed Church in South Africa is
the Nederduitse Gereformeerde Kerk (NGK). As John de
Gruchy explains, the NGK

> with its million-and-a-half white members is quite
> clearly the dominant church in terms of its access to the
> policy makers of the nation. Included within its ranks
> are most of the members of Parliament and of the pro-
> vincial councils. Its members virtually control many of
> the town councils throughout the land. The vast ma-
> jority of people employed by the government in various
> capacities and institutions, including the police and the
> military, belong to the DRC [i.e., the NGK].[57]

After 1948, *predikants* inexorably became deeply involved in the policies of the government. The General Synod of the NGK meets every four years. Majorities in successive synods adopted a conservative approach to the burning political issues of the *apartheid* state, interpreting Scripture as upholding the essential unity of mankind but claiming that ethnic diversity is in accordance with the will of God; rejecting racial injustice and discrimination in principle but accepting the policy of separate development. The synods of the Nederduitsch Hervormde Kerk (NHK)—a Transvaal church—were still more rigidly conservative, and the NHK leadership was strongly supportive of Andries Treurnicht's Conservative Party. The Gereformeerde Kerk van Suid Afrika (GKSA) produced some dissent; but it was the smallest of the three Afrikaans churches and its influence had declined since the days when Paul Kruger, president of the old South African Republic, had been an active member. The cost of this pervasive conservatism was the alienation of the Afrikaans churches from the rest of institutional Christianity, in South Africa and abroad.[58]

As early as 1948, most of the other Christian churches in South Africa issued statements criticizing *apartheid*.[59] Often, indeed, their behavior did not match their rhetoric; the stipends of white clergy were usually higher than those of black clergy. Nevertheless, many of their clergy and congregations were deeply concerned. A dramatic example of clerical anguish occurred in 1957, when Geoffrey Clayton, Anglican archbishop of Cape Town, died of a heart attack within hours of signing a letter to Prime Minister Verwoerd saying that he could not counsel members of his church to obey pending legislation which would make it unlawful for black people to attend church services in "white" areas.[60] In 1968 the South African Council of Churches published a "Message to the People of South Africa" showing how *apartheid* and separate development were contrary to the Christian gospel. The government's response was predictable: it denounced its clerical critics for demeaning their pulpits "into becoming political platforms to attack the Government and the National Party."[61]

Initially, the World Council of Churches tried to play a mediating role in South Africa. In 1960 it arranged a "consultation" on Christian race relations and social problems at Cottesloe in the Transvaal. Delegates of the NGK took part in the consultation and accepted a statement criticizing several aspects of *apartheid*. However, Prime Minister Hendrik Verwoerd and other Nationalist politicians, and conservative clergy including Andries Treurnicht, proceeded to put strong pressure on members of the NGK provincial synods, which then rejected the statement.[62] Subjected to further political pressures, the clerical conservatives managed to maintain control of successive synods, including the General Synods of the NGK, which meet every four years.

Despite these pressures, several *predikants* were moved by conscience to denounce the pernicious effects of the government's racial policies. As early as 1956 the Reverend B. B. Keet, a widely respected Stellenbosch University theologian, raised the question whether *apartheid*, or separate development, could be applied in a just manner as claimed by the NGK.[63] Five years later, after Sharpeville and the banning of the ANC and the PAC, he and eight other Afrikaner theologians answered that question with a resounding No![64] In the following year the Reverend C. F. Beyers Naude, a former member of the Broederbond and moderator of the NGK in the Transvaal, founded a Christian Institute, which brought African, Coloured, and white Christians of various denominations together, launched a series of studies of "Christianity in Apartheid Society," and espoused increasingly radical responses to official policies.[65] In October 1977, in its crackdown after the Soweto disturbances, the government banned Beyers Naude, the Christian Institute, and its journal *Pro Veritate*. Nevertheless, the South African Council of Churches maintained its interdenominational opposition to *apartheid*, and by the 1980s it had become quite widely representative of South African Christians, led by an African general secretary—an Anglican bishop, Desmond Tutu.[66]

Nineteen eighty-two was a crisis year for the Afrikaans churches. The NGK had withdrawn from the World Council of Churches in the aftermath of the Cottesloe Consultation in 1960 but had retained membership in the World Alliance of Reformed Churches (WARC). At its Ottawa meeting in 1982, however, the WARC decided that *apartheid* is a heresy, suspended the membership of the NGK and its sister church, the NHK, and elected as president Allen Boesak, a member of the Coloured Mission Church affiliated with the NGK. Boesak's church synod concurred with the WARC's estimate of *apartheid*, and by the end of the year it had joined the South African Council of Churches. Meanwhile, in June, 123 Afrikaner *predikants* and theologians had published an open letter roundly condemning the practice of segregation in church and state. Nevertheless, when the General Synod of the NGK met in October 1982 its conservative establishment retained control. The synod elected as president a *predikant* who, like his predecessor, spoke for resistance to change, and it was reported to have listened to speeches by a security officer about the "total onslaught" on South Africa. Although the synod granted that racism has no scriptural basis, it refrained from recommending that the laws against mixed marriages and sexual relations should be repealed and paid virtually no attention to the brutal effects of official racism. Finally, a majority of the members of the synod supported a motion to leave the WARC, but the motion was not carried because it did not receive the two-thirds majority that was required for such a change; consequently the NGK remained a suspended member of the WARC.[67]

The Afrikaans press was filled with heated discussions of these religious disputes. It often published letters from Afrikaners criticizing racist behavior. Much of this was directed at specific actions by individual clergy. For example, during 1982, when the *predikant* at Clanwilliam in the Cape Province obliged a Coloured schoolmaster to write an examination for an external degree of the University of South Africa in the kitchen of the church hall while the three white candidates wrote the same examination in the church consistory, there was a flood of correspondence, largely critical of the *predikant*'s action. The decisions of the General Synods of the NGK also evoked a vast amount of press comment. In November 1982, "Afrikaner," describing himself as a member of the NGK and a Nationalist, wrote to the editor of *Die Burger*, the major Afrikaans daily in Cape Town, to inquire, "If I arrive in heaven some day, will there be separate provision for the white Afrikaner members of the NGK and other conveniences for 'other races'. . . ? I am ashamed of these decisions and cannot support my Church in the world outside."[68] Willem de Klerk, an influential journalist, used his column in the Afrikaans weekly *Rapport* to complain about the inaction of the 1982 General Synod of the NGK and to call for effective leadership in the church.[69] Nevertheless, the editorials in the Afrikaans press always expressed a cautious establishment point of view on religious issues. For example, *Die Transvaler* editorialized as follows in the aftermath of the 1982 General Synod:

> The violent attack, domestic and foreign, against the Afrikaans churches is there for all to see. It is perhaps not so strange, because it is the one terrain where the Afrikaner is perhaps most vulnerable, because he has

the highest esteem for his church. Certainly, everyone who attacks the Afrikaans churches in the name of Christianity must not be condemned without more ado, because many do so in deep and earnest sincerity. Also, one must not assume innocence, because fault is to be found here too. But many of those who raise the loudest voice in condemnation are clearly themselves condemned by the words from their own mouths that are nothing else but politics.[70]

It was inevitable that this theological debate should hone in on the Covenant. Each December the Afrikaans press included extensive discussions of the subject. "How should the day of the vow be celebrated?" asked *Die Kerkbode*, the organ of the NGK, early in December 1983. The editorial answer emphasized the religious character of the *voortrekkers* and treated the Blood River victory as a miracle:

The vow speaks of people in need, people with a realization of deep dependence on and a firm belief in God. . . . If among the Voortrekkers it was only a consciousness of need and dependence, we would not have had much cause to be proud of them. Their firm and immovable faith in the power and mercy of God, stamps them however as people who are an example and inspiration for any people—and therefore people of whom and with whom we can be rightly proud. In the Victory Commando there was no doubt that the Lord was completely able to give them the victory if it pleased Him. For the victory no praise and honor should be claimed, because it should only be regarded as a miracle. And for that all honor and thanks to Him. At our Day of the Vow celebrations this striking faith of the Voortrekkers must be clearly emphasized—not to glorify people, but to glorify God, who performed the miracle.[71]

In conclusion, the *Kerkbode* editorial linked the behavior of the *voortrekkers* with the contemporary political scene: "The firm faith in God that the vow bespeaks must be an inspiration for the present generation in the dangers and onslaughts in which we find ourselves in the present day world."[72]

In the secular Afrikaans press the debates about the Covenant reflected the passion that had aroused Terreblanche and his Afrikaanse Weerstandbeweging to tar and feather Professor van Jaarsveld. Was December 16 an Afrikaner ethnic festival or a national festival? Should English-speaking white South Africans be encouraged to join in the celebrations? And Coloureds? And Africans? "Lojale Burger" (Loyal citizen) argued as follows:

I consider that the Geloftefees [Festival of the Vow] is not limited to the Afrikaner volk. That day comes from a victory that God allowed to happen and not so much the victory that a group of white men achieved over a horde of black men. God willed that the white Christian trekkers, who were the bearers of the Bible, should appear as missionaries and progress to Blood River, where the taking of the vow was arranged and the fight had to take place, so that the various races could live in peace in the future. The celebration of Geloftedag is thus not limited to a certain group of people in the country. The gelofte is not intended to raise certain people and to open wounds in others, but that all inhabitants of the country shall honor God for the mercy and prosperity that are received since the Battle of Blood River. The bearers of the Word could thereafter go forth with their service among the natives. Today we still reap the fruits of it. All racial and language groups must have a part in the commemoration of that day and it must not be limited to white Afrikaans-speakers or the Afrikaner volk, seeing that the white Christian trekkers were not limited to a certain language group.[73]

Other correspondents expressed the traditional view. As "Patriot" put it: "I believe that the day is ours, Afrikaners, alone. We are bound by the blood bond. . . . Let the rest of the country get on with their work, since others are not concerned with Geloftedag."[74] Many writers made specific linkages with the present. In a special article in *Die Transvaler*, Professor Arrie van Rensburg of the University of Pretoria wrote:

> The day of the vow tells us that the Great Trek has still not come to an end. . . . The Great Trek cut the Afrikaner off from his source in Europe and made a white African nation of him. . . . Today, South Africa stands like a White Giant with his back to the southern Ocean. . . . and the realities of his existence in a populous black continent oblige him to look northwards again and anew, like the Voortrekkers a century and a half ago, to achieve peaceful coexistence and to draw out a message that will make us a people of the future. . . . Let us accept the challenge of Africa to be great: great of character, great of spirit, great of faith.[75]

By the 1980s Afrikaner editors were adopting a very different line from the exclusive ethnicity of the previous generation. The editorial in the Transvaal daily, *Die Beeld*, on 15 December 1983, which was repeated almost word for word in the Cape Town daily *Die Burger* the next day, admitted that "some interpretations of Geloftedag that were given in the past are simply not tenable." Geloftedag "is associated with a universal experience with God that all peoples know if they call on His Name, but which acquired concrete meaning for us in a specific historical event." Moreover, with hindsight, we can see that the victory paved the way for the evangelization of all the people in the South African interior. Thus, Geloftedag is much more than an Afrikaner festival: "It concerned the communal welfare of all peoples and groups in our land. . . . We have often politicized and ideologized the day. We have used it as an opportunity to talk about the black peril ('swart gevaar') and the menace of 'our enemies.' And we have often misperceived the appeal of the day: that we in this land must serve the kingdom of God for the good of all people."[76]

V

In 1983, the celebrations of the Day of the Vow were overshadowed by the latest wave of African sabotage.[77] For members of the African resistance movement, 16 December 1983 was the twenty-second anniversary of the founding of the ANC fighting arm, Umkhonto we Sizwe, rather than the one hundred and forty-fifth anniversary of the Battle of Blood River. The morning newspapers that day reported the forty-second attack by ANC saboteurs since the beginning of the year—a bomb blast that destroyed the Johannesburg offices of the Department of Foreign Affairs—as well as three separate bomb blasts in Durban.[78]

Die Vaderland listed twenty-nine places where celebrations were to be held and the names of the principal speakers at each place.[79] In most cases the attendance was sparse: many Afrikaners and nearly everyone else in the country ignored the celebrations. Those who did attend were confronted with considerable ideological confusion.

Government supporters, who controlled the platforms at most places, departed widely from the view that the vow had created a special relationship between God and the Afrikaner "nation" and justified exclusive Afrikaner domination of South Africa. Instead, they used the occasion to promote the constitutional changes that were to be introduced in 1984, providing limited participation in the political process to Coloured and Asian people, but none to Africans. Addressing about two thousand people at Hartenbos in the Cape Province, Prime Minister P. W. Botha appealed to Afrikaner cultural organizations to help other "minority groups" come closer to the Afrikaner, so that the Afrikaner could share his "fine language and culture" with them. This was necessary if the Afrikaner was to continue to exist in South Africa. Hatred and prejudice were not preconditions for being a good Afrikaner. The victory at Blood River was not a victory of Whites over Blacks but of God's omnipotence over all. The prime minister explicitly denied that Afrikaners should be regarded as a Chosen People.[80]

In a widely reported speech in Cape Town, F. W. de Klerk, minister of internal affairs, warned his listeners: "As in 1838, the white South African today again faces a moment of truth—not because a political leader creates it, but because the objective facts demand it." He said that,

> internally, all the elements existed which made South Africa a fertile breeding ground for tension and growing collision. These were that the white minority group was more prosperous, possessed the most land, the most attractive homes, the most power—and the black majority was being prompted that it was wronged, that it could progress only if the Whites' prosperity and freedom were taken away. . . . [However] Whites did not have cause to feel guilty about their prosperity or freedom. Mistakes had been made and they were not free of selfishness but in general they had attempted to rec-

oncile their prosperity and freedom with fairness to other groups.

De Klerk concluded: "This beautiful country, this land of milk and honey, this country bought so dearly—if we do not act correctly and in time—can be changed into a country of blood and hatred, revolution and crisis."[81]

The government made sure that right-wing Afrikaner dissidents were excluded from most of the platforms. This led to a confrontation at the Voortrekker Monument near Pretoria. The organizers allowed only five hundred invited guests onto the grounds where the official ceremonies were being televised by the South African Broadcasting Corporation. Several hundred people, including women wearing traditional *voortrekker* bonnets (*kappies*), were denied admission. " 'Why must we stand outside the gate like blacks?' the Kappies shouted at the guards, and one guard was on the receiving end of pointed invective. 'You look just like the Zulu king Dingaan with your fat stomach,' the protesters shouted at him. The 500 people inside were traitors, the Kappie leader, Mrs Marie van Zyl, said and were 'using the Bible of the anti-Christ.' "[82]

Where right-wing dissidents did obtain a hearing, their speeches received much less space in the Afrikaans press, all of which was controlled by the ruling National Party. No newspaper paid much attention to a speech made by Andries Treurnicht at Vegkop, in the Orange Free State, the site of an Ndebele attack on *voortrekkers* in 1837. Treurnicht's typed notes for that speech run to eleven pages and constitute a lucid exposition of the conservative Christian nationalist view of the Covenant and its relevance for the 1980s.[83] It is the speech of a person steeped in Christian fundamentalism. Races and nations are ineluctable human categories. The history of the events of 1838 as purveyed by nationalist scribes is literally true. The policy of separate development as enunciated by Verwoerd is a just and sufficient response to the problems of South Africa. The modifications being introduced by the Botha government are the thin end of a wedge that will inexorably lead to the collapse of the *volk*. Treurnicht said not a word about the historic role of black people in the economy of colonial and postcolonial South Africa.

Unlike normal Sundays, said Treurnicht, Geloftedag is the day when Afrikaners "thank our God for deliverance" and "commemorate a particular historical battle in which our people survived and which brought us to safety." Whereas the nineteenth-century Africans fought "pitiless wars of conquest, which depopulated vast areas," the *voortrekkers* "made treaties with black peoples and assured them protection and survival when they were threatened with extermination."

> I think I can rightly say: the Voortrekkers strove after a dispensation of orderly neighborly existence for peoples—for territory for their own people and good neighborliness. They wanted to live and let live in freedom! So different from what happened in America and Australia. The trekkers gave something permanent to South Africa. And that is: the claim of a people to be itself; the right not to be dominated or oppressed. The right to be free and the right of self-determination.

And again:

> As spiritual descendants of the Trekkers we stand on the side of those who seek the freedom of different peoples, each within its own living space. We grant it for others! We demand it for ourselves! He who wipes out boundary lines, destroys the rights of different communities. He who forces different sorts together, commits tyranny!

Treurnicht then made a still more pointed reference to contemporary politics:

> There comes an hour when you must stop making concessions if you want to maintain your freedom and self-respect. You must be able to offer resistance, to refuse those who demand that you must be so yielding that everyone is satisfied with you; otherwise everyone will deride you. . . . I say to you, on the day when we have changed and reformed so much . . . that the liberalists and Marxists will be satisfied with us, we shall have deteriorated. Then they can bury us. And it will be a burial without honor. . . . There is a difference between surviving in shame and misery and oppression, and survival in freedom and honor and autonomy— survival that will be a blessing! A person can well survive . . . but with treason towards your past and your people! You can survive as an individual and yet renounce and lose your national existence! You can say, I remain White, while the Whites collectively lose their power! [Here Treurnicht inserted the word Rhodesians in brackets in his notes.] You can stay alive . . . in moral decay and sin! You can survive as a despicable cringer and without true manliness and honor!

Treurnicht then praised the *voortrekkers* as agents of civilization: "Theirs was a civilizing task, a missionary task, the vocation of a trustee to lead the native peoples to greater independence and self-determination. Therefore, there stands at Dingaan's village today a great cross and a church through which the descendants of the trekkers account to the Zulu people and the world for their Christian faith and their responsibility even towards their former enemies." He went on to emphasize the religious behavior of the Victory Commando: Pretorius's suggestion that they make a vow; Cilliers's agreement; the approval of "everyone"; the taking of the vow; its repetition "every evening"; and the miraculous outcome of the battle against overwhelming odds. "A surrounded and threatened people, in its hour of utmost need, in a struggle for life and death, placed its dependence in belief in God, and He saved them." Toward the end of his speech, Treurnicht again linked his perception of the events of 1838 with his Christian nationalist view of the present:

> Today our people are still a surrounded people. Everyone has the right to self-determination, but, say some, we must disappear in *veelrassigheid* [literally, many-raceness]. We are busy writing the greatest chapters in the history of a people's liberation, but because it is us, it is suddenly racism and we are answered with sanctions resolutions of the U.N. We lead peoples to independence but it is not allowed for ourselves! For a surrounded people there is only one way out! Childlike trust in God; submission to God's commands; justice towards other peoples; moral and spiritual discipline; battle readiness against the enemy.

In publishing brief notices of the speeches by Treurnicht and several other right-wing Afrikaners, the English newspapers selected their more bizarre components. They informed their readers that Carel Boshof, who was the son-in-law of former Prime Minister Hendrik Frensch Verwoerd and who had recently resigned from the chairmanship of the Broederbond in disagreement with the government's constitutional plans, compared Afrikanerdom to "a building that had to be fortified against the onslaughts of the age."[84] A speech by Almaar Swart, delivered at the site of the Blood River battle, attracted much attention. He was reported to have said that the Whites no longer had a future in South Africa. Their only salvation lay in a white homeland, where no black man would be allowed at all; and every white family in the homelands should have eight children. Several hundred people walked out of the hall at Blood River when Swart expressed these pessimistic views.[85]

The most remarkable theological justification for racism came from a *predikant*, the Reverend J. A. Kriel, who was reported to have told a small gathering in the Cape Town suburb of Rondebosch that "discrimination, injustice and suffering will always exist until Christ comes again, and then Christ will remove them. Through fighting against discrimination now, people are trying to take God's task over from Him, and thus open the way for the Antichrist. 'He who wants to do more than what God wants him to do, commits suicide, as will happen to the United Nations and the world powers.' "[86]

VI

By the 1980s, the political mythology that had developed around the turn of the century to bolster the Afrikaner nationalist cause fell far short of satisfying the three criteria that we have identified for the assessment of a political mythology.[87] The specific myths that we have examined are known to contain distortions of the historical events that they purported to describe: ancestors of the African population of southern Africa have been living in the region since early in the Christian era; the Boers who took up arms against the Cape colonial government in 1815 were unheroic figures whose behavior conflicted with the norms that Afrikaners respect; and we do not know precisely what happened in the 1838 commando against the Zulu, but we do know that the *voortrekkers* themselves failed to honor any vow that some of them may have made. Second, biologists have discarded the taxonomy according to which the human species comprises a series of distinct "races," each with peculiar, indelible cultural as well as physical qualities. Finally, racism has also been losing its respectability. Outside South Africa it is no longer expedient to apportion rights and duties on a racial basis.

In these circumstances, the entire racist paradigm has come under unprecedented strain in South Africa. Strain has become evident within the white population as well as the black, among Afrikaners as well as English-speaking Whites. The tensions in the Dutch Reformed churches have already been described. Philosophers and historians of impeccable Afrikaner antecedents, such as André du Toit and Hermann Giliomee, have demonstrated that the government's racial policies do not represent the only, or the best, Afrikaner political tradition.[88] Critiques of the racial order dominate white South African literature and drama, as in the works of André Brink, J. M. Coetzee, Nadine Gordimer, Alan Paton, and Athol Fugard.[89] They also permeate the poetry and novels of black South Africans, notably Dennis Brutus, Mafika Gwala, Es'kia Mphahlele, Oswald Mtshali, Mbulelo Mzamane, Sipho Sepamla, Mongane Serote, and Miriam Tlali.[90]

Nevertheless, the racist mythology dies hard in white South African society. It is true that the Slagtersnek myth, formerly a particularly potent contributor to Afrikaner political consciousness, is being eased out of the lexicon, and that the myth of the covenant is the source of lively debate among Afrikaners. However, official South Africa remained wedded to a modified version of the cluster of myths concerning the vacant land, the unassimilable races, and the ten black nations. The 1978 and 1983 editions of the massive *Official Yearbook of the Republic of South Africa* pay some attention to recent scholarship but end up with contradictory and muddled statements. They say:

> The Blacks, according to modern evidence, came from the north in waves, first as early as the 10th or 11th

century, followed by others in the 13th and 14th century. They started settling in the northern parts of the country during the 17th century—more or less at the same time as the first white people began settling at the southern tip of the country.[91]

There is also a variant of the old claim that white hegemony is justified by superior technology:

The Xhosas, like all other Black tribes with whom Whites came into contact later, practised a kind of shifting agriculture to tide them over from one season to the next, and relied heavily on hunting and their cattle. Generally, in moving about Southern Africa they selected the best-watered regions and as soon as one parcel of land was exhausted they trekked further in search of virgin soil. Thus, Black settlements in South Africa at that time were not purposive or permanent in the European sense.[92]

The *Yearbooks* also perpetrate a classic muddle between genetic and cultural factors, and attribute all vital creative processes in precolonial sub-Saharan Africa to "Hamites": "those Bantu-speaking negroids in whom Hamitic pastoralism was the strongest cultural influence would have spread more quickly and farther afield than those whose Negro-derived horticulture permitted a more settled way of life."[93] This "Hamitic myth" has long since been discarded by historians of Africa.[94]

South African schoolchildren continue to labor under an old-fashioned, pigmentocratic history syllabus. The version that has been used in senior classes in South African schools since 1974 starts with this statement: "The general aim of the teaching of History at school is to convey to the pupils a knowledge and understanding of the past, especially in respect of the history of his own country, the manner in which the conduct of public affairs in his own country has evolved, and the history of the major events and movements which affect life in South Africa today."[95] In each of the last three school years, half the syllabus is exclusively South African; all the rest is exclusively European in standard 8 (1789–1848) and standard 9 (1848–1918), while the syllabus for standard 10 (1919–70), the final year, also includes sections on international relations, the Far East, the Middle East, and tropical Africa.

The textbooks that have been authorized to be used in South Africa to cover the syllabus have recently been studied by Johanna Maria du Preez, a graduate of the Afrikaans-medium University of Potchefstroom and lecturer in communications at the University of South Africa, Pretoria, who describes herself as "a loyal, proud Afrikaner" and "a loyal South African."[96] In a master's thesis written originally in Afrikaans for the University of South Africa, du Preez's key concept is "master symbols," defined as "symbols with which the individual or the community are strongly identified and which are inherently capable of manipulating the behavior of people."[97] Reviewing the political background, she notes:

> The official premise is that all education in South Africa must be Christian National; a system that was introduced by the Afrikaner in his resistance to British cultural imperialism. The orthodox Afrikaner sees no conflict between Christian and National demands. He regards the two as one. The Afrikaner sees his history as a great national epic struggle in which his entire existence, all his ideals and institutions, were realised.[98]

From her content analysis of fifty-three textbooks prescribed for use in the final five years in both black and white sec-

ondary schools in 1980 and 1981, she deduces that the textbooks are riddled with master symbols that justify the
existing order in South Africa. In summary, she concludes
that twelve master symbols appear repeatedly in the textbooks, starting with the following four: "Legitimate authority is not questioned"; "Whites are superior; Blacks are
inferior"; "The Afrikaner has a special relationship with
God"; and "South Africa rightfully belongs to the
Afrikaner."[99]

VII

The history of Afrikaner nationalist mythology has shown
that a political mythology may include several different types
of myths. There are specific secular myths, which may be
readily abandoned in the light of changing circumstances
without weakening the ideological legitimacy of the regime.
There are specific myths that include strong religious content,
which cannot be abandoned so easily, because religious attitudes are especially slow to change. There are also myths
that form an integral part of the ideology. Such myths cannot
be abandoned without stripping the regime of its legitimacy,
though they may be modified as policy adapts to the changing material context.

Of the examples studied, the Slagtersnek myth is of the
first type. It is derived from a specific historical event—a
secular event that had scarcely any religious connotations.
By the 1980s, as a result of the waning of British power and
influence, and of the need to turn English-speaking white
South Africans into allies against the "total onslaught" from
black South Africans and their foreign supporters, the anti-
British thrust of the Slagtersnek myth ceased to be functional
for Afrikaner nationalism. Consequently, that myth was
eased out of the lexicon without much difficulty.

The Covenant is a myth of the second type. It, too, is derived from a specific historical event, but it has a strong religious content. Religion is still a significant element in Afrikaner culture, and, as events in countries such as Iran and Northern Ireland demonstrate, a religious ideology, supported by a mythology cast in religious terms, can still be a very potent force in the modern world. Consequently, despite the fact that modern Afrikaner historians have access to information that casts doubt on several aspects of the myth, it has remained a vital part of the nationalist lexicon; but Afrikaners themselves differ sharply as to how they should interpret and celebrate the Covenant in their context in the 1980s.

The set of myths concerning the origin and more particularly the culture of the African population of southern Africa is of the third type. As those myths developed during the nineteenth century and the first half of the twentieth century, they were unashamedly racist. They posed a clearcut dichotomy between Whites and Blacks, especially Africans. Whites formed a superior race, Africans an inferior one; and the differences among Africans were not very significant. Since the Afrikaner nationalist government came into power in 1948, however, this simple set of myths has been substantially modified to meet the changing political context; but the modified version is still essentially a racial interpretation of history and society.

As we have seen, somewhat fuzzy concessions have been made to archaeologists' findings that ancestors of the African population were present in southern Africa early in the Christian era. More important, profound changes have been made in the interpretation of the quality of African culture and the structure of precolonial African society in the region. Although the textbooks lag behind, as du Preez has shown, the official mythology has shifted from a hierarchical view of the human species with Whites at the top and Blacks near the bottom, to the view that Whites are not necessarily superior to Blacks. However, this is at best a "separate but equal" doctrine. It is racist on two counts. First, the modified mythology still treats "races" as fundamental divisions of mankind, distinguished from one another by permanent cultural differences. Second, the modified mythology lays great stress on the ethnic distinctions among Africans. This is an innovation that has accompanied the unfolding of the policy of separate development, which compulsorily divides the African population into ten different nations with ten different "homelands."

These modifications in the mythology represent a shift from strict and elementary racism to a policy of racial manipulation. The government's constitutional program has the same effect. Strict racist dogma prevailed throughout the 1950s and the 1960s, when the government went to inordinate lengths to overcome constitutional obstacles to the exclusion of Coloured people from participation in the central political system.[100] By 1984, domestic and global pressures made it expedient to attempt to appease the Coloured and Asian communities so as to prevent them from forming alliances with Africans. Racial manipulation was the hallmark of the new constitution that the government then introduced, because, although it gives Coloureds and Asians legislative bodies alongside the white legislature, it also ensures that ultimate power remains in white hands, and it leaves untouched the rest of the laws discriminating against Coloured and Asian people, for example, by making them live in segregated areas and attend segregated schools and colleges. Above all, the 1984 constitution does nothing for Africans, who continue to be denied the right to participate in the central political system and to be subjected to pervasive segregation and discrimination, including draconian controls over their movements and their efforts to achieve economic security, on the pretext that they possess adequate rights as citizens of their homelands.

The Afrikaners who are most involved in coping with the erosion of the nationalist political mythology and adapting it to the changing material context are the intellectuals. As the successors of the people who created the mythology around the turn of the century, they are its natural custodians. Moreover, the role of intellectuals in creating and propagating myths is more significant in an authoritarian society such as South Africa than in a democratic society. The Afrikaner intelligentsia cannot ignore this problem. However, as Robert Jervis has shown, people invoke a series of mechanisms when their basic attitudes are challenged by new information. They may fail to see that the new information might contradict their beliefs. They may recognize that the information is discrepant but reject its validity—by discrediting the source, by seeking fresh information in support of their views, or by sloughing off the parts that are causing attitudinal conflict. Only when all such mechanisms fail do people change their views. Even then, people start by modifying their views on the least important questions and only gradually change their opinions on subjects that are fundamental to them.[101]

By the 1980s, Afrikaner intellectuals differed widely about how to cope with the historical, scientific, and normative attacks on the established political mythology, and they conducted their disputes with acrimony. Some adhered passionately to the mythology as it had been propounded in 1938, during the celebrations marking the centenary of the Great Trek. A few rejected that mythology root and branch, at the cost of ostricization from the *volk*. Most adopted some sort of compromise, often involving contradictory behavior in different contexts. For example, after the tarring and feath-

ering incident, Floris van Jaarsveld published an essay criticizing another element in the established mythology.[102]
Nevertheless, van Jaarsveld's demythologizing did not ex-
tend to the racial myths that are at the very core of the
mythology: his textbooks continued to be steeped in racial
mythology.[103] Among the intellectuals who continued to
claim their ethnic identity as Afrikaners, the so-called *oor-
verligtes* ("over-enlightened ones") came closest to complete
rejection of the mythology. Hermann Giliomee and André
du Toit, the leading lights of that group, published documents on the history of *Afrikaner Political Thought* that highlighted the writings of Afrikaners who have opposed racism
in its crudest forms.[104]

For other classes in Afrikaner society the specific myths
are less important. As with nonintellectual people in other
industrialized countries, most modern white South Africans
are not much concerned with the specifics of history. Their
mode of life is quite different from that of earlier generations,
and they do not depend on detailed historical underpinnings
for their beliefs or their behavior. Moreover, in South Africa
as elsewhere, by the 1980s fewer students were taking history as a university subject than in earlier years, and in many
schools history was being replaced by subjects containing a
mixture of history, geography, and civics. Nevertheless, most
Afrikaners of the younger as well as the older generation
retain from their schooling a generalized assumption that
racial and ethnic categories are fundamental, a strong sense
of identity as Afrikaners and as white South Africans, and,
indeed, a belief in the "master symbols" that Johanna Maria
du Preez has identified.

Crawford Young has pointed out that ethnic conflict is
capable of triggering more potent "emotions, anxieties, fears,
and insecurities" than all other types of conflicts.[105] Young's
judgment is confirmed by contemporary events among cul-

tures as diverse as those in tropical Africa and Ulster, Lebanon and the Basque country, and the Canadian province of Quebec. Moreover, during the 1980s racism was still a potent influence over the thought and behavior of millions of white Americans and Europeans, despite the fact that overt expression of racism was confined to fringe groups such as the Ku Klux Klan. In this sense, as has been said of Americans, "the past takes a long while to be over."[106] Racial and ethnic assumptions thrive without specific historical corroboration. In South Africa, where official racial classification still molds a person's life, these assumptions are confirmed by experience of life on the upper side of the color bar. During the last quarter century they have also been strengthened by the effects of in and out migration: the exodus of Whites who reject the racial order, and the influx from Mozambique and Zimbabwe of large numbers of people of Portuguese and British origin, seething with animus against the new regimes in tropical Africa.

CONCLUSION

My case study has illuminated the role of political myth in the modern world. In the late nineteenth century Afrikaner politicians, clergy, and writers sought to create ethnic solidarity among an unsophisticated rural people who were scattered over a vast area from the Cape to the Zambezi and whose cultural and material interests were being threatened by British imperialism. To that end, they fashioned a political mythology out of the historical materials at hand. Their product was primarily a liberatory mythology that assisted in the survival and solidification of Afrikaner ethnicity despite Britain's conquest of their republics and subsequent attempt to reconstruct South African society in an imperial mold.

However, if anti-imperialism was the warp of early Afrikaner mythology, its woof was the racism that was then endemic in Western culture. By the middle of the twentieth century, however, the context had changed. British power was ebbing and the black inhabitants of South Africa, incorporated as a laboring class into a dynamic regional economy, constituted the major challenge to white hegemony. The mythology was then modified to place less stress on its anti-British element and more on its racist element.

By the last quarter of the twentieth century the context had changed still further. The European imperial era was over; mainstream Western scholars were rejecting scientific racism; the judiciary was outlawing segregation in the United

States; and it was ceasing to be expedient for politicians in any country outside South Africa to espouse racism. In the same period, Afrikaner nationalists, having gained control of the South African state, were making it the only state in the world where race was still the primary determinant of a person's social, economic, and political rights. In that context, Afrikaner nationalists needed the support of English-speaking white South Africans to cope with foreign pressures and increasingly formidable resistance from the black population. Further modifications were then made in the mythology. Myths that had originally inculcated anti-British emotions were abandoned, or reinterpreted to exemplify the errors of foreign critics of the structure of South African society; and myths that had formerly illustrated the superiority of white people were modified to legitimate the homelands policy by emphasizing the differences among Africans as well as the differences between the "races."

This book provides a striking demonstration of the human capacity to modify mythologies in response to changes in the local and global environments. But are there limits to the adaptability of a mythology? What happens if its component myths are contradicted by historical research? If it is at odds with contemporary science? And if it conflicts with values that have the respect of contemporary humanity? The Afrikaner nationalist mythology is in bad shape in all three respects. By the mid-1980s, Andries Treurnicht and his conservative colleagues could claim to be the authentic custodians of an uncorrupted mythology, but it was a mythology that had become patently obsolete, while P. W. Botha's ruling party was placing far less reliance on mythological legitimation. In the last resort, can a regime expect to endure without a credible political mythology? Or, when a regime is under extreme stress, can it transform its mythology into one that legitimates a policy of survival, regardless of intellectual and moral defects?

The Nazi precedent is instructive to a point. The racist element in the official mythology of the Third Reich was an extreme elaboration of ideas that were deeply rooted in the European mentality, notably the Aryan myth. However, although its intellectual and moral defects were transparent and its effects were diabolical, these shortcomings did not seriously affect the capacity of the Third Reich to fight for survival to the bitter end. Will that be the outcome in South Africa? Not necessarily, for there are fundamental differences in the racial structure of German and South African societies: in the former case, the vast majority of the population were Germans, for whom the war was a patriotic war rather than a racial war; in South Africa, the regime's patriotic symbols cannot conceal the fact that the reality is a racial hegemony.

This raises the controversial question of the role of ideas in history. Idealists have exaggerated the power of ideas, but, while attacking them, historical materialists have never managed to handle this problem very efficiently. Their concept of reciprocal interaction between material base and ideological superstructure, with the forces of the base prevailing "ultimately," "in the last resort," is vague: the last resort is not defined. Our study of political mythology helps us to add a historical dimension to the role of ideas. We have found that the Afrikaner nationalist case exemplifies the process whereby political mythologies are created, sustained, and modified by interest groups at particular times to further particular goals. Once a regime has entrenched its mythology in the symbols of the state, and in its educational and communications institutions, the mythology becomes an independent conservative force, which limits the capacity of the regime to make substantial changes that conflict with it. Thus, when the dominant faction in the National Party decided that it was expedient to modify the Verwoerdian program by creating a limited role in the central political institutions for the Coloured and Asian people, and also by giving limited rights of urban domicile to a small proportion of the African population, this was too much for many Afrikaners who were steeped in the racist mythology. In Marxist terms, the new official ideological "superstructure" was out of step with the material "base" of lower middle-class Afrikaners who had been the historical mainstay of the party, and the Afrikaner nationalist movement went into disarray.

I should point out that I have not discussed the political mythology of the English-speaking white South Africans. Although there is much common ground between them and Afrikaners on racial matters, English-speakers tend to make Afrikaners the historical scapegoats for anything that they consider to have gone wrong in the country. Sixty years ago, jingoism was still rampant in some circles: British rule had been wise and just; Afrikaners—Boers—were crude, uncouth people. In the 1920s, when South African postage stamps were printed in Afrikaans as well as English versions for the first time, children at an elementary school in Natal carefully put the Afrikaans version upside down on the envelope. Later, as racism became the dominant element in Afrikaner mythology, South Africans of British descent represented themselves as having always been more humane in their dealings with black people. In their mythology Afrikaners were the cruel ones; it was Afrikaners who invented segregation, as well as *apartheid*. More recently, Anglo–South African mythology has emphasized the achievements of the economic sector as contrasted with the Afrikaner-dominated political sector. There is a prophetic element in this mythology: given time, economic growth will create prosperity and justice for all—contrary to the experience of the last century and more.

Nor has this book described the radical mythology that has been developing among the black population in South Africa. Reacting against the racist order and ideology, the subject peoples have been creating a liberatory mythology which, ironically, has much in common with the anti-imperialist element that was formerly dominant in Afrikaner nationalism. There are several different tendencies within this mythology. One version gives precedence to the African tradition of *ubuntu* (humaneness) as well as the Christian tradition that was introduced by European missionaries and the Hindu tradition that was injected into the African nationalist movement by Mohandas Gandhi. Second, there is a version that stresses African cultural identity, harking back to the achievements of precolonial Africans and shaped by the Pan-Africanist Congress and the Black Consciousness movement, with borrowings from black America. The third version is Marxist—a European import that did not penetrate deeply into black South African society before the Second World War but that has been gaining ground in recent years, during which the South African regime has been claiming to be presiding over a free enterprise capitalist economy and has been receiving diplomatic and material support from conservative sources in the West. By the 1980s, after nearly forty years of *apartheid,* the emphasis on common humanity was losing ground; Black Consciousness had become a powerful force, and it in turn was being challenged by Marxism-Leninism. The longer the white minority regime persists in its racist policies, the greater the likelihood that black South African mythology will become overwhelmingly anti-capitalist and anti-Western.

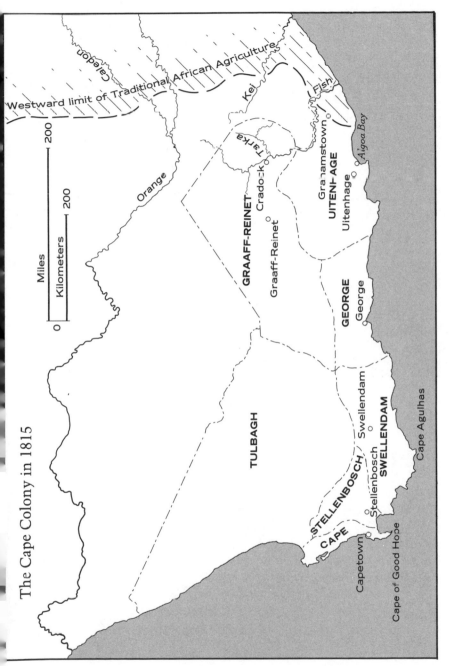

The Cape Colony in 1815

Westward limit of Traditional African Agriculture

Caledon

Orange

Tarka

Kel

Fish

Gra`amstown

Aigoa Bay

GRAAFF-REINET

Cradock

UITENHAGE

Graaff-Reinet

Uitenhage

Miles

Kilometers

200

200

0

GEORGE

George

TULBAGH

Swellendam

SWELLENDAM

STELLENBOSCH

Swellendam

Stellenbosch

CAPE

Stellenbosch

Capetown

Cape of Good Hope

Cape Agulhas

MAP 1

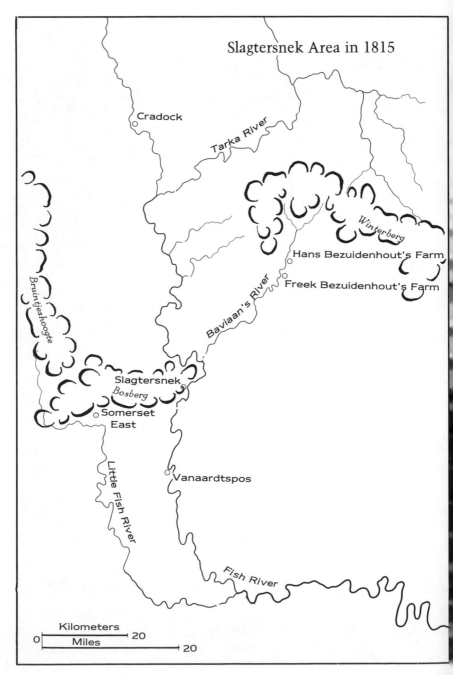

Slagtersnek Area in 1815

Cradock

Tarka River

Winterberg

Hans Bezuidenhout's Farm

Freek Bezuidenhout's Farm

Bruintjeshoogte

Baviaan's River

Slagtersnek

Bosberg

Somerset
East

Little Fish River

Vanaardtspos

Fish River

Kilometers
0   20
Miles
          20

MAP 2

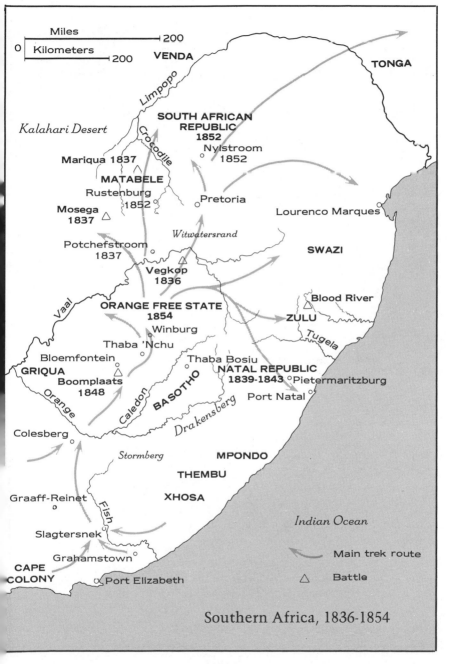

Southern Africa, 1836-1854

MAP 3

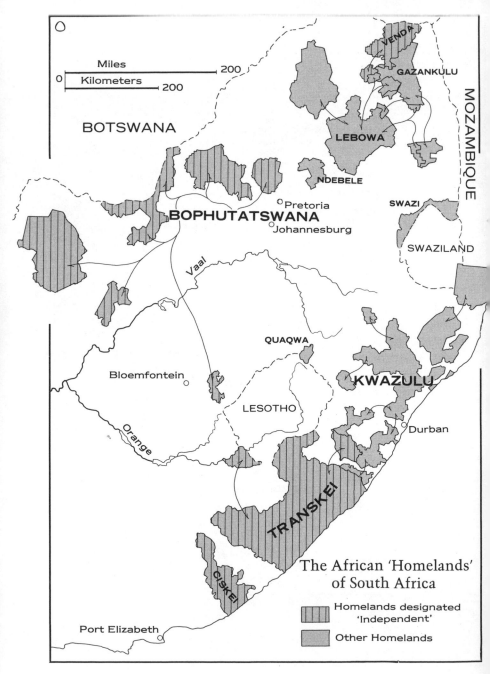

BOTSWANA

MOZAMBIQUE

VENDA

GAZANKULU

LEBOWA

NDEBELE

○Pretoria

BOPHUTATSWANA

○Johannesburg

SWAZI

SWAZILAND

Vaal

QUAQWA

Bloemfontein ○

KWAZULU

LESOTHO

○Durban

Orange

TRANSKEI

CISKEI

Port Elizabeth ○

Miles   200
0
Kilometers   200

The African 'Homelands'
of South Africa

Homelands designated
'Independent'

Other Homelands

MAP 4

Modern Southern Africa

Miles 500
0 Kilometers 500

MAP 5

CHRONOLOGY

Millennia B.C.	Ancestors of the Khoisan (San and Khoikhoi: "Bushmen" and "Hottentots") living in South Africa
Before A.D. 300	Ancestors of the Bantu-speaking African population begin to settle in South Africa
1652	The Dutch East India Company founds a refreshment station at the Cape of Good Hope
1652–1795	Genesis and expansion of the Afrikaners ("Boers"); conquest of the Khoisan; importation of slaves
1795	Britain takes the Cape Colony from the Dutch
1803	The Dutch (Batavian Republic) regain the Cape Colony by treaty
1806	Britain reconquers the Cape Colony
1809	Colonial proclamation re status of "Hottentots"
1811–12	British and colonial forces expel Africans from the territory west of the Fish River
1815	Rising of frontier Boers (later known as the Slagtersnek rebellion)
1816–28	Shaka creates the Zulu kingdom; warfare among Africans in southeastern Africa (the Mfecane)
1828	The Cape Colony liberates "Hottentots and other free persons of colour" from legal disabilities

1834–35	Frontier war between Xhosa and the Cape Colony
1834–38	The British parliament emancipates the slaves
1836–40	Five thousand Boers (later known as *voortrekkers*) leave the Cape Colony with their Coloured clients (a movement later known as the Great Trek)
December 1838	An Afrikaner commando defeats the Zulu: the Covenant and the Battle of Blood River
1843	Britain annexes Natal
1852–54	Britain recognizes the South African Republic (Transvaal) and Orange Free State as independent Afrikaner states
1856	Publication of Henry Cloete's *Five Lectures on the Emigration of the Dutch Farmers*
1867	Diamond mining begins in Griqualand West
1868	Britain annexes Basutoland (Lesotho)
1873–74	Publication of G. M. Theal's first substantial work: *Compendium of South African History and Geography*
1876	Publication of H. J. Hofstede's *Geschiedenis van den Oranje-Vrijstaat* (History of the Orange Free State)
1877	Britain annexes the Transvaal
	Publication of S. J. du Toit's *Geskiedenis van Ons Land in die Taal van ons Volk* (History of our land in the language of our people)
1880–81	Transvaal Afrikaners regain independence in the First Boer War, or the First War of Freedom
1882	Publication of F. Lion Cachet's *De Worstelstrijd der Transvalers* (The struggle of the Transvalers)
1883	Publication of C. P. Bezuidenhout's *De Geschiedenis van het Afrikaansch Geslacht* (The history of the Afrikaans race)
1886	Gold mining begins on the Witwatersrand

1895–96   Leander Starr Jameson's unsuccessful filibustering raid into the Transvaal

1897   Publication of James Bryce's *Impressions of South Africa* and of J. W. G. van Oordt's *Slagtersnek*

1898   Transvaal forces conquer the Venda, completing the white conquest of the African population of South Africa

           Publication of J. F. van Oordt's *Paul Kruger en de Opkomst der Zuid-Afrikaansche Republiek* (Paul Kruger and the rise of the South African Republic)

1899   Publication of J. C. Voigt's *Fifty Years of the Republic in South Africa* and of the fifth edition of G. M. Theal's *South Africa* in the Story of the Nations series

1899–1902 The (Second) Boer War or the Second War of Freedom: Britain conquers the Afrikaner republics

1900   Publication of F. W. Reitz's *A Century of Wrong*

1902   Publication of the official records of *The Rebellion of 1815, Generally Known as Slachters Nek*, ed. H. C. V. Leibbrandt

1910   The Cape Colony, Natal, the Transvaal, and the Orange Free State join to form the Union of South Africa, a white-controlled, self–governing British dominion

1912   Publication of G. M. Theal's *Ethnography and Condition of South Africa before* A.D. *1505*

           Foundation of the African National Congress (ANC)

1913   Natives Land Act limits African landownership to the reserves

1914   J. B. M. Hertzog forms the first Afrikaner National Party

1914–19   As a member of the British Empire, South Africa participates in the First World War

1918   Publication of second edition of J. H. Malan's *Boer en Barbaar* (Boer and barbarian)

1918–38   Publication of *Voortrekkermense* (Voortrekker people), 6 vols., ed. G. S. Preller

1919   Publication of G. B. A. Gerdener's *Sarel Cilliers*

1924–33   J. B. M. Hertzog heads a National Party government

1929   Publication of A. T. Bryant's *Olden Times in Zululand and Natal* and W. M. Macmillan's *Bantu, Boer and Briton*

1933   Publication of C. J. Langenhoven's *Die Pad van Suid-Afrika* (The path of South Africa)

1933–38   J. B. M. Hertzog heads a fusion government, then a United Party government; D. F. Malan forms the new Afrikaner National Party

1937   Publication of I. D. MacCrone's *Race Attitudes in South Africa*, and *The Bantu-speaking Tribes of South Africa*, ed. Isaac Schapera

1938   Publication of E. G. Jansen's *Die Voortrekkers in Natal*
1939   Publication of *Bloedrivierse Eeufees-Gedenkboek* (Blood River centenary memorial book), ed. A. G. du Toit and Louis Steenkamp

1939–45   South Africa participates in the Second World War on the Allied side, with J. C. Smuts heading a United Party government

1941   Publication of C. W. de Kiewiet's *History of South Africa: Social and Economic*, and *Ons Republiek* (Our republic), ed. J. Albert Coetzee et al.

1945   Publication of G. Cronje's *'n Tuiste vir die Nageslag* (A home for posterity)

1948   D. F. Malan's National Party wins general election and begins to apply its policy of *apartheid*

1952   The ANC and allies launch a passive resistance campaign against unjust laws

1955   Publication of the *Summary of the Report of the [Tom-linson] Commission*

1960   Police kill 67 African anti-pass law demonstrators at Sharpeville

            The government bans African political organizations

1961   South Africa becomes a republic and leaves the Commonwealth

1964   Publication of F. A. van Jaarsveld's *The Afrikaner's Interpretation of South African History*

1966–68   Lesotho, Botswana, and Swaziland become independent states and members of the United Nations

1969   Publication of *Five Hundred Years: A History of South Africa,* ed. C. F. J. Muller.

1969–71   Publication of *The Oxford History of South Africa,* 2 vols., ed. Monica Wilson and Leonard Thompson

1973   Publication of J. A. Heese's *Slagtersnek en sy Mense* (Slagtersnek and its people)

1975   Publication of Leonard Thompson's *Survival in Two Worlds: Moshoeshoe of Lesotho, 1786–1870*

1975–76   Mozambique and Angola become independent states and members of the United Nations

1976–77   At least 575 people die in disturbances in Soweto and other African townships

1976–81   South Africa grants "independence" to the Transkei, Bophuthatswana, Venda, and Ciskei "Homelands," but they are not recognized abroad

1977   The UN Security Council imposes a mandatory embargo on the supply of arms to South Africa

            Publication of Richard Elphick's *Kraal and Castle: Khoikhoi and the Founding of White South Africa,* and B. J. Liebenberg's *Andries Pretorius in Natal*

1979   Publication of *The Shaping of South African Society,* ed. Richard Elphick and Hermann Giliomee

1980   Zimbabwe (previously Rhodesia) becomes indepen-
            dent and a UN member

            Publication of *Economy and Society in Pre-Industrial
            South Africa,* ed. Shula Marks and Anthony Atmore;
            F. A. van Jaarsveld's "A Historical Mirror of Blood
            River," in *The Meaning of History,* ed. A. Konig and
            H. Keane; and Marianne Cornevin's *Apartheid: Power
            and Historical Falsification*

1981   The National Party wins its ninth successive general
            election

1981–82   South African raids on Maputo (Mozambique) and
            Maseru (Lesotho)

1982–   ANC guerrilla bombings in Pretoria, Johannesburg,
            Pietermaritzburg, and Durban

1982   Publication of Charles van Onselen's *Studies in the
            Social and Economic History of the Witwatersrand*

1983   Publication of J. M. du Preez's *Africa Afrikaner: Master
            Symbols in South African School Textbooks*

1984   South Africa and Mozambique sign a peace pact

            A new constitution gives Asians and Coloured people
            but not Africans limited participation in the South
            African political system

            Start of prolonged and widespread resistance in black
            South African townships and violent government
            reactions

            Bishop Desmond Tutu awarded the Nobel Prize for
            Peace and elected Anglican bishop of Johannesburg

NOTES

Chapter 1

1. James Oliver Robertson, *American Myth, American Reality* (New York, 1980), p. 11, summarizes the myth as propounded by Mason Weems in his pamphlet biography, which was published in 1800, the year after Washington's death.

2. Geoffrey Moorhouse, *India Britannica* (New York, 1983), pp. 45–46.

3. Leszek Kolakowski, *Main Currents of Marxism*, 3 vols., trans. P. S. Falla (Oxford and New York, 1981), 3:94.

4. Henry Tudor, *Political Myth* (London, 1972), chap. 3.

5. Robertson, *American Myth, American Reality*, p. 26. See also Frances FitzGerald, *America Revised: History Schoolbooks in the Twentieth Century* (Boston, 1979).

6. Monica Wilson, "The Pagan Reaction," in *The Oxford History of South Africa*, 2 vols. (Oxford, 1969, 1971), ed. Monica Wilson and Leonard Thompson, 1:256–60.

7. As in Immanuel Wallerstein, *The Capitalist World-Economy* (Cambridge, England, 1979), pp. 35–36, 65, 117–18, 129–30, 136–37.

8. Tzvetan Todorov, *The Conquest of America*, trans. Richard Howard (New York, 1984), p. 147.

9. Ibid., p. 148. See also Lewis Hanke, *The Spanish Struggle for Justice in the Conquest of America* (Philadelphia, 1949), pp. 31–35, and *Aristotle and the American Indians* (London, 1959), pp. 15–16.

10. Ernst Cassirer, *The Myth of the State* (New Haven and London, 1946), p. 3.

11. Ibid., p. 280.

12. Geoffrey Barraclough, *Main Trends in History* (New York, 1979), p. 211.

13. Bronislaw Malinowski, *Myth in Primitive Psychology* (New York, 1926), p. 19.

14. Tudor, *Political Myth*, p. 35.

15. George Barany has drawn attention to this: "On Truth in Myths," *East European Quarterly* 15, no. 3 (1981), 348.

16. For example, Marianne Cornevin, *Apartheid: Power and Historical Falsification* (Paris, 1980).

17. Tudor, *Political Myth*, pp. 65–90.

18. Marina Warner, *Joan of Arc: The Image of Female Heroism* (New York, 1981), p. 255.

19. Ibid., pp. 255–56.

20. Ibid., p. 265.

21. *Main Currents of Marxism*, 3:95.

22. Ibid.

23. Stephen Fischer-Galati, "Myths in Romanian History," *East European Quarterly*, 15, no. 3 (1981), p. 333. Piotr Wandycz drew my attention to this article.

24. Ibid., p. 327.

25. Leon Poliakov, *The Aryan Myth: A History of Racist and Nationalist Ideas in Europe*, trans. Edmund Howard (New York, 1977).

26. Henry Hatfield, "The Myth of Nazism," in *Myth and Mythmaking*, ed. Henry Murray (Boston, 1968); Raphael Patai, *Myth and Modern Man* (Englewood Cliffs, 1972), chap. 6.

27. Richard Elphick, "Methodology in South African Historiography: A Defence of Idealism and Empiricism," *Social Dynamics* (Cape Town), 9, no. 1: 1–17.

28. Among the vast literature on scientific racism, for American racism see especially the works of Stephen Jay Gould, notably *The Mismeasure of Man* (New York and London, 1981), and for British racism, Nancy Stepan, *The Idea of Race in Science: Great Britain, 1800–1960* (London, 1982). See also Thomas S. Kuhn, *The Structure of Scientific Revolutions*, 2d ed. (Chicago, 1970), and R. C. Lewontin, Steven Rose, and Leon J. Kamin, eds., *Not in Our Genes* (New York, 1984).

29. Gould, *Mismeasure*, p. 232.

30. *We Europeans* (London), 1935.

31. Francis Jennings, *The Invasion of North America: Indians, Colonialism, and the Cant of Conquest* (Chapel Hill, N.C., 1975).

32. *Idea of Race*, p. 176.

33. Ibid., p. 189.

34. Arthur Jensen, "Race and Mental Ability," in *Racial Variation in Man*, ed. F. J. Ebling (London, 1975), pp. 71–108, and *Bias in Mental Testing* (New York, 1980); H. J. Eysenck, *The I.Q. Argument: Race, Intelligence, and Education* (New York, 1971); John E. Baker, *Race* (London, 1974).

35. *Idea of Race*, p. 182.

36. *Main Currents of Marxism*, 3: 102–03, 137–38.

37. *The Republic*, trans. Benjamin Jowett (Oxford, 1908), 3. 414–15.

38. *Aristotle's Politics*, trans. Benjamin Jowett (Oxford, 1908), 1. 5.

39. Tudor, *Political Myth*, pp. 124–25.

40. William H. McNeill, "Make Mine Myth," *New York Times*, 28 December 1981.

Chapter 2

1. See the chronology on pp. 245–50. Surveys of South African history include C. W. de Kiewiet, *A History of South Africa: Social and Economic* (Oxford, 1941, and many reprints), T. R. H. Davenport, *South Africa: A Modern History*, 2d ed. (London and Toronto, 1979), and Monica Wilson and Leonard Thompson, eds., *The Oxford History of South Africa*, 2 vols. (Oxford, 1969, 1971). Most of the first volume of the *Oxford History* has been reprinted, with a new preface, as *A History of South Africa to 1870* (Cape Town, 1982). There is a useful historical bibliography, C. F. J. Muller et al., *South African History and Historians: A Bibliography* (Pretoria, 1979). For comparisons with the American experience, see John W. Cell, *The Highest Stage of White Supremacy: The Origins of Segregation in South Africa and the American South* (Cambridge, England, 1982), George M. Fredrickson, *White Supremacy: A Comparative Study in American and South African History* (Oxford, 1981), and Howard Lamar and Leonard Thompson, eds., *The Frontier in History: North America and Southern Africa Compared* (New Haven, 1981). Surveys of South African politics include Leonard Thompson and Andrew Prior, *South African Politics* (New Haven, 1982).

2. By 1961, when the Union of South Africa became the Republic of South Africa, the government had proclaimed a large number of scattered lands, totaling less than 13 percent of the area of the country, to be "Native Reserves," and made it unlawful for Africans to own land elsewhere in South Africa. Since then, the government has amended the boundaries of these reserves—a process involving forced removals of hundreds of thousands of people, mainly Africans, from their homes— and grouped the reserves into ten clusters of land. It treats each such cluster as the "Homeland" of a specific African "nation" and has encouraged the Homeland governments, which are economically dependent on South Africa, to seek "independence," on condition that their people lose their claim to citizenship of South Africa. By 1980, three Homelands had accepted such independence: Transkei, Bophuthatswana, and Venda; but they were not recognized by any other members of the international community. According to the 1980 census, the population of the Republic

of South Africa, excluding the three "independent" Homelands, was (in thousands):

	Total	White	Coloured	Asian	Black
White areas	18,050	4,514	2,601	799	10,122
National states [i.e., 7 homelands]	6,836	14	11	7	6,802
Total R.S.A.	24,886	4,528	2,613	806	16,924

At that time, the populations of the three "independent Homelands" were estimated to total 3,963,000, nearly all of whom were African. *South Africa 1983: Official Yearbook of the Republic of South Africa* (Johannesburg, 1983), prints the above table on page 33, and tabulates the home languages of Asians, Coloureds, and Whites in 1970 on page 31. The estimates of the populations of the three independent Homelands are from South African Institute of Race Relations, *Survey of Race Relations in South Africa 1982*, ed. Peter Randall (Johannesburg, 1983), p. 45.

3. T. Dunbar Moodie, *The Rise of Afrikanerdom: Power, Apartheid, and the Afrikaner Civil Religion* (Berkeley and Los Angeles, 1975), pp. 110–11.

4. J. C. Kannemeyer, *Geskiedenis van die Afrikaanse Literatuur*, vol. 1 (Cape Town and Pretoria, 1978), pp. 48–57, 63–65; F. A. van Jaarsveld, *The Awakening of Afrikaner Nationalism 1868–1881* (New York, 1961), pp. 106–21.

5. D. W. Kruger, *Paul Kruger*, 2 vols. (Johannesburg, 1963).

6. Irving Hexham, *The Irony of Apartheid* (Toronto, 1981), pp. 56–69.

7. Joshua Slocum, *Sailing Alone Around the World* (London, 1950), pp. 222–23.

8. Moodie, *Afrikanerdom*, pp. 26–28.

9. C. P. Bezuidenhout, *De Geschiedenis van het Afrikaansch Geslacht van 1688 tot 1882* (Bloemfontein, 1883), p. 1.

10. F. Lion Cachet, *De Worstelstrijd der Afrikaners* (Amsterdam, 1882), p. 5.

11. J. F. van Oordt, *Paul Kruger en de Opkomst der Zuid–Afrikaansche Republiek* (Amsterdam and Cape Town, 1898); C. N. J. du Plessis, *Uit de Geschiedenis van de Zuid-Afrikaansche Republiek en van de Afrikaanders* (Pretoria and Amsterdam, 1898); J. C. Voigt, *Fifty Years of the Republic in South Africa (1795–1845)* (London, 1899).

12. Also published as "A Century of Injustice," in *The Story of the Boers*, ed. C. W. van der Hoogt (New York and London, 1900). The quotations are from pages 75 and 164 of this edition.

13. *De Vriend des Volkes*, 23 March 1906, cited in Hexham, *Irony*, p. 179.

14. The Reverend H. S. Bosman, cited in Leonard M. Thompson, *The Unification of South Africa, 1902–1910* (Oxford, 1960), p. 19.

15. Hexham, *Irony*, pp. 100–16; Moodie, *Afrikanerdom*, pp. 52–57.

16. Cited in Thompson, *Unification*, p. 20.

17. Kannemeyer, *Literatuur*, 1:113–17; Hexham, *Irony*, pp. 36–46.

18. Hexham, *Irony*, p. 37.

19. Cited in Ibid., p. 40.

20. Ibid., pp. 46–53, 137–41; Kannemeyer, *Literatuur*, 1:168–69.

21. Cited in Moodie, *Afrikanerdom*, p. 47.

22. Kannemeyer, *Literatuur*, pp. 146–49.

23. Ibid., pp. 170–80.

24. Since the Union of South Africa was founded in 1910, its ruling parties and prime ministers were as follows: 1910–24, South African Party, Prime Ministers Louis Botha and Jan Smuts; 1924–33, Coalition of the first National Party (founded 1914) and the Labour Party, Prime Minister J. B. M. Hertzog; 1933–34, Coalition of the National Party and the South African Party, Prime Minister Hertzog; 1934–39, United Party (product of fusion of the National Party and the South African Party), Prime Minister Hertzog; 1939–48, United Party, Prime Minister J. C. Smuts; 1948–84, second National Party (founded 1934), Prime Ministers D. F. Malan, J. G. Strijdom, H. F. Verwoerd, B. J. Vorster, and P. W. Botha. In 1984, P. W. Botha became president under a new constitution.

25. *South Africa 1983*, p. 112.

26. In his autobiography, D. F. Malan regarded the outcome of the flag controversy as one of his greatest achievements: *Afrikaner-volkseenheid en my ervarings op die pad daarheen* (Cape Town, 1959).

27. Moodie, "The Centenary of Geloftedag: Highpoint of the Civil Faith," in *Afrikanerdom*, pp. 175–96.

28. Ivor Wilkins and Hans Strydom, *The Super-Afrikaners* (Johannesburg, 1978), pp. 104–05.

29. *Die Groot Trek: Gedenkuitgawe van die Huisgenoot*, December 1938, p. 9.

30. In a referendum, the white electorate had endorsed the proposal that South Africa should become a republic in the expectation that, following the Indian precedent of 1947, the country would continue to be a member of the Commonwealth. However, at the subsequent Commonwealth Conference in London Prime Minister H. F. Verwoerd withdrew South Africa's application when he encountered severe criticisms of South Africa's racial policies.

31. When the National Party came into power in 1948, it received distinctly fewer votes than the United Party, primarily because the constitution ensured that rural electoral districts should contain fewer voters

than urban electoral districts. In subsequent elections it fared progressively better, partly by eliminating all African and Coloured voters, but also by gaining the support of an increasing majority of the Afrikaner voters and, by 1981, of a substantial minority of the English-speaking white voters. In a general election in 1981, the National Party won 131 of the 165 seats in the House of Assembly.

32. Brian Willan, *Sol Plaatje: South African Nationalist 1876–1932* (Berkeley and Los Angeles, 1984); André Odendaal, *Vukani Bantu! The Beginnings of Black Protest Politics in South Africa to 1912* (Cape Town, South Africa, and Totowa, N.J., 1984); Peter Walshe, *The Rise of African Nationalism in South Africa: The African National Congress 1912–1952* (Berkeley and Los Angeles, 1971); Thomas Karis and Gwendolen Carter, eds., *From Protest to Challenge: A Documentary History of African Politics in South Africa*, 4 vols. (Stanford, 1972–77).

33. W. M. Macmillan, *The Cape Colour Question: A Historical Survey* (London, 1927).

34. Malan, *Afrikaner-volkseenheid*; C. M. van den Heever, *Generaal J. B. M. Hertzog* (Johannesburg, 1946); W. K. Hancock, *Smuts*, 2 vols. (Cambridge, England, 1962, 1968).

35. Cited in W. A. de Klerk, *The Puritans in Africa* (Harmondsworth, 1976), p. 204.

36. Ibid., p. 214.

37. J. Albert Coetzee, "Republikanisme in die Kaapkolonie," in *Ons Republiek*, ed. J. Albert Coetzee, P. Meyer, and N. Diederichs (Bloemfontein, 1941), p. 7.

38. G. Eloff, *Rasse en Rasvermenging* (Bloemfontein, 1942), p. 104.

39. G. Cronjé, *'n Tuiste vir die Nageslag* (Cape Town, 1945), p. 79.

40. H. F. Verwoerd, election day statement, 18 October 1961, cited by Verwoerd in Parliament, 25 January 1963: *House of Assembly Debates*, 1963, col. 231.

41. H. F. Verwoerd, speech in London in May 1961, cited by Eric H. Louw in his speech to the UN General Assembly on 6 November 1962: *The Case for South Africa*, ed. H. H. H. Biermann (New York, 1963), p. 147.

42. Wilkins and Strydom, *Super-Afrikaners*; J. H. P. Serfontein, *Brotherhood of Power* (London, 1979); Ernst G. Malherbe, *Education in South Africa*, 2 vols. (Cape Town, 1925, 1977), 2:663–90.

43. Wilkins and Strydom, *Super-Afrikaners*, p. 379.

44. Malherbe, *Education*, 2:674.

45. Richard Pollak, *Up Against Apartheid* (Carbondale and Edwardsville, Ill., 1981); *South Africa, 1983*, pp. 819–22.

46. Pollak, *Up Against Apartheid*.

47. Ibid.; John C. Laurence, *Race Propaganda and South Africa* (London, 1979); Leonard Thompson and Andrew Prior, *South African Politics* (New Haven, 1982), pp. 137–48. *Die Transvaler* ceased publication in 1984.

48. Laurence, *Race Propaganda;* Thompson and Prior, *South African Politics*, pp. 137–48. The *Rand Daily Mail* ceased publication in 1985.

49. Cited in Malherbe, *Education*, 2:101.

50. Cited in Wilkins and Strydom, *Super-Afrikaners*, pp. 258–59.

51. Leo Marquard, *The Peoples and Policies of South Africa*, rev. ed. (London, 1969), pp. 190–219; Malherbe, *Education*, 2:1–151.

52. Federasie van Afrikaanse Kultuur-Verenigings, *Christelike Nasionale Onderwys Beleid* (Johannesburg, 1948).

53. National Education Advisory Council Act, No. 86 of 1962; National Education Policy Act, No. 39 of 1967; Minister of National Education proclamation, 16 May 1969. Malherbe, *Education*, 2:696–98; Brian Rose and Raymond Tumner, eds., *Documents in South African Education* (Johannesburg, 1975), pp. 60–81.

54. Nevertheless, this law was never strictly applied in the Transvaal. Virtually all the private schools in South Africa are church-related English-medium schools.

55. Malherbe, *Education*, 2:538–76; Rose and Tumner, *Documents*, pp. 201–80.

56. Union of South Africa, *The Economic and Social Conditions of the Racial Groups in South Africa*, U.G. 53/1948, pp. 54–74.

57. Union of South Africa, *House of Assembly Debates*, 1953, col. 3576.

58. Loraine Gordon, ed., *Survey of Race Relations in South Africa, 1980* (Johannesburg, 1981), p. 460. After some of the African "homelands" became "independent," starting with the Transkei in 1976, they became responsible for their educational systems. However, being poor and economically dependent territories, they were not able significantly to raise the quality of their education.

59. Malherbe, *Education*.

60. Cited in F. E. Auerbach, *The Power of Prejudice in South African Education* (Cape Town and Amsterdam, 1965), p. 109.

61. R. F. M. Immelman, "George McCall Theal: A Biographical Sketch," in Theal, ed., *Basutoland Records*, vol. 1, *1833–1852*, new ed. (Cape Town, 1964), pp. 1–19, which includes a bibliography of Theal's publications. See also Christopher Saunders, "The Making of an Historian: The Early Years of George McCall Theal," *South African Historical Journal*, 13 (November 1981), 1–19.

62. Theal, *History of South Africa*, vol. 5, p. v. References to Theal's multivolume history of South Africa are complicated by the fact that the

volumes originally appeared in three separate series and were frequently reprinted, with or without amendment. My references are to the consecutively numbered 11-volume Star edition published in London from 1919 to 1926 and subsequently reprinted in Cape Town. This quotation is from the preface to the fourth edition of volume 5, dated 1915.

63. Theal, *History*, 3:464–65.

64. J. S. Marais, *Maynier and the First Boer Republic* (Cape Town, 1944), p. vi.

65. Andrew Prior and Clive Keegan obtained for me some data from Maskew Miller, the publishers of the Fowler and Smit series. It seems that fifteen thousand copies were printed in 1953, half in each official language. The data are somewhat confusing, but the 1953 figures seem to have been about average. In the 1960s Maskew Miller was also publishing a separate edition for Natal schools.

66. C. de K. Fowler and G. J. J. Smit, *Maskew Miller's New Senior History Course* (Cape Town, n.d. [1932]), p. 74.

67. C. de K. Fowler and G. J. J. Smit, *Senior History: Written for the 1969 Syllabus* (Cape Town, n.d.), pp. 242–52.

68. Auerbach, *Power of Prejudice*, p. 57.

69. Ibid., p. 99.

70. Ibid., p. 96.

71. Ibid., p. 117, citing J. F. E. Havinga, C. F. Robbertse, and A. G. Roodt, *Geskiedenis Vir Std. 6* (1958), p. 65.

72. Ibid., p. 121, citing Christian Education, *Race Studies in Transvaal Secondary Schools* (Johannesburg, May 1960).

73. Ibid., p. 122.

74. Ibid., p. 129.

75. F. A. van Jaarsveld, *New Illustrated History, Standard 8* (Johannesburg, 1974), p. 90.

76. C. J. Joubert, *History for Standard 10* (Johannesburg, 1979).

77. E. H. W. Lategan and A. J. de Kock, *History in Perspective, Std. 7* (Parow, 1978), p. 47.

78. Elizabeth Dean, Paul Hartmann, and May Katzen, *History in Black and White: An Analysis of South African School History Textbooks: A Report to UNESCO* (Centre for Mass Communication Research, Leicester University, December 1981), pp. 153–58.

79. J. A. Heese, *Slagtersnek en sy Mense* (Cape Town, 1973), unnumbered page in the introduction.

80. A. N. Boyce, *Europe and South Africa, Part 2: A History for Standard 10* (Cape Town, 1974); M. S. Geen, *The Making of South Africa, 7th ed.* (Cape Town, 1982).

81. P. A. W. Cook, *South African History for Natives* (London, 1932), p. vii.

82. Ibid., p. 7.

83. Ibid., p. 135.

84. L. B. Hurry, H. A. Mocke, H. C. Wallis, and G. Englebrecht, *Social Studies Standard 6, Social Studies Standard 7,* and *Social Studies Standard 8* (Goodwood, Cape, 1980).

85. On African school education, see the *Survey of Race Relations in South Africa,* published annually by the South African Institute of Race Relations, Johannesburg; e.g., the volume for 1982, ed. Peter Randall, pp. 469–81.

86. S. M. Molema, *The Bantu Past and Present: An Ethnographical and Historical Study of the Native Races of South Africa* (Edinburgh, 1920), p. 194.

87. Karis and Carter, eds., *Protest to Challenge,* 4:94–95.

88. Monica Wilson, ed., *Freedom for My People: The Autobiography of Z. K. Matthews: Southern Africa, 1901 to 1968* (London and Cape Town, 1981), pp. 58–59. The passage cited was dictated by Matthews during 1952 or 1953.

89. Willan, *Plaatje,* pp. 259–93.

90. Private communication.

91. Nosipho Majeke, *The Role of the Missionaries in Conquest* (Johannesburg, 1952); "Mnguni," *Three Hundred Years,* 3 vols. in 2 (Lansdowne, Cape, 1952).

92. Gail M. Gerhart, *Black Power in South Africa: The Evolution of an Ideology* (Berkeley and Los Angeles, 1978), and John A. Marcum, *Education, Race, and Social Change in South Africa* (Berkeley and Los Angeles, 1982).

Chapter 3

1. Cited in W. A. de Klerk, *The Puritans in Africa: A Story of Afrikanerdom* (Harmondsworth, 1976), p. 246.

2. Ibid., p. 247.

3. Ibid.

4. *South African Digest,* 22 January 1982, citing an article in the *Boca Raton News,* n.d.

5. Foreign Policy Study Foundation, *South Africa: Time Running Out* (Berkeley and Los Angeles, 1981), pp. 274–75.

6. P. J. Marshall and Glyndwr Williams, *The Great Map of Mankind: Perceptions of New Worlds in the Age of Enlightenment* (Cambridge, Mass., 1982).

7. R. Raven-Hart, ed., *Before van Riebeeck: Callers at South Africa from 1488 to 1652* (Cape Town, 1967).

8. Facsimile reprint of the original, which was published in Amsterdam in 1652 (Cape Town, 1952), ed. P. Serton, with English translation by L. C. van Oordt.

9. Ibid., English translation, pp. 25–29.

10. Raven-Hart, ed., *Before van Riebeeck,* pp. 19, 46.

11. Ibid., p. 46.

12. *Great Map of Mankind.* Winthrop D. Jordan, *White over Black: American Attitudes toward the Negro, 1550–1812* (Chapel Hill, 1967), starts with a chapter that stresses the disposition of Europeans, especially the English, to racist attitudes, even before they had begun to meet Africans.

13. Raven-Hart, ed., *Before van Riebeeck,* pp. 177–78.

14. R. Raven-Hart, ed., *Cape of Good Hope, 1652–1702: The First 50 Years of Dutch Colonization as Seen by Callers,* 2 vols. (Cape Town, 1971), 1:118.

15. Richard Elphick, *Kraal and Castle: Khoikhoi and the Founding of White South Africa* (New Haven, 1977), p. xv.

16. Elphick (*Kraal and Castle,* p. xv) draws attention to this definition.

17. I. D. MacCrone, *Race Attitudes in South Africa: Historical, Experimental and Psychological Studies* (London, 1937).

18. Elphick, *Kraal and Castle;* C. R. Boxer, *The Dutch Seaborne Empire, 1600–1800* (London, 1965); Richard Elphick and Hermann Giliomee, eds., *The Shaping of South African Society, 1652–1820* (Cape Town and London, 1979); Lamar and Thompson, eds., *Frontier in History.*

19. This was the origin of the word *commando,* which was subsequently incorporated into the English language.

20. Peter Kolben, *The Present State of the Cape of Good Hope,* trans. Guido Medley (London, 1731), p. 46.

21. *Shaping of South African Society,* pp. 133, 327; Robert Ross, *Adam Kok's Griquas* (Cambridge, 1976).

22. *Present State,* p. 31.

23. H. B. Thom, ed., *Journal of Jan van Riebeeck 1651–1662,* 3 vols. (Cape Town and Amsterdam, 1952–58), 1:380–81, 3:8, 12, 73, 281–83, 285–86.

24. C. R. Boxer, ed., *The Tragic History of the Sea, 1589–1622,* Hakluyt Society, 2d series, no. cxii (Cambridge, 1959).

25. John Bird, *The Annals of Natal, 1495–1845,* 2 vols. (Pietermaritzburg, 1888), 1:27–32, 35–53; also in Donald Moodie, *The Record,* 3 vols. (Cape Town, 1838–41) 1:415–22, 424–28, 430–33.

26. Bird, *Annals of Natal,* 1:41–42.

27. Ibid., 1:46–47.

28. Ibid., 1:45–46.

29. Lamar and Thompson, eds., *Frontier in History;* Wilson and Thompson, eds., *Oxford History of South Africa,* 1: chaps. 6, 8, 9; 2: chap. 5. Studies of African resistance to conquest include Shula Marks, *Reluctant Rebellion: The 1906–1908 Disturbances in Natal* (Oxford, 1970); Terence Ranger, *Revolt in Southern Rhodesia, 1896–97: A Study in African Resistance* (London, 1967); Leonard Thompson, *Survival in Two Worlds: Moshoeshoe of Lesotho, 1786–1870* (Oxford, 1975); and J. J. Guy, *The Destruction of the Zulu Kingdom: The Civil War in Zululand, 1879–1884* (London, 1979).

30. J. D. Omer-Cooper, *The Zulu Aftermath: A Nineteenth Century Revolution in Bantu Africa* (Madison, 1966); D. R. Morris, *The Washing of the Spears: A History of the Rise of the Zulu Nation under Shaka and Its Fall in the Zulu War of 1879* (New York, 1965).

31. Stanley B. Greenberg, *Race and State in Capitalist Development* (New Haven, 1980); Leonard Thompson, *The Unification of South Africa* (Oxford, 1960).

32. Retief's "Manifesto," *Grahamstown Journal*, 2 February 1837, reprinted in G. W. Eybers, *Select Constitutional Documents Illustrating South African History, 1795–1910* (London, 1918), pp. 143–45, is summarized in numerous other South African history textbooks.

33. Natal Government, *Proceedings of the Commission Appointed to Inquire into the Past and Present State of the Kafirs in the District of Natal and to Report upon Their Future Government*, 6 parts (Natal, 1852–53).

34. Ibid., 6:30–31.

35. Ibid., 1:53.

36. Ibid., 6:32.

37. Ibid., 1:55–56.

38. Ibid., 3:42.

39. Ibid., 1:57.

40. Ibid., 6:49.

41. [S. J. du Toit], *Die Geskiedenis van Ons Land in die Taal van Ons Volk* (Cape Town, 1877), pp. 9–14.

42. F. Lion Cachet, *De Worstelstrijd der Transvalers*, 2d ed. (Amsterdam, 1883), pp. 80–82.

43. J. F. van Oordt, *Paul Kruger en de Opkomst van de Zuid-Afrikaansche Republiek* (Amsterdam and Cape Town, 1898), p. 13.

44. Cited in Sidney Mendelssohn, *South African Bibliography*, 2 vols., 3d ed. (London, 1968), 2:556.

45. J. C. Voigt, *Fifty Years of the History of the Republic in South Africa, 1795–1845*, 2 vols. (London, 1899), 1:14.

46. Ibid., 1:15.

47. Ibid., 2:298.

48. John Barrow, *An Account of Travels into the Interior of Southern Africa*, 2 vols. (London, 1801, 1804), 2:117.

49. Nancy Stepan, *The Idea of Race in Science: Great Britain, 1800–1960* (London, 1982), pp. 1–20.

50. Barrow, 1:205–06.

51. Thomas Pringle, *Narrative of a Residence in South Africa* (London, 1835), p. 266.

52. William F. Lye, ed., *Andrew Smith's Journal of His Expedition into the Interior of South Africa, 1834–36* (Cape Town, 1975), p. 77.

53. Richard Godlonton, *Introductory Remarks to a Narrative of the Irruption of the Kafir Hordes into the Eastern Province of the Cape of Good Hope, A.D. 1834–35* (Graham's Town, 1835), pp. 212–15.

54. Captain William Cornwallis Harris, *The Wild Sports of Southern Africa*, 5th ed. (London, 1852), p. 288.

55. *Proceedings of the Commission*, 3:36.

56. Ibid., 6:85. On Shepstone, see David Welsh, *The Roots of Segregation: Native Policy in Colonial Natal, 1845–1910* (Cape Town, 1971).

57. This was a reference to a proclamation issued by the Cape colonial governor, Sir Benjamin D'Urban, on 29 May 1835, which described Xhosa chiefs as "treacherous and irreclaimable savages." See W. M. Macmillan, *Bantu, Boer and Briton: The Making of the South African Native Problem*, rev. ed. (Oxford, 1963), p. 135.

58. *Proceedings of the Commission*, 3:63, 4:7,12.

59. Ibid., 6:96.

60. Ibid., 5:45, 55.

61. W. H. I. Bleek, "Researches into the Relations between the Hottentots and the Kaffirs," *Cape Monthly Magazine*, 1 (1857) :199–212, 289–96; *A Comparative Grammar of South African Languages*, 2 parts (Cape Town and London, 1862, 1869).

62. George W. Stow, *The Native Races of South Africa*, ed. George McCall Theal (London, 1905). Stow completed his manuscript in 1880 and died soon afterward; Theal used it in his own work but did not see it into print before 1905.

63. Theal's ideas on this subject matured during the 1890s, as demonstrated in his volume *South Africa* in *The Story of the Nations Series*, 5th ed. (London, 1899). He amplified them at great length in the first volume of his 11-volume *History of South Africa*, entitled *Ethnography and Condition of South Africa before A.D. 1505* (London, 1st ed., 1912; 2d ed., 1922).

64. Ethnography, 2d ed., p. 28.

65. Ibid., pp. 83ff.

66. Ibid., pp. 395ff.

67. Ibid., p. 310.

68. Ibid.

69. Ibid., p. 418.

70. A. Wilmot, *The Story of the Expansion of South Africa*, 2d ed. (London, 1895), pp. 2–3.

71. James Bryce, *Impressions of South Africa* (New York, 1897), pp. 56, 95–96.

72. Ibid., pp. 80–81.

73. Ibid., pp. 401, 420–21.

74. C. P. Lucas, *South and East Africa, Part 1, Historical: Being Vol. IV of A Historical Geography of the British Colonies* (Oxford, 1897), pp. 38, 39, 152, 188.

75. S. M. Molema, *The Bantu Past and Present: An Ethnographical and Historical Study of the Native Races of South Africa* (Edinburgh, 1920).

76. J. H. Malan, *Boer en Barbaar of Die Geskiedenis van die Voortrekkers tussen die jare 1835–1840 en verder van die Kaffernasies met wie hulle in aanraking gekom het*, 2d ed. (Bloemfontein, 1918), p. 50.

77. D. J. J. de Villiers, G. H. P. de Bruin, and J. J. Muller, *Geskiedenis vir Senior-Sertifikaat* (Cape Town, n.d. [ca. 1920]), 8th imp., p. 17.

78. W. Fouché, *Darter se Geskiedenis van die Unie van Suid-Afrika* (Cape Town and Stellenbosch, 1930), 9th imp., p. 1.

79. Ibid., p. 11. Fouché gives further details re the origins and migrations of the precolonial peoples in appendix A, pp. 441–50.

80. Robert Russell, *Natal: The Land and Its Story*, 12th (and final) ed. (Pietermaritzburg, 1911), p. 124.

81. Ibid., pp. 124, 126–27.

82. George McCall Theal, *Catalogue of Books and Pamphlets Relating to Africa South of the Zambesi* (Cape Town, 1912), p. 259. Theal's comments refer specifically to the first edition of Russell's book, dated 1891; they relate equally to all later editions.

83. *History of the Basuto: Ancient and Modern*, compiled by D. Fred. Ellenberger and written in English by J. C. Macgregor (London, 1912), pp. xxii, xviii.

84. A. T. Bryant, *Olden Times in Zululand and Natal* (London, 1929), p. 3 n.

85. Ibid., p. ix.

86. Ibid., p. 11.

87. Raymond A. Dart, "Racial Origins," in *The Bantu-speaking Tribes of South Africa*, ed. I. Schapera (Cape Town, 1937), pp. 1–31.

88. Ibid., p. 14.

89. Dart's references are to G. Sergi, *L'Uomo* (Turin, 1911), F. Frassetto, *Lezioni di antropologia* (Bologna, 1909–18 [sic]), and S. Sergi, *Crania habessenica* (Rome, 1912): ibid., pp. 15, 19. Anders Retzius, whose work Dart did not identify, was a mid-nineteenth-century Swedish anatomist; in 1859 he published "The Present State of Ethnology in Relation to the Form of the Human Skull," *Smithsonian Institution Reports*, 7 (1859): 251–70.

90. Ibid., p. 28.

91. Ibid., pp. 8, 9, 10.

92. N. J. van Warmelo, "Grouping and Ethnic History," in *Bantu-speaking Tribes*, p. 46.

93. Stephen Jay Gould, *The Mismeasure of Man* (New York and London, 1981); Stepan, *Idea of Race*.

94. C. G. Seligman, *Races of Africa*, 3d ed. (London, 1957), p. 85.

95. Ibid., p. 10.

96. Ibid., p. 85. In the first edition Seligman acknowledged the help and advice of D. C. Meek and others. The publishers listed as contributing

to the revision for the third edition, which was issued after Seligman's death, the following renowned anthropologists: E. E. Evans-Pritchard, P. Bohannan, D. Forde, M. Fortes, P. Kaberry, J. H. Beattie, G. W. B. Huntingford, L. P. Mair, M. Douglas, and (for South Africa) Isaac Schapera, the editor of *The Bantu-speaking Tribes of South Africa:* ibid., publisher's note. The Hamitic myth was demolished in the 1960s: e.g., Wyatt MacGaffey, "Concepts of Race in the Historiography of Northeast Africa," *Journal of African History,* 7, no. 1 (1966), 1–17; Edith R. Sanders, "The Hamitic Hypothesis: Its Origin and Functions in Time Perspective," *Journal of African History,* 10, no. 4 (1969), 521–32.

It is curious that the original "Hamitic" myth was derogatory. Derived from Genesis 9:21–27, where God cursed the progeny of Canaan, son of Ham, who had seen his father Noah drunk and disrobed on his couch, it had Hamites doomed to inferiority, as hewers of wood and drawers of water. See William McKee Evans, "From the Land of Canaan to the Land of Guinea: The Strange Odyssey of the Sons of Ham," *American Historical Review,* 85, no. 1 (February 1980), 15–43.

97. Cited by Frantz Fanon, *The Wretched of the Earth,* trans. Catherine Farrington (Harmondsworth, 1977), p. 243. Neil Lazarus drew my attention to this reference.

98. Ibid., pp. 244–45. On Carothers and the "Mau-Mau," see Carl Rosberg and John Nottingham, *The Myth of Mau Mau: Nationalism in Kenya* (New York, 1966).

Chapter 4

1. P. J. van der Merwe, *Die Trekboer in die geskiedenis van die Kaapkolonie, 1657–1842* (Cape Town, 1938), *Trek: Studies oor die Mobiliteit van die Pioniersbevolking aan die Kaap* (Cape Town, 1945); Hermann Giliomee, "Processes in Development of the Southern African Frontier," Christopher Saunders, "Political Processes in the Southern African Frontier Zones," and Robert Ross, "Capitalism, Expansion, and Incorporation on the Southern African Frontier," in *The Frontier in History: North America and Southern Africa Compared,* ed. Howard Lamar and Leonard Thompson (New Haven, 1981), pp. 76–119, 149–71, 209–33.

2. There can be no doubt that some Boers were brutal in dealing with Khoikhoi serfs as well as with imported slaves. Comments by European travelers include those of François le Vaillant, *Travels from the Cape of Good Hope into the Interior Parts of Africa,* trans. Elizabeth Helme, 2 vols. (London, 1790), 2:150–51; John Barrow, *Travels into the Interior of Southern Africa in the Years 1797 and 1798,* 2 vols. (London, 1801–04), 2:96ff., 404ff.; and Henry Lichtenstein, *Travels in Southern Africa in the Years 1803, 1804, 1805 and 1806,* 2 vols., trans. Anne Plumptre (London, 1812, 1815; reprint, Cape Town, 1928, 1930), 1:447–48, 453ff. John Philip, super-

intendent of the London Missionary Society stations in South Africa from 1819 to 1851, was especially scathing thoughout his *Researches in South Africa*, 2 vols. (London, 1828). Before the 1820s, furthermore, the high court in the colony consisted of men without legal training, and many of their sentences were extremely lenient to white prisoners who were guilty of murdering slaves and Khoikhoi: Sir John Cradock, governor of the Cape Colony, to Lord Bathurst, secretary of state, 15 April 1814, *Records of the Cape Colony,* ed. George McCall Theal, vol. 10 (Cape Town, 1902), pp. 1–60.

3. J. S. Marais, *Maynier and the First Boer Republic*, (reprint, Cape Town, 1962); Hermann Giliomee, "The Eastern Frontier, 1770–1812," and "The Burgher Rebellions on the Eastern Frontier, 1795–1815," in *The Shaping of South African Society, 1652–1820,* ed. Richard Elphick and Hermann Giliomee (Cape Town, 1979), pp. 291–356.

4. J. S. Marais, *The Cape Coloured People, 1652–1937,* (Johannesburg, 1957), pp. 109–31; W. M. Macmillan, *The Cape Colour Question: A Historical Survey* (London, 1927); Susan Newton-King, "The Labour Market of the Cape Colony, 1807–28," in *Economy and Society in Pre-Industrial South Africa,* ed. Shula Marks and Anthony Atmore (London, 1980), pp. 171–207.

5. P. J. Venter, *Landdros en Heemrade, 1682–1827: Archives Year Book for South African History,* 3, no. 2 (1940); G. W. Eybers, *Select Constitutional Documents Illustrating South African History, 1795–1910* (London, 1918).

6. *Records of the Cape Colony,* 9:54–128.

7. L. Duly, *British Land Policy at the Cape, 1795–1844* (Durham, N.C., 1968).

8. A. J. Smithers, *The Kaffir Wars, 1779–1877* (London, 1973); W. M. Macmillan, *Bantu, Boer and Briton: The Making of the South African Native Problem,* rev. ed. (Oxford, 1963); Giliomee, "Eastern Frontier."

9. Marais, *Cape Coloured People,* pp. 131–34.

10. In this narrative I follow the account in the first chapter of J. A. Heese, *Slagtersnek en sy mense* (Slagtersnek and its people) (Cape Town, 1973), pp. 1–41, which is based on thorough and careful research and contains much fresh material. The fullest earlier account is in George Cory, *The Rise of South Africa* (London, 1910), 1:323–68. The records of the trial of the rebels are published in H. C. V. Leibbrandt, ed., *The Rebellion of 1815, Generally Known as Slachters Nek* (Cape Town, 1902), which includes a summary of the events in the report of the judges who conducted the trial, dated 21 September 1816, pp. 858–68. C. W. Hutton, ed., *The Autobiography of the Late Sir Andries Stockenström,* 2 vols. (Cape Town, 1887), contains a partisan and self-serving statement written many years after the event by a man who played a leading part in the suppression of the rebellion. By 1815, many "Khoikhoi" were of mixed descent—i.e., "Coloured."

11. Heese, pp. 90–162, provides a full description of the actors in these events.

12. Ibid., pp. 10–11.

13. Ibid., chap. 4.

14. Interrogation of Adriaan Laubscagne, 22 December 1815, in Leibbrandt, p. 352.

15. Evidence of Hendrik Nouka, 11 January 1816, in Leibbrandt, p. 743.

16. Hendrik Fredrik Prinsloo to Jacobus Krugel, 9 November 1815, in Leibbrandt, p. 134.

17. The name Slachter's Nek, Slagter's Nek, or Slagtersnek, meaning Butcher's Neck or Butcher's Mountain Pass, is apparently derived from Slachter's Knecht, meaning Butcher's Agent, and originally connoted a place where butchers' agents from Cape Town bought sheep and cattle from frontier Boers: Heese, "Inleiding," unnumbered page.

18. Heese, pp. 28–29.

19. Leibbrandt.

20. Ibid., pp. 80–114.

21. J. G. Cuyler to the colonial secretary, Cape Town, 18 March 1816, in Leibbrandt, p. 824.

22. Ibid.

23. C. I. Latrobe, *Journal of a Visit to South Africa in 1815 and 1816* (London, 1818), pp. 147–48. Latrobe is certainly wrong in saying that twenty-four people were "condemned to die," and probably wrong in suspecting that the ropes had been "intentionally cut" and also that "other halters" were procured. In other respects his report of Herold's account of the hangings rings true and is more detailed than Herold's official statement in Leibbrandt, pp. 116–17.

24. Leibbrandt, p. 853.

25. Ibid., p. 861.

26. Cape Colony, *Sententie en Uitspraak gewijzigd door Raad van Justitie, 19.2.1816* (Cape Town, 1886).

27. C. W. Hutton, ed., *The Autobiography of the Late Sir Andries Stockenstrom,* 2 vols. (Cape Town, 1887), p. 93.

28. Latrobe, pp. 231–33.

29. Thomas Pringle, *Narrative of a Residence in South Africa* (London, 1835; new ed., Cape Town, 1966), pp. 72, 75.

30. Ibid., p. 302. Pringle has much more to say about white attitudes and atrocities; e.g., on pp. 232–64 (re the "Hottentots") and 265–321 (re the "Caffers").

31. George Thompson, *Travels and Adventures in Southern Africa,* 2 vols. (London, 1827; Van Riebeeck Society reprint, Cape Town, 1967, 1968), 1:31.

32. William J. Burchell, *Travels in the Interior of Southern Africa*, 2 vols. (London, 1822, 1824; reprint, Cape Town, 1967); John Philip, *Researches in South Africa*, 2 vols. (London, 1828: reprint, New York, 1969).

33. For example, Saxe Banister, *Humane Policy: Or Justice to the Aborigines of New Settlements* (London, 1830); R. Godlonton, *A Narrative of the Irruption of the Kaffir Hordes into the Eastern Province of the Cape of Good Hope*, 2 vols. (Graham's Town, 1836; reprint in 1 vol., Cape Town, 1965); Justus (Beverley Mackenzie), *The Wrongs of the Caffre Nation* (London, 1837); Stephen Kay, *Travels and Researches in Caffraria* (London, 1833); Andrew Steedman, *Wanderings and Adventures in the Interior of Southern Africa*, 2 vols. (London, 1835); J. Centlivres Chase, *The Cape of Good Hope and the Eastern Province* (London, 1843; reprint, Cape Town, 1967).

34. Heese, p. 89.

35. Eybers, *Select Constitutional Documents*, pp. 143–45.

36. Daniel Pieter Bezuidenhout in the *Orange Free State Monthly Magazine*, December 1879, cited in English translation in John Bird, *The Annals of Natal*, vol. 1 (Cape Town, n.d. [1885]), pp. 367–76; Anna Elizabeth Steenkamp, née Retief, in the *Cape Monthly Magazine*, September 1876, reprinted in Bird, 1:459–68.

37. J. D. Kestell in the Bloemfontein *Express*, 20 September 1892, cited in F. A. van Jaarsveld, *The Awakening of Afrikaner Nationalism, 1868–1881* (New York, 1961), p. 226, n. 2.

38. Henry Cloete, *Three Lectures on the Emigration of the Dutch Farmers* (Pietermaritzburg, 1852), reprinted in *Five Lectures on the Emigration of Dutch Farmers* (Cape Town, 1856), and again reprinted in *The History of the Great Boer Trek and the Origin of the South African Republics*, ed. W. Brodrick Cloete (London, 1899). The quotation is from page 29 of the 1899 edition.

39. Heese, p. 51. The only statement that I have found by a *voortrekker* asserting that Slagtersnek was a reason for his leaving the Cape Colony is by a grandson of the executed rebel, Theunis de Klerk: "Herinneringe van Lourens Christian de Klerk," in Gustav S Preller, ed., *Voortrekkermense* (Cape Town and Bloemfontein, 1918), 1:214.

40. Cloete, 1899 ed., p. 26. Heese has established the points made in this paragraph on pages 40, 50, 62–63, and 65 of his book.

41. Pringle, *Narrative*, pp. 66–75; Heese, "Inleiding," unnumbered page.

42. A. Wilmot and John Centlivres Chase, *History of the Colony of the Cape of Good Hope* (Cape Town, 1869), pp. 259–60.

43. John Noble, *South Africa Past and Present* (London and Cape Town, 1877), pp. 33, 34.

44. John Nixon, *The Complete Story of the Transvaal from the Great Trek to the Convention of London* (London, 1885), p. 15.

45. James Bryce, *Impressions of South Africa* (London, 1897; reprint, New York, 1969), p. 113.

46. W. Basil Worsfold, *A History of South Africa* (London, 1900), pp. 42–48.

47. C. W. de Kiewiet, *British Colonial Policy and the South African Republics, 1848–1872* (London, 1929); Leonard Thompson, *Survival in Two Worlds: Moshoeshoe of Lesotho, 1786–1870* (Oxford, 1975).

48. André du Toit informs me that *De Tijd*, 22 July 1868, reported the production of the play *Willem Nel*, by H. W. Teengs. For the letter, see F. A. van Jaarsveld, *The Awakening of Afrikaner Nationalism, 1868–1881* (New York, 1961), p. 87.

49. C. W. de Kiewiet, *The Imperial Factor in South Africa* (Cambridge, 1937; reprint, London, 1965).

50. Anonymous [S. J. du Toit], *Die Geskiedenis van ons Land in die Taal van ons Volk* (Cape Town, 1877; reprint, Cape Town, 1975). See chap. 2 for a general discussion of the origins of Afrikaner nationalist historiography.

51. *Geskiedenis van ons Land*, pp. 89–90, trans. T. Dunbar Moodie, in *The Rise of Afrikanerdom* (Berkeley, 1975), p. 4.

52. Africanus [J. D. Kestell], *Slagtersnek, een Verhaal uit het Grensleven van 1815* (Cape Town, 1880).

53. Leinad [J. D. Kestell], *The Struggle for Freedom: Or, the Rebellion of Slagters Nek* (London, 1881), pp. 11–12. André du Toit drew my attention to this curious drama and sent me a copy.

54. Heese, p. 54.

55. C. P. Bezuidenhout, *De Geschiedenis van het Afrikaansch Geslacht van 1688 tot 1882* (Bloemfontein, 1883), pp. 3–5. This book identifies the Afrikaners with the Israelites: "Just as the old Israel was planted in Canaan and was protected, so our people, through God's providence, are planted in Africa from Holland, France and Germany, according to Psalm 80:9–16 and Isaiah 27:1–3" (p. ii).

56. J. W. G. van Oordt, *Slagtersnek: Een Bladzijde uit de Voorgeschiedenis der Zuid Afrikaansche Republiek* (Amsterdam and Pretoria, 1897); D'Arbez [J. F. van Oordt], *Liefde en Plicht: En Historisch Verhaal uit de Jaren 1815* (Amsterdam and Pretoria, 1897).

57. Jean van der Poel, *The Jameson Raid* (London, 1951); J. S. Marais, *The Fall of Kruger's Republic* (Oxford, 1961).

58. In the Cape Colony, political rights were color-blind in form; in practice, no Coloured man or African ever became a member of the Cape parliament, and the white voters were never fewer than 85 percent of the total electorate. See Leonard Thompson, *The Unification of South Africa* (Oxford, 1960), pp. 109–26; Phyllis Lewsen, "The Cape Liberal Tradition: Myth or Reality?" *Race*, 13, no. 1 (July 1971), 65–80; and Stanley Trapido, " 'The Friends of the Natives': Merchants, Peasants and the Political and

Ideological Structure of Liberalism in the Cape," in *Economy and Society in Pre-Industrial South Africa* (London, 1980), pp. 247–74.

59. J. W. G. van Oordt, pp. 136–40.

60. J. F. van Oordt, *Paul Kruger en de Opkomst van de Zuid-Afrikaansche Republiek* (Amsterdam and Cape Town, 1898), p. 16.

61. C. N. J. du Plessis, *The Transvaal Boer Speaking for Himself,* selected and trans. R. Acton, 2d ed. (London, 1899), p. 94.

62. J. C. Voigt, *Fifty Years of the History of the Republic of South Africa (1795–1845),* 2 vols. (London, 1899; reprint, New York, 1969), 1:129.

63. Ibid., pp. 134–35.

64. Ibid., p. 144.

65. Ibid., p. 152.

66. F. W. Reitz, *Een Eeuw van Onrecht* (Dordrecht, 1900), and *A Century of Wrong* (London, 1900); also "A Century of Injustice," in C. W. van der Hoogt, *The Story of the Boers* (New York and London, 1900). The quotation is from the version in *The Story of the Boers,* pp. 78–79. This brilliant, hastily written polemic contained several factual errors: e.g., five, not six people were hanged, and no wives or children were compelled to attend the executions. For its authorship, see W. K. Hancock, *Smuts,* vol. 1, *The Sanguine Years* (Cambridge, 1962), pp. 108–10 and 569, n. 4.

67. On Theal, see pp. 54–57, 133–36, and 182–83. His bibliography fills 16 pages of *Mendelssohn's South African Bibliography,* vol. 2, pp. 472–88.

68. *South Africa,* 6th imp., 6th ed. (London, 1899), pp. 148–50.

69. *History of South Africa,* 11 vols., vol. 5, 4th ed. (London, 1915), pp. 289–90.

70. Ibid., 5:297–98.

71. Ibid., 5:298.

72. Ibid., 5:301.

73. G. E. Cory, *The Rise of South Africa* (London, 1910), 1:324, 368.

74. D. J. J. de Villiers et al., *Geskiedenis vir Senior-Sertifikaat,* 6th imp. (Cape Town, n.d.), pp. 54–55.

75. I have consulted four books in the Fowler and Smit series: *Maskew Miller's New Senior History Course* (Cape Town, 1932); *New History for Senior Certificate and Matriculation* (Cape Town, n.d. [ca. 1944]); *Geskiedenis vir die Kaaplandse Senior Sertifikaat* (Cape Town, 1956); and *Senior History,* 9th ed. (Cape Town, "*Written for 1969 Syllabuses*"). The quotations are from the 1932 version, pp. 213, 214; the same passages, with one inconsequential verbal alteration, occur in the edition published in ca. 1944, pp. 153, 154.

76. W. Fouché, *Darter se Geskiedenis van die Unie van Suid-Afrika,* 9th imp. (Cape Town and Stellenbosch, 1930), pp. 192, 204.

77. C. J. Langenhoven, *Versamelde Werke* (Collected works), 5th ed. (Cape Town, 1973), 7:25–28. This is my translation, checked and slightly amended by André du Toit.

78. Ibid., pp. 31–34.
79. T. R. H. Davenport, "The South African Rebellion, 1914," *English Historical Review*, 78, no. 306 (1963), 73–94.
80. Heese, pp. 205–06.
81. Ibid., p. 207; Langenhoven, p. 34.
82. Heese, pp. 82–86.
83. Ibid., "Inleiding," unnumbered page.

Chapter 5

1. Act 5 of 1952, Act 72 of 1980. According to the *Standard Encyclopaedia of Southern Africa* (Cape Town, 1972), 5:562, the name Dingaan's Day was dropped because it "conveyed the impression to the uninitiated that it involved esteem for Dingaan, or that it could rouse antipathy among the Bantu against the Whites."
2. A. P. Treurnicht, notes for a speech delivered on 16 December 1983: copy supplied by a South African correspondent.
3. *Sunday Times* (Johannesburg), 1 April 1979.
4. G. W. Eybers, *Select Constitutional Documents Illustrating South African History, 1795–1910* (London, 1918), pp. 109–12, 114–19.
5. W. M. Macmillan, *The Cape Colour Question* (London, 1927), and *Bantu, Boer and Briton*, rev. ed. (Oxford, 1963); J. S. Marais, *The Cape Coloured People, 1652–1937*, 2d ed. (Johannesburg, 1957).
6. C. F. J. Muller, *Die Oorsprong van die Groot Trek* (Cape Town, 1974); André du Toit and Hermann Giliomee, *Afrikaner Political Thought: Analysis and Documents*, vol. 1, *1780–1850* (Berkeley and Los Angeles, 1983), pp. 14–22.
7. Macmillan, *Bantu, Boer and Briton*.
8. Eybers, pp. 143–45.
9. *Cape Monthly Magazine*, September 1876, republished in John Bird, *The Annals of Natal, 1495 to 1845*, 2 vols. (Pietermaritzburg, 1888), 1:459.
10. Leonard Thompson, "Co-operation and Conflict: The Zulu Kingdom and Natal," and "Co-operation and Conflict: The High Veld," in *The Oxford History of South Africa* [*OHSA*], 2 vols., ed. Monica Wilson and Leonard Thompson (Oxford, 1969, 1971), 1:334–446. Eric A. Walker, *The Great Trek*, 5th ed. (London, 1965), is still useful.
11. J. D. Omer-Cooper, *The Zulu Aftermath* (London, 1966).
12. *OHSA*, 1:355–61.
13. Ibid., pp. 361–62.
14. *S. A. Archival Records: Notule van die Natalse Volksraad, 1838–1845*, ed. J. H. Breytenbach (Cape Town, n.d. [ca. 1958]), pp. 270–73, 282–85, 290, 293–94. There are English versions of the first and the last of these documents in *The Annals of Natal*, 1:453–58, but several passages in Bird's translations are inaccurate. In citing these documents and the

one identified in the next note, I have treated the Dutch versions as authentic and have corrected the English translations by Bird and the *Zuid Afrikaan* (see n. 18) as requisite.

15. *Notule*, pp. 273–82; Bird, 1:438–52.

16. According to one of the emigrants, Bantjes was "'n bruine jonkman" (literally, a brown young man): "Dagboek van Erasmus Smit," entry for 1 January 1837, in Gustav Preller, ed., *Voortrekkermense*, 6 vols. (Cape Town, 1918–38), 2:79. This seems to mean that he was regarded as being a Coloured man. However, his descendants are classified White in modern South Africa, and Afrikaner scholars consider that he was "a young white man with a swarthy complexion": personal communication. In his introduction to his edition of the Bantjes report, Gustav Preller made use of the Smit diary, which he had previously published, but he omitted Smit's statement that Bantjes was "'n bruine jonkman": *Voortrekkermense*, 6:54–56. The article on Bantjes in W. J. de Kock, ed., *Dictionary of South African Biography* (Cape Town,1970), 1:50–52, also ignores the subject of Bantjes's ethnic category.

17. *Notule*, pp. 273–74.

18. I am grateful to Nancy Clark, William Worger, and André du Toit for sending me xerox copies of these *Zuid Afrikaan* sheets, which appeared as special supplements of the newspaper. William Worger and Nancy Clark have also examined the problem in the South African Archives, Pretoria, and conclude that the original manuscripts no longer exist and that no other contemporary eyewitness reports are available. The *Zuid Afrikaan* supplements include English as well as Dutch versions of these documents. The Dutch versions would probably have been copied from the original manuscripts, and the English versions would probably have been translations made by the editorial staff. The *Notule* use the Dutch versions in the *Zuid Afrikaan*, so I am treating them as the most authentic forms of the only contemporary eyewitness reports on the Wenkommando. See also n. 14.

19. *Notule*, p. 277.

20. Ibid., pp. 277–78.

21. Ibid., p. 280.

22. Ibid., pp. 271, 272, 273.

23. Ibid., pp. 10, 42, 92, 131, 163, 286. H. B. Thom, "Die Geloftekerk," in *Die Geloftekerk en Ander Studies oor die Groot Trek* (Cape Town, 1949).

24. Barbara Buchanan, *Pioneer Days in Natal* (Pietermaritzburg, 1934), p. 18.

25. B. J. Liebenberg, *Andries Pretorius in Natal* (Pretoria and Cape Town, 1977), p. 130.

26. Ibid.

27. G. B. A. Gerdener, *Sarel Cilliers: Die Vader van Dingaansdag* (Cape Town, 1919), p. 86.

28. P. S. de Jongh, *Die Lewe van Erasmus Smit* (Cape Town, 1977), p. 182.

29. Liebenberg, p. 130.

30. Gerdener, p. 86.

31. *Notule van die Natalse Volksraad,* p. 268. On British policy in this respect, see John S. Galbraith, *Reluctant Empire: British Policy on the South African Frontier, 1834–1854* (Berkeley and Los Angeles, 1963).

32. Major Charters to Sir George Napier, governor of the Cape Colony, 5 January 1839, in *Annals of Natal,* 1:493.

33. Eybers, p. 144.

34. See pp. 116–18.

35. De Kock, ed., *Dictionary of South African Biography,* 1:195.

36. Henry Lichtenstein, *Travels in Southern Africa,* 2:447. Other Europeans reported similar experiences in Boer households, e.g., John Barrow, *Travels into the Interior of Southern Africa in the Years 1797 and 1798,* 2 vols. (London, 1801, 1804; reprint, London and New York, 1968), 1:82–83, and Rev. James Archbell to the editor, *Grahamstown Journal,* September 1841, in Bird, *Annals of Natal,* 1:654–55.

37. Lichtenstein, 2:107–14.

38. Adulphe Delegorgue, *Voyage dans l'Afrique australe,* 2 vols. (Paris, 1847), 1:215–18, 2:130–31. Bird, 1:469–72, and 2:553–76, contains extracts from Delegorgue in English translation.

39. Edwin W. Smith, ed., *The Life and Times of Daniel Lindley, 1801–80* (London, 1949), pp. 162–63. Nestorianism, the doctrine that Christ had two distinct persons, human and divine, was condemned at the Council of Ephesus in 431, but the Nestorian Church has survived.

40. Ibid., pp. 159–60.

41. Ibid., chap. 6.

42. I. D. MacCrone, *Race Attitudes in South Africa* (Johannesburg, 1937); Sheila Patterson, *The Last Trek: A Study of the Boer People and the Afrikaner Nation* (London, 1957); T. Dunbar Moodie, *The Rise of Afrikanerdom: Power, Apartheid, and the Afrikaner Civil Religion* (Berkeley and Los Angeles, 1975); W. A. de Klerk, *The Puritans in Africa* (London, 1975). James A. Michener's historical novel *The Covenant* rests on the same assumption about Afrikaner religion in the early nineteenth century.

43. André du Toit, "No Chosen People: The Myth of the Calvinist Origins of Afrikaner Nationalism and Racial Ideology," *American Historical Review,* 88 (October 1983), 920–52. Du Toit's comments on an early draft of this chapter have been exceptionally valuable.

44. J. S. Marais, *Maynier and the First Boer Republic* (reprint, Cape Town, 1962).

45. H. C. V. Leibbrandt, ed., *The Rebellion of 1815, Generally Known as Slachters Nek* (Cape Town, 1902), pp. 864–65.

46. Gustav S. Preller, ed., *Voortrekkermense,* 6 vols. (Cape Town, 1918–38), 1:300.

47. S. J. du Toit, pp. 162–63; G. M. Theal, *Compendium of South African History and Geography,* 2 vols., 2d ed. (Lovedale, Cape Colony, 1876), 2:94–95; Liebenberg, p. 130; F. A. van Jaarsveld, "A Historical Mirror of Blood River," in *The Meaning of History,* ed. A. Konig and H. Keane (Pretoria, 1980), p. 11.

48. F. Lion Cachet, *De Worstelstrijd der Transvalers,* 2d ed. (Amsterdam, 1883), p. 201. The first edition was published in 1882.

49. Ibid.

50. H. J. Hofstede, *Geschiedenis van den Oranje-Vrijstaat* (The Hague, 1876).

51. F. A. van Jaarsveld, *The Awakening of Afrikaner Nationalism, 1868–1881* (New York, 1961), pp. 91–92.

52. Hofstede, p. 50. The Cilliers "Journaal" follows on pages 50–66. There is an English translation in Bird, *Annals of Natal,* 1:238–52. In the quotations that follow I have used the Bird translation, which is substantially accurate.

53. Bird, p. 244.

54. Ibid.

55. Ibid., pp. 244–45.

56. Ibid., p. 245.

57. Ibid., p. 247.

58. C. P. Bezuidenhout, *De Geschiedenis van het Afrikaansch Geslacht van 1688 tot 1882* (Bloemfontein, 1883), pp. 8–9.

59. J. H. Breytenbach, ed., *Notule van die Volksraad van die S.A. Republiek, S.A. Argiefstukke, Transvaal, no. 5,* p. 73, cited by F. A. van Jaarsveld in "Historical Mirror" in *The Meaning of History,* p. 11.

60. C. W. de Kiewiet, *The Imperial Factor in South Africa* (Cambridge, 1937); D. M. Schreuder, *The Scramble for Southern Africa, 1877–1895* (Cambridge, 1980); Peter Delius, *The Land Belongs to Us: The Pedi Polity, the Boers and the British in the Nineteenth-century Transvaal* (Berkeley and Los Angeles, 1984).

61. Van Jaarsveld, "Blood River," p. 11.

62. D. W. Kruger, *Die Viering van Dingaansdag* (Cape Town, n.d. [1935]).

63. André du Toit, "No Chosen People."

64. Ibid., pp. 939–47.

65. Irving Hexham, *The Irony of Apartheid: The Struggle for National Independence of Afrikaner Calvinism against British Imperialism* (New York, 1981); Moodie, *Rise of Afrikanerdom.* On Paul Kruger and the Doppers, see also pp. 131–32.

66. D. W. Kruger, *Paul Kruger,* 2 vols. (Johannesburg, 1961, 1963).

67. Ibid., 1:263–64.

68. Ibid., 1:xxx.

69. Sir John Robinson, *A Life Time in South Africa: Being the Recollections of the First Premier of Natal* (London, 1900), pp. 63, 65, 66.

70. F. A. van Jaarsveld, "Die Ontstaangeskiedenis van die begrippe 'Voortrekkers' en 'Groot Trek,' " in *Lewende Verlede* (Johannesburg, 1962), pp. 173–200; Muller, *Oorsprong*, pp. 19–20.

71. Preller, *Voortrekkermense*, 3: preface.

72. Bird, 1:453–58 (Pretorius); 1:438–52 (Bantjes); 1:238–52 (Cilliers).

73. For example, George McCall Theal, *South Africa*, 5th ed. (London, 1899); C. P. Lucas, *South and East Africa, Part I, Historical* (Oxford, 1897); James Bryce, *Impressions of South Africa* (London, 1897); A. Wilmot, *The Story of the Expansion of South Africa*, 2d ed. (London, 1895); W. Basil Worsfold, *A History of South Africa* (London, 1900).

74. W. J. Pretorius in English in Bird, 1:230–37; P. van Gass in *Voortrekkermense*, 1:1–102; D. Bezuidenhout in *Voortrekkermense*, 3:148ff., and in English translation in Bird, 1:367–76.

75. This question is discussed at length by E. G. Jansen in "Is die Gelofte op Danskraal afgelê?" in *Die Voortrekkers in Natal* (Cape Town, 1938), pp. 56–74. He concludes that Bantjes's account is to be accepted and that the location was on the banks of the stream previously known as Blyrivier but thereafter known as Wasbankrivier. B. J. Liebenberg agrees with Jansen: *Andries Pretorius in Natal* (Pretoria, 1977), pp. 29–32.

76. Preller, *Voortrekkermense*, 3:99.

77. Ibid., 1:186–87.

78. Ibid., 3:113–14; 4:12, 47–48.

79. Ibid., 2:27–48; English translation in Bird, 1:459–68, citing the *Cape Monthly Magazine*, September 1876.

80. Preller, *Voortrekkermense*, 2:54ff.

81. Cachet, *De Worstelstrijd.*

82. J. C. Voigt, *Fifty Years of the History of the Republic in South Africa*, 2 vols. (London, 1899), 2:87.

83. Ibid., p. 91.

84. The document is entitled "A Century of Injustice," in *The Story of the Boers* (New York and London, 1900).

85. George M. Theal, *Compendium of South African History and Geography*, 2d ed. (Lovedale, Cape Colony, 1876).

86. Theal, *South Africa* (1899), pp. 213–14.

87. Alexander Wilmot, *The Story of the Expansion of South Africa*, 2d ed. (London, 1895), p. 123.

88. Lucas, *South and East Africa, Part 1, Historical*, p. 111.

89. James Bryce, *Impressions of South Africa* (London, 1899), pp. 117, 121.

90. Ibid., p. 421.
91. Kruger, *Viering van Dingaansdag*, p. 50.
92. Ibid., p. 52.
93. See pp. 35–37, 39–40.
94. Gustav S. Preller, *Piet Retief: Lewensgeskiedenis van die grote Voortrekker*, 10th ed. (Cape Town, 1930); ed. *Voortrekkermense*, 6 vols. (Cape Town, 1918–38); ed. *Dagboek van Louis Trichardt, 1836–1838* (Cape Town, 1938); *Andries Pretorius: Lewensbeskrywing van die Voortrekker Kommandant-Generaal*, 2d ed. (Johannesburg, 1940).
95. *Andries Pretorius*, pp. 37–38.
96. Cited by F. A. van Jaarsveld, *The Afrikaner's Interpretation of South African History* (Cape Town, 1964), p. 79. Van Jaarsveld provides a judicious assessment of the work of Preller (pp. 78–87).
97. J. H. Malan, *Boer en Barbaar, of Die Geskiedenis van die Voortrekkers tussen die jare 1835–1840, en verder, van die Kaffernasies met wie hulle in aanraking gekom het*, 2d ed. (Bloemfontein, 1918), p. 396.
98. Ibid., pp. 342–43.
99. Gerdener, *Cilliers*, p. 3.
100. Ibid., pp. 92–109.
101. H. S. Pretorius et al., eds. *Voortrekker-argiefstukke, 1819–1849* (Pretoria, 1937); Kruger, *Viering van Dingaansdag;* Carel Potgieter and N. H. Theunissen, *Kommandant-generaal Hendrik Potgieter* (Johannesburg, 1938); E. G. Jansen and P. Nel, eds., *Uit die Voortrekkertyd: Herinneringe van Louis Jacobus Nel* (Pretoria, 1939); E. G. Jansen, *Die Voortrekkers in Natal: Opstelle* (Cape Town, 1938); I. D. Bosman et al., eds., *Voortrekker-gedenkboek van die Universiteit van Pretoria* (Pretoria, 1938).
102. George McCall Theal, *History of South Africa*, 11 vols., vol. 7, 4th ed. (London, 1927), p. 297.
103. Ibid., vol. 6, 5th ed. (London, 1926), p. 381.
104. C. de K. Fowler and G. J. J. Smit, *Maskew Miller's New Senior History Course* (Cape Town, 1932), pp. 311-12; *New History for Senior Certificate and Matriculation* (Cape Town, n.d. [ca. 1944]), p. 260; *Geskiedenis vir die Kaaplandse Senior Sertifikaat* (Cape Town, 1956), p. 308; *Senior History, "Written for 1969 Syllabuses"* (Cape Town, n.d.), pp. 279–80.
105. D. J. J. de Villiers, G. H. P. de Bruin, and J. J. Muller, *Geskiedenis vir Senior-Sertifikaat* (Cape Town, n.d. [ca. 1920]), pp. 84–85.
106. W. Fouché, *Darter se Geskiedenis van die Unie van Suid-Afrika* (Cape Town and Stellenbosch, 1930), p. 301.
107. See pp. 39–40.
108. Moodie, *Rise of Afrikanerdom*, pp. 175–207; A. G. du Toit and Louis Steenkamp, eds., *Bloedrivierse Eeufees-Gedenkboek* (Pietermaritzburg, 1939).
109. Moodie, p. 179. Klopper's version of the vow, as translated by Moodie, who cites *Die Gedenkboek van die Ossewaens op die Pad van Suid-*

Afrika (Cape Town, 1940), pp. 112–13, is the Cilliers version as published in H. J. Hoftstede, *Geschiedenis van den Oranje-Vrijstaat* (The Hague, 1876), pp. 57–58, as translated by me (above, p. 167), with minor variations.

110. Du Toit and Steenkamp, eds., *Eeufees-Gedenkboek*, p. 16.

111. Ibid., p. 22.

112. Ibid., pp. 30, 31, 32.

113. Ibid., p. 37.

114. Ibid., pp. 123–24.

115. Ibid., p. 124.

116. M. C. Botha, ed., *Die Huldejaar 1949* (Johannesburg, 1952).

117. Ibid., pp. 271–77.

118. Ibid., p. 272.

119. There are photographs of these panels (ibid., pp. 11–13). The Covenant lives on thus in South African school textbooks of the 1970s and 1980s: e.g., A. N. Boyce, *Europe and South Africa: A History for South African High Schools*, 3d imp. (Cape Town, 1970), p. 175; C. de K. Fowler and G. J. J. Smit, *Senior History*, 9th ed., 3rd imp. (Cape Town, 1969), p. 279; E. H. W. Lategan and A. J. de Kock, *History in Perspective: Standard 8* (Johannesburg, 1979), pp. 120–21; M. C. E. van Schoor et al., *Senior History for South African Schools, Standard 8* (Goodwood, Cape Province, 1980), p. 102; C. J. Joubert, *History for Standard 8*, 2d imp. (Johannesburg, 1980), pp. 134–35; A. P. van Niekerk, F. Stander, and H. G. J. Lintvelt, *Ons Lewende Verlede: Geskiedenis vir Standerd 6*, 7th imp. (Cape Town, 1981), p. 101.

120. *The Voortrekker Monument: Official Guide* (Pretoria, n.d. [ca. 1960]), p. 49.

Chapter 6

1. On contemporary South Africa, see Foreign Policy Study Foundation, *South Africa: Time Running Out* (Berkeley and Los Angeles, 1981), which focuses on American policy toward South Africa, and Leonard Thompson and Andrew Prior, *South African Politics* (New Haven, 1982). R. W. Johnson, *How Long Will South Africa Survive?* (London, 1977), and John de St. Jorre, *A House Divided: South Africa's Uncertain Future* (Washington and New York, 1977), are still useful. Publications of the South African government include the annual *Yearbook* and the weekly *South African Digest*. The South African Institute of Race Relations, Johannesburg, publishes the annual *Survey of Race Relations in South Africa*. The United Nations Centre against Apartheid, New York, publishes numerous documents. Africa Research Ltd., Exeter, England, produces the monthly *Africa Research Bulletin* in two series, *Political, Social and Cultural* and *Economic*.

2. Leonard Thompson, "The Parting of the Ways in South Africa," in *The Transfer of Power in Africa*, ed. Prosser Gifford and Wm. Roger Louis (New Haven, 1982), pp. 417–44.

3. Heribert Adam and Hermann Giliomee, *Ethnic Power Mobilized: Can South Africa Change?* (New Haven and London, 1979); Hermann Giliomee and Heribert Adam, *Afrikanermag: Opkoms en Toekoms* (Stellenbosch and Grahamstown, 1981); Dan O'Meara, *Volkskapitalisme: Class, Capital and Ideology in the Development of Afrikaner Nationalism, 1934–1948* (Cambridge, England, and New York, 1983).

4. Baruch Hirson, *Year of Fire, Year of Ash: The Soweto Revolt: Roots of a Revolution?* (London, 1979); *Africa Research Bulletin: Political, Social and Cultural Series*, March 1980, pp. 5613–14, summarizes the official report on the Soweto events.

5. Thomas G. Karis, "Revolution in the Making: Black Politics in South Africa," *Foreign Affairs*, 62 (Winter 1983/84): 378–406.

6. Richard Leonard, *South Africa at War: White Power and the Crisis in Southern Africa* (Westport, Conn., 1983).

7. *Republic of South Africa Constitution Act, No. 110, 1983.*

8. Numerous reports of these forced removals have appeared in the American and European press.

9. For the background to the right-wing revolt from the National Party, see the works listed in n. 3.

10. Union of of South Africa, *Report of Native Economic Commission, 1930–1932: U.G. 22/1932* (Pretoria, 1932); *Report of the Native Laws Commission 1946–48: U.G. 28/1948* (Pretoria, 1948); *The Native Reserves and Their Place in the Economy of the Union of South Africa: U.G. 32/1946* (Pretoria, 1946).

11. Technically, the printed document, consisting of xviii plus 213 pages plus 64 pages of maps, is merely the *Summary of the Report of the Commission for the Socio-Economic Development of the Bantu Areas within the Union of South Africa* (U.G. 55/1955). The full report, consisting of 3,755 pages as well as 589 tables and an atlas of 66 large-scale maps, was never published.

12. Ibid., p. 10.

13. Ibid.

14. Ibid., p. 13.

15. Ibid., p. 1.

16. Ibid., p. 14.

17. *Official Yearbook of the Union of South Africa and of Basutoland, Bechuanaland Protectorate, and Swaziland, No. 5—1922* (Pretoria, 1923), pp. 9, 11.

18. *Official Yearbook of the Union of South Africa and of Basutoland, Bechuanaland Protectorate, and Swaziland, No. 22—1941* (Pretoria, 1941), p. 1151.

19. *South Africa 1976: Official Yearbook of the Republic of South Africa,* 3d ed. (Johannesburg, n.d.), p. 202. This massive volume of xxiii plus 1,013 pages was "distributed by the South African Department of Information, its various offices abroad and regional representatives within the Republic" (p. iv).

20. Ibid., p. 78.

21. Ibid., p. 210.

22. Ibid., p. 200.

23. Ibid., pp. 85, 89.

24. Ibid., p. 28.

25. "A New South Africa: Black States: Consolidation and Development," *South African Digest,* 25 July 1980, p. 1.

26. D. Ziervogel, "Appendix I: The Natives of South Africa," in *Five Hundred Years: A History of South Africa,* ed. C. F. J. Muller (Pretoria and Cape Town, 1969), p. 430.

27. Ibid., p. 434.

28. C. de K. Fowler and G. J. J. Smit, *Senior History,* 9th ed. (Cape Town, 1969), pp. 397–98.

29. M. C. E. van Schoor et al., *Senior History for South African Schools Standard 8* (Goodwood, Cape Province, 1980), pp. 81–82; similarly the chapter entitled "The Southward Migration of the Southern Blacks" in C. J. Joubert, *History for Standard 8* (Johannesburg and Cape Town, 1977), pp. 102–19. Both textbooks were available in both Afrikaans and English.

30. L. B. Hurry, H. A. Mocke, H. C. Wallis, and G. Engelbrecht, *Social Studies Standard 6, Social Studies Standard 7,* and *Social Studies Standard 8* (Goodwood, 1980).

31. William M. Macmillan, *The Cape Colour Question: A Historical Survey* (London 1927), and *Bantu, Boer and Briton: The Making of the South African Native Problem* (London, 1929; rev. ed., Oxford, 1963); Cornelis W. de Kiewiet, *British Colonial Policy and the South African Republics, 1848–1872* (London, 1929), *The Imperial Factor in South Africa: A Study in Politics and Economics* (Cambridge, 1937), and *A History of South Africa: Social and Economic* (Oxford, 1941).

32. Monica Wilson and Leonard Thompson, eds., *The Oxford History of South Africa* (Oxford, 1969, 1971), 1:vii–x.

33. For example, Shula Marks and Anthony Atmore, eds., *Economy and Society in Pre-Industrial South Africa* (London, 1980); Shula Marks and Richard Rathbone, eds., *Industrialisation and Social Change in South Africa* (London, 1982); Charles van Onselen, *Studies in the Social and Economic History of the Witwatersrand, 1886–1914,* 2 vols. (London, 1982).

34. Richard Elphick, *Kraal and Castle: Khoikhoi and the Founding of White South Africa* (New Haven, 1977).

35. David William Cohen, *Womunafa's Bunafu: A Study of Authority in a Nineteenth-Century African Community* (Princeton, 1977); Robert W.

Harms, *River of Wealth, River of Sorrow: The Central Zaire Basin in the Era of the Slave and Ivory Trade, 1500–1891* (New Haven, 1981).

36. Jeff Guy, "Ecological Factors in the Rise of Shaka and the Zulu Kingdom," and William Beinart, "Production and the Material Base of Chieftainship: Pondoland, c. 1830–80," in Marks and Atmore, eds., *Economy and Society*, pp. 102–47.

37. Leonard Thompson, *Survival in Two Worlds: Moshoeshoe of Lesotho, 1786–1870* (Oxford, 1975). For Bantu-speaking farmers in Kenya, this theme is developed in Charles Ambler, "Central Kenya in the Late Nineteenth Century: Small Communities in a Regional System," Ph.D. diss., Yale University, 1983.

38. Chief Gatsha Buthelezi of KwaZulu made this point effectively in an interview with J. T. Kruger, minister of justice, police, and prisons, at the Union Buildings in Pretoria, on 19 September 1977: transcript in my possession.

39. *The Journal of African History* frequently publishes lists of carbon-14 dates and descriptive articles by archaeologists: e.g., Tim Maggs, "The Iron Age Sequence South of the Vaal and Pongola Rivers: Some Historical Implications," *JAH*, 21, no. 1 (1980), 1–15. There is a summary in R. R. Inskeep, *The Peopling of Southern Africa* (Cape Town and London, 1978).

40. Marianne Cornevin, *Apartheid: Power and Historical Falsification* (Paris, 1980).

41. For example, Slagtersnek is scarcely mentioned in the later versions of the widely used high school textbooks written by C. de K. Fowler and G. J. J. Smit: *Geskiedenis vir die Kaaplandse Senior Sertifikaat* (Cape Town, 1956), and *Senior History: Written for 1969 Syllabuses*, 9th ed. (Cape Town, n.d.).

42. M. A. S. Grundlingh in A. J. H. van der Walt, J. A. Wiid, and A. L. Geyer, eds., *Geskiedenis van Suid-Afrika*, 2 vols. (Cape Town, 1951), pp. 232–34.

43. C. R. Kotze in C. F. J. Muller, ed., *Five Hundred Years: A History of South Africa* (Pretoria and Cape Town, 1969), pp. 113–14.

44. D. J. Kotze, "Slachter's Nek Rebellion," in D. J. Potgieter, ed., *Standard Encyclopaedia of Southern Africa* (London, 1973), 3:655–56.

45. Heese, *Slagtersnek*, "Voorwoord," unnumbered page.

46. Ibid., "Inleiding," unnumbered page.

47. Ibid., p. 86.

48. Ibid., p. 73.

49. Ibid., p. 87.

50. Hermann Giliomee, "The Burgher Rebellions in the Eastern Frontier, 1795–1815," in *The Shaping of South African Society 1652–1820*, ed. Richard Elphick and Hermann Giliomee (London, 1979), pp. 338–56, and "Processes in Development of the Southern African Frontier," in *The Frontier in History: North America and Southern Africa Compared*, ed. How-

ard Lamar and Leonard Thompson (New Haven, 1981), pp. 76–119. See also Martin Legassick, "The Frontier Tradition in South African Historiography," in Marks and Atmore, eds., *Economy and Society*, pp. 44–79.

51. Giliomee, "Processes in Development," p. 88.

52. *The Meaning of History*, ed. A. Konig and H. Keane (Pretoria, 1980).

53. *Sunday Times* (Johannesburg), 1 April 1979. Subsequently, Eugene Terreblanche informed a reporter: "I led 40 members into the hall with my braided whip in hand. I was prepared to horsewhip anyone who mocked us. . . . On what grounds can Prof. Van Jaarsveld question Sarel Cilliers's vow that the Day of the Covenant would always remain a day of reverence? God fulfilled His part of the contract. What right has anyone, particularly the Afrikaner, to desanctify this day? . . . I want to warn others that if they do not toe the line, their punishment will be as swift. We want to reunite South Africa in one great Afrikanerdom" (ibid., 8 April 1979).

54. *Meaning of History*, pp. 8–59.

55. John W. de Gruchy, *The Church Struggle in South Africa* (Cape Town, 1979); John de Gruchy and Charles Villa-Vicencio, eds., *Apartheid Is a Heresy* (Cape Town, 1983); T. Dunbar Moodie, *The Rise of Afrikanerdom: Power, Apartheid, and the Afrikaner Civil Religion* (Berkeley, 1975); Marjorie Hope and James Young, *The South African Churches in a Revolutionary Situation* (Maryknoll, N.Y., 1981).

56. *Rapport*, 8 and 15 January 1984. I have studied numerous extracts from five leading Afrikaans newspapers over parts of 1982 and 1983.

57. De Gruchy, *Church Struggle*, p. 69.

58. Ibid., pp. 69–85. In 1980, about 1,693,640 white people were members of the NGK, 246,340 of the NHK, and 128,360 of the GKSA; their separate mission churches, nearly all of them NGK mission churches, had a combined total of about 1,103,560 African members, 678,380 Coloured members, and 3,940 Asian members. See Republic of South Africa, *South Africa 1983: Official Yearbook of the Republic of South Africa* (Johannesburg, 1983), pp. 782–83.

59. *The Churches' Judgment on Apartheid* (Cape Town, 1948).

60. Alan Paton, *Apartheid and the Archbishop: The Life and Times of Geoffrey Clayton, Archbishop of Cape Town* (Cape Town, 1973).

61. De Gruchy, *Church Struggle*, pp. 118–22 (quotation, p. 119); Hope and Young, *Churches in a Revolutionary Situation*, pp. 86–104.

62. De Gruchy, *Church Struggle*, pp. 65–69; A. H. Luckhoff, *Cottesloe* (Cape Town, 1978).

63. B. B. Keet, *Whither South Africa?* (Stellenbosch, 1956).

64. B. B. Keet et al., *Delayed Action* (Pretoria, 1961).

65. De Gruchy, *Church Struggle*, pp. 103–15; Hope and Young, *Churches in a Revolutionary Situation*, pp. 76–85. Richard Turner, the author of one of these publications, *The Eye of the Needle: An Essay on Participatory*

Democracy (Johannesburg, 1972), was subsequently shot dead in his home in Durban, and nobody was ever charged with the crime.

66. De Gruchy, *Church Struggle*, pp. 115–27.

67 Alan Paton, *Sunday Times* (Johannesburg), 10 October 1982; Ivor Wilkins, ibid., 17 October 1982; *Rand Daily Mail* editorials, 22 and 27 October 1982.

68. *Die Burger*, 22 November 1982.

69. *Rapport*, 31 October 1982.

70. *Die Transvaler*, 22 October 1982.

71. *Die Kerkbode*, 2 December 1983.

72. Ibid.

73. *Die Burger*, 23 December 1982.

74. Ibid., 29 December 1982.

75. *Die Transvaler*, 15 December 1982.

76. *Beeld*, 15 December 1983; *Die Burger*, 16 December 1983. The *Beeld* version is signed Dr. Willie Jonker.

77. The following passage is based on reports concerning the events of 16 December 1983 that were supplied by correspondents in South Africa. They include cuttings from three Cape Town newspapers, *Die Burger*, the *Cape Argus*, and the *Cape Times*; the East London *Daily Despatch*; three Natal papers, the *Natal Witness*, the *Natal Mercury*, and the *Sunday Tribune*; and seven Transvaal papers, the *Sunday Times*, the *Rand Daily Mail*, the *Star*, *Beeld*, *Die Vaderland*, the *Citizen*, and *Rapport*. The Conservative Party's only newspaper, *Die Patriot*, ceased publication on 2 December 1983, after which all Afrikaans newspapers were supporters of the National Party government. The English press was, in varying degrees, anti-NP, except for the *Citizen*, which was subsidized by the government.

78. The *Rand Daily Mail*, 16 December 1983, with a banner headline on the front page: TERROR IN THE CITY CENTRE. Also the *Star*, 16 and 17 December 1983, and *Beeld*, 16 December 1983. The South African Institute of Strategic Studies reported 44 attacks by ANC saboteurs in 1983, 39 in 1982, 55 in 1981, and 19 in 1980. Those in 1983 included bomb damage to the Supreme Court buildings in Pietermaritzburg, the Southern Orange Free State administration offices in Bloemfontein, the headquarters of the Air Force and the National Intelligence Services in Pretoria, the offices of the Department of Internal Affairs in Roodepoort near Pretoria, the offices of the Port Natal Administration Board near Durban, and several electric power pylons and railway lines. See *Africa News* (Durham, N.C.), 20 February 1984, pp. 5–6.

79. *Die Vaderland*, 15 December 1983.

80. *Rapport* and the *Sunday Times*, 18 December 1983.

81. The *Star*, 17 December 1983; the *Daily Despatch*, 17 December 1983; the *Cape Argus*, 16 December 1983.

82. The *Sunday Tribune*, 18 December 1983.

83. A South African correspondent sent me a copy of these notes. The xerox shows that the original was signed A. P. Treurnicht. In translating this speech, I have used the English words *people* and *peoples* for the Afrikaans words *volk* and *volke*. These are the nearest equivalents; nevertheless, the English words do not convey the strong nationalist overtones of the Afrikaans originals.

84. The *Citizen*, 17 December 1983.

85. *Rapport*, 18 December 1983.

86. *Die Burger*, 17 December 1983.

87. My criteria for evaluating political myths are described in chapter 1.

88. André du Toit and Hermann Giliomee, *Afrikaner Political Thought: Analysis and Documents: I; 1780–1850* (Berkeley and Los Angeles, 1983); André du Toit, "No Chosen People: The Myth of the Calvinist Origins of Afrikaner Nationalism and Racial Ideology," *American Historical Review* 88 (1983): 920–52.

89. André Brink, *Kennis van die Aand, Gerugte van Reën, 'n Droe Wit Seisoen;* J. M. Coetzee, *Dusklands, In the Heart of the Country, Waiting for the Barbarians;* Nadine Gordimer, *The Conservationist, July's People;* Alan Paton, *Cry the Beloved Country, Too Late the Phalarope;* Athol Fugard, *Statements, Notebooks.*

90. Many black South African poets and novelists went into exile in the 1960s and 1970s, notably the poets Dennis Brutus and Mazisi Kunene, and the novelist Alex La Guma. Works by black authors who were living in South Africa in the mid-1980s include novels by Mongane Serote, *To Every Birth Its Blood*, Mbulelo Mzamane, *The Children of Soweto*, and Miriam Tlali, *Amandla;* and poetry by Mafika Gwala, Oswald Mtshali, Sipho Sepamla, and Mongane Serote, which is published in Robert Royston, ed., *Black Poetry in South Africa*. Es'kia Mphahlele, author of *Down Second Avenue* and other works, returned to South Africa in 1980 after a long absence.

91. Republic of South Africa, *South Africa 1983: Official Yearbook of the Republic of South Africa* (Johannesburg, 1983), p. 23. The passage in the 1978 edition is identical. There is another version on p. 78: "It is now generally accepted that the Bantu-speaking Blacks of South Africa are the descendants of Iron Age farmers who reached this region in the 11th and 12th centuries. Some authorities view this migration as having a swirling rather than a constant directional pattern. This is supported by Iron Age datings in the northern Transvaal as early as the third and fourth centuries."

92. Ibid., p. 196. This statement is peculiar because in the frontier conflict in question many Afrikaner frontiersmen were more nomadic than the Xhosa people, who were relatively sedentary because they were cultivators as well as pastoralists.

93. Ibid., p. 78.

94. Philip Curtin, Steven Feierman, Leonard Thompson, and Jan Vansina, *African History* (Boston, 1978), p. 121.

95. Hermann Giliomee supplied me with copies of the officially prescribed syllabuses in use in senior schools in South Africa since 1974. There are no significant differences between the syllabuses used in schools for the different "races," except that more appropriate syllabuses are being introduced in some of the "homelands," notably Bophuthatswana.

96. *Cape Argus*, 4 April 1984.

97. J. M. du Preez, *Africana Afrikaner: Master Symbols in South African School Textbooks* (Alberton, 1983), p. 6.

98. Ibid., p. 21.

99. Ibid., p. 71.

100. Thompson and Prior, *South African Politics*, pp. 85–87.

101. Robert Jervis, *Perception and Misperception in International Politics* (Princeton, 1976), pp. 288–315.

102. F. A. van Jaarsveld, *Die Afrikaners se Groot Trek na die Stede en ander Opstelle* (Johannesburg, 1982).

103. F. A. van Jaarsveld, A. P. J. van Rensburg, and P. H. Kapp, *New Illustrated History STD. 10* (Johannesburg, 1984). See also André du Toit, "Captive to the Nationalist Paradigm: Prof. F. A. van Jaarsveld and the Historical Evidence for the Afrikaner's Ideas on His Calling and Mission," *South African Historical Journal*, no. 16 (1984), 49–80, and van Jaarsveld's reply, ibid., p. 81.

104. The first volume was published in 1983; see n. 88.

105. Crawford Young, "Patterns of Social Conflict: State, Class, and Ethnicity," *Daedalus* 111 (Spring 1982), 93.

106. Philip Larken, *Times Literary Supplement*, 13 January 1984, p. 29.

INDEX

African languages, 47, 91

African National Congress (ANC), 66, 194, 217, 223

Africans: conquest of, 26, 79–81, 164, 223; white myths of early history of, 70–72, 77–78, 82–100, 234–35; modern ethnic communities, 78–79; first studies of southern African precolonial history, 91; Theal's views of origins of, 91–92; Afrikaner attitudes toward, 120–21, 129–33; nationalism of, 146; resistance to changes in racial laws, 195; official publications' views of, 195, 197–200; depiction in modern textbooks, 200; models of precolonial history of, 201–03; languages of, 204; scientific evidence of origins of, 205; and *1984* Constitution, 241; urban domicile of, 242; political mythology of, 242–43. *See also* Homelands; Textbooks; *names of African communities*

Afrikaans language: and Dutch, 27, 36, 50, 76; features, 30–31; attempts to create literature, 35; historiography, 37; SABC broadcasts, 47; press, 48; use in schools, 49–51, 58–60; textbooks, 58–60, 183. *See also* Christian National Education; Education; Textbooks

Afrikaans newspapers, 215, 219–23

Afrikaner frontiersmen, 105–43 passim

Afrikaner historiography: first attempts to formulate, 30–31; state of by *1899*, 32–33; Great Trek as centerpiece, 36,

180; and Slagtersnek, 126–33, 208–12; and the Covenant, 165–68, 173–76, 180–82; textbooks, 200–01, 207–08. *See also* Textbooks; *names of individual historians*

Afrikaner nationalism: and Dutch Reformed churches, 31–35; and Second Anglo-Boer War, 33–34; national anthem, 37–40; national flag, 38, 40; Great Trek celebrations, 39–40, 141, 144, 183–86; norms of 63; and Slagtersnek, 126–33, 142, 206, 212; and the Covenant, 145–46, 168–76, 178–80, 183–88, 211–13; and British imperialism, 168–69, 173, 178–80; and Chosen People theology, 169–72. *See also* Afrikaner historiography; British imperialism; Chosen People; Covenant; Dutch Reformed churches; Education; Slagtersnek

Afrikaner nationalist mythology: mobilizing function, 26–29; racist theme, 28–30, 40–43, 69; liberatory thrust, 29–30; in nineteenth century, 30–33, 239; in twentieth century, 33–41, 239–40; influence of German National Socialism, 42–43; propagation by schools, 49–54; propagation by textbooks, 54–62; assumptions about precolonial African history, 70; centrality of unassimilable races myth, 105; and Slagtersnek, 126–33; and the Covenant, 168–76, 183–88; failure of, 229–30; types of, 233; effects of *1948* National Party victory,

285

① Stephen Jay Gould
   1981 "The Mismeasure of Man"

② Malinowski, Myth in Primitive
              Psychology.